ROUTLEDGE LIBRARY EDITIONS:
THE MEDIEVAL WORLD

Volume 17

ENGLISH MEDIAEVAL PILGRIMAGE

ENGLISH MEDIAEVAL PILGRIMAGE

D. J. HALL

LONDON AND NEW YORK

First published in 1965 by Routledge & Kegan Paul

This edition first published in 2020
by Routledge
2 Park Square, Milton Park, Abingdon, Oxon OX14 4RN

and by Routledge
52 Vanderbilt Avenue, New York, NY 10017

Routledge is an imprint of the Taylor & Francis Group, an informa business

© 1965 D. J. Hall

All rights reserved. No part of this book may be reprinted or reproduced or utilised in any form or by any electronic, mechanical, or other means, now known or hereafter invented, including photocopying and recording, or in any information storage or retrieval system, without permission in writing from the publishers.

Trademark notice: Product or corporate names may be trademarks or registered trademarks, and are used only for identification and explanation without intent to infringe.

British Library Cataloguing in Publication Data
A catalogue record for this book is available from the British Library

ISBN: 978-0-367-22090-7 (Set)
ISBN: 978-0-429-27322-3 (Set) (ebk)
ISBN: 978-0-367-20519-5 (Volume 17) (hbk)
ISBN: 978-0-367-20524-9 (Volume 17) (pbk)
ISBN: 978-0-429-26200-5 (Volume 17) (ebk)

Publisher's Note
The publisher has gone to great lengths to ensure the quality of this reprint but points out that some imperfections in the original copies may be apparent.

Disclaimer
The publisher has made every effort to trace copyright holders and would welcome correspondence from those they have been unable to trace.

English Mediaeval Pilgrimage

by
D. J. HALL

Readers Union
Routledge & Kegan Paul
1967

© D. J. Hall 1965

This Readers Union edition was produced in 1967 for sale to its members only by Readers Union Limited at Aldine House, 10 - 13 Bedford Street, London W.C. 2, and at Letchworth Garden City, Herts. Full details of membership may be obtained from our London address.

This book is set in 11/12pt Baskerville and has been printed by Bookprint Limited.

It was first published by Routledge & Kegan Paul.

CONTENTS

I	PILGRIMAGE AND THE MEDIAEVAL MIND	*page*	1
II	SAINT WINEFREDE OF HOLYWELL		18
III	THE SHRINES OF GLASTONBURY		45
IV	SAINT CUTHBERT OF LINDISFARNE AND DURHAM		76
V	THE SHRINE OF OUR LADY OF WALSINGHAM		104
VI	SAINT THOMAS BECKET OF CANTERBURY		130
VII	SAINT EDWARD THE CONFESSOR		166
VIII	SAINT ALBAN THE PROTOMARTYR		185
IX	THE HOLY ROOD OF BROMHOLM		201
X	CONCLUSION		213
	INDEX		227

ILLUSTRATIONS

1 Initial P (Paratum cor meum). [From   *page*   1
Codex Vossianus, Winchester, 10th C. 2nd quarter.
MS. Junius 27. Bodleian 146/112.]

2 Pilgrim, setting out, puts on a gambeson,   *page*   5
a quilted coat which pricks him and symbolizes
patience. [From *Le Pelerinage de la Vie Humaine.*
French, Early 15th C. Flemish. Bodleian MS.
Douce 300 (168J/13).]

3 Sainte Winefrede – dressed as an abbess.   *page*   22
[From a *Book of Hours* (Sarum Use) Norman
1430–40. Bodleian.]

4 Satan and his daughter Heresy spreading   *page*   30
traps for the unwary pilgrim. [From *Pilgrimage of
the Life of Man* by John Lydgate; first half 15th C.
B.M. Cott. Tib. A Vii f.51v.]

5 Charity addresses a group of kneeling   *page*   33
pilgrims. [*Le Pelerinage de la Vie Humaine.* Early
15th C. French. Bodleian. Douce 300 f.24v.
(163C/4).]

6 Joseph of Arimathaea before Pilate.   *page*   56
[*Hours of the Blessed Virgin.* Flemish 1500. B.M.
Add: 24098.f.12v.]

7 King Arthur: his shield carrying his arms   *page*   57
of the Virgin and Child. [Early 14th C. From part
of the introductory matter to the *Chronicle of
England* by Peter of Langtoft written in French
verse, probably in the time of Edward II (1307–
1327) B.M. Royal MS. 20A. ii f. iv.]

Illustrations

8   Lancelot taken prisoner in error on the   *page*   58
    bridge of Pomparles (pons periculosus: pont
    perdu). [From *Lancelot du Lac*, North French
    c. 1320–30. Bodleian MS. Rawl. Q.b.6.]

9   Dunstan catching the Devil with his   *page*   66
    tongs. [Early 14th C. written in Italy for French
    use. *Decretals* of Gregory IX. B.M. Royal 10 E.IV.
    f. 250 v.]

10 Angel healing Cuthbert's knee after his   *page*   79
    accident. [Bede's *Life of Cuthbert*. 12th C. MS.
    Univ. Coll. Oxford (Bodleian Ref: 167H/2).]

11 Cuthbert after a night in the sea, having   *page*   80
    his feet dried by sea creatures. [Bede's *Life of
    Cuthbert*. 12th C. MS. Univ. Coll. Oxford
    (Bodleian Ref: 167H/10).]

12 Pilgrims, one paralysed, at St Cuthbert's   *page*   94
    shrine. [Bede's *Life of Cuthbert*. 12th C. MS.
    Univ. Coll. Oxford (Bodleian Ref: 167H/10).]

13 Second Seal of Walsingham.   *page*   106
    Obverse: The priory church, from the South:
    Sigillum. ecclie:beate:Marie:de Walsingham.
    Reverse: The Crowned Virgin with Holy Child on
    left knee: fleur-de-lis Sceptre in right hand.
    ✠ *Ave.Marie:Gracie: plena: dominus: tecum.*
    [B.M. lxix, 31, 32. Ackn. of Supr (P.R.O.)
    112.]

14 Pride dressed as a Jester. [*Vision of Piers*   *page*   115
    Plowman. England 1427. Bodleian MS. Douce
    104 (168I No. 3).]

15 Hare, sheep and fox dressed as pilgrims.   *page*   121
    [*Romance of Renart and Isengrim*. 1339. Douce
    360 f. 72 Bodleian (140b/4).]

16 Argument between Henry II and Becket   *page*   140
    (over Constitutions of Clarendon?) with armed
    knights in the background. [From a collection of
    English historical documents. Appears to have
    been written in England in the 14th C. B.M.
    Cott: MS. Claudius. D ii.]

Illustrations

17 Quarrel between Henry and Becket. *page* 142
[Early 14th C. From part of the introductory matter to the *Chronicle of England* by Peter of Langtoft written in French verse. Probably in the time of Edward II (1307–1327) B.M. Royal MS. 20 A. ii 7 v.]

18 Murder of Becket. [*Franciscan Missal I.* *page* 147
French 14th C. Bodleian Douce 313 f.xxi. (158B/20).]

19 Edward touching for the King's Evil *page* 167
and curing the scrofulous woman. [*La Estoire de Saint Aedward le Rei.* Ca. 1250. C. Univ. Lib. Ee. 3. 59. No. 37. p. 38.]

20 St Peter re-crossing Thames after dedi- *page* 171
cating Westminster; instructing fisherman who on right gives best salmon to Bishop Mellitus. [*La Estoire de Saint Aedward le Rei.* Ca. 1250. C. Univ. Lib. Ee. 3.59. No. 31. p. 32.]

21 Cures at the tomb. Pilgrims creeping in *page* 176
and out of the enclosure which permits them to touch the coffin. [*La Estoire de Saint Aedward le Rei.* C. Univ. Lib. Ca. 1250. Ee. 3.59. No. 60. p. 61.]

22 Building the Abbey. [*Vie de Seint Auban.* *page* 186
Matthew Paris. Ca. 1240. MS. Trinity Coll. Dublin. E. i. 40.]

23 Martyrdom of Alban. The executioner *page* 189
catches his own eyes as they fall out, and Alban's soul flies upwards as a haloed bird. [*Vie de Seint Auban.* Matthew Paris. Ca. 1240. MS. Trinity Coll. Dublin. E.i.40.]

24 Invention of St Alban. The discovery of *page* 193
the *ossa martiris* by Offa. Monk praises God; bishop on far right holds his nose. [*Vie de Seint Auban.* Matthew Paris. Ca. 1240. MS. Trinity Coll. Dublin E. i. 40.]

Illustrations

25 Illuminated card showing Rood of   page 206
Bromholm. [Stuck to a page of a late 14th C. or early 15th C. *Hours of Our Lady* Lambeth Palace Library MS. 545. Actual size 5" × 2$\frac{7}{16}$".]

26 Miniature of 'The Holy Rood of Brom-   page 207
holm'. [From Prayer Roll in Latin and English. (Approx. 4' 6" × 7$\frac{1}{2}$") East Anglia late 15th C. Actual size of miniature 5$\frac{1}{4}$" × 5$\frac{1}{4}$".]

27 Initial I. (Iubilate deo) [From *Codex*   page 214
Vossianus, Winchester 10th C. 2nd quarter. MS. Junius 27. Bodleian 146/104.]

ACKNOWLEDGEMENTS

A GREAT PART OF MY ENJOYMENT in writing this book has come from the conversations I have had with all those who have helped me. In the first place of course I am greatly indebted to the Keepers and staff of the Reading Room and the Department of Manuscripts of the British Museum, who, as always, showed unflagging enthusiasm. At the Bodleian Library I am particularly grateful to Dr W. O. Hassall and his staff in the Department of Western Manuscripts for their help in selecting illustrations from their remarkable collection of transparencies. I must thank Dr A. N. L. Munby, the Librarian of King's College, Cambridge for the Roxburghe Club facsimile editions edited by Dr W. R. James which made easier the illustrations to the chapters on St Edward and St Alban, as well as for his stimulating company at Walsingham and Bromholm. Dr William Urry, Cathedral Librarian, Canterbury, Mr Lawrence E. Tanner, C.V.O. Keeper of the Muniments at Westminster Abbey, the reverend Father David of St Winefrede's, Holywell, Dr A. I. Doyle of Durham University Library, and many other college and borough librarians, especially Mr Stanley Horrocks of Reading, were ready always to give every assistance in my research. I appreciate too the permission given by Dawsons of Pall Mall to reproduce a miniature from the Bromholm prayer-roll in their possession as well as that given by Lambeth Palace Library. Finally, and to me most important, I thank my wife for the illustrations to this book, line drawings from Illuminations of mediaeval manuscripts.

Forth, pilgrim, forth! Forth, beste, out of they stal!
Know they contree, look up, thank God of al;
Hold the hye wey, and lat thy gost thee lede:
And trouthe shal delivere, hit is no drede.

GEOFFREY CHAUCER: *Balade de bon conseyl*

I

PILGRIMAGE AND THE MEDIAEVAL MIND

PILGRIMAGE IS AN EVOCATIVE WORD. A vision forms of the lame, the halt and the blind making their painful progress under a lowering or a burning sky encouraged by the prayers of the religious with them, or there come Chaucer's men and women setting forth in that mediaeval springtime, which to us seems like the spring of the world, wiling away the hours of their pilgrimage to Canterbury with tales as entertaining to-day as they were more than five hundred years ago. There pass before the eye the ceremonial processions, the grand ritual accompanying a special festival at a saint's shrine; or, in contrast, the lonely pilgrim with his scallop-shell of quiet and staff of faith in a green and empty landscape.

These pictures are all true but only as projections on the wide screen of the imagination; the figures emerge, cross and disappear in all reality, but there is no beginning nor fulfilment apparent, nor has the picture any depth. Pilgrimage in the middle ages was more than a religious exercise, a custom, a habit, an escape, an entertainment or an act of profound faith. Simply because it contained all these qualities in varying degrees it cannot be viewed in isolation. It interweaves the whole of the social as well as religious life of the people from king to beggar. The different attitudes towards pilgrimage are an expression of the different attitudes towards living, towards every aspect of the temporal and spiritual worlds.

The story of mediaeval pilgrimage in England can only be understood when seen as an integral part of the whole history of the country: sometimes it is the cause, sometimes the outcome, of social or historical events, occasionally it is incidental. The devious veins of chance and intent, folk-lore and religion, which led pilgrims to a variety of shrines are an arterial system for mediaeval man with each shrine a heart. Giving out and being constantly renewed, these carry the whole flow of life.

It seemed to me that to write a straight history or account of pilgrimage would require so many digressions to deal with the innumerable aspects touched by it that the essence would be lost. I have chosen instead to take a number of shrines each of which speaks for itself through its own idiosyncratic history. This prefatory chapter is only to avoid as far as possible the need to interpret some of the attitudes and doctrines which in every case will arise.

To begin with, there are two imponderables: the eternal impulse to pilgrimage and the mediaeval mind which was circumscribed by time. While the idea of pilgrimage is as old as man the act is a parable of the particular pilgrim's life. Whatever the reasons for setting out, they spring commonly from a mixture of curiosity and faith which impels him to search for what may benefit him spiritually, materially, mentally or physically, with the belief that he will find this in some special place or through some special action outside his usual experience. From the very beginning there has been a deeply-rooted belief that certain places are favoured by the Godhead; and this acquires a personal quality from the customary urge to visit places where greatly admired and loved men have lived and died. This was the origin of Christian pilgrimage. Early Christianity had no sanctuaries nor temples; God was to be worshipped in spirit and in truth anywhere. It was the memory of Jesus that made shrines of the places which marked stages of His life. From this, with the development of the Church and its doctrines, grew the veneration of saints and the multiplication of pilgrimage.

The second imponderable, the mediaeval mind, is far more

Pilgrimage and the Mediaeval Mind

difficult to comprehend. It was both the creator and the product of its age, a period itself hard to define but usually taken as between the 5th and the 15th century. There was nothing static about this millennium and the people living in it would certainly not have recognized the compartment in time allocated by historians for their own arguable convenience. The historians borrowed the term 'middle ages' from the humanists of the Renaissance who set a dark interval between the end, for them, of the classical world and their own enlightenment. The first half of the period up to the 10th century was indeed dark, a seemingly losing struggle with barbarism; but the second was an emergence into light, the growth of culture and the arts, and the beginnings of the modern state. The papacy as the most important single authority during those thousand years, if only from the fact of its indestructibility, parallelled this development. After the brilliance of Gregory the Great at the end of the 6th century its power dwindled, and then in the 11th century under Gregory VII gathered a tremendous strength which reached its peak at the end of the 13th.

Consideration of this influence of Rome is vital to a reckoning with the mediaeval mind which believed in the unity of the human race. The possibility of so splendid a concept being fulfilled depended on the unity of Church and State and Gregory VII went far towards building the theocracy. The later disrepute of the papacy must never be allowed to obscure this earlier pursuit of a world which would be a City of God in which nationalist passions had no place.

Here then is a basic assumption of the mediaeval mind: the unity of mankind. To-day this remains an aspiration, recognized by many as man's only hope, but so hedged with argument and qualification that it is largely ignored. The assumption, like almost every mediaeval assumption, was basically religious. An assumption does not admit pastel qualifications, and the colours of the middle ages were violent and partisan. For centuries men lived with the firm belief that the end of the world was near and they also believed without question in the reality of Hell: from the pictures they saw and the descriptions given by the Church they were well acquainted with its inhabitants and the torments they practised. Their minds were therefore continually called upon to cope with situations in which their natural desires caused these beliefs to conflict. The expectancy of life being short, they were impelled to indulge their passions to the full; awareness of the awful fate which was the reward of sin drove them to almost any religious extravagance that might possibly bring redemption.

Violent antithesis is the essence of the middle ages. The contrast between rich and poor was vast, often as great as between men and beasts even though the conduct of both might be similar. For everyone life was precarious; hygiene was non-existent and horrible diseases were widespread; murder and robbery were everyday risks, the poor struggled desperately to survive and the rich were constantly on guard to protect their position or trying to destroy before being destroyed. If overhanging death brought terror of another world and opportunity for pleasure inspired extravagant joy, it was natural for these highly charged emotions to be expressed in everyday affairs: outbursts of rage, weeping, wild abuse or hysterical laughter were publicly indulged and often on most solemn occasions. When in 1176 Roger Archbishop of York strode furious into a legatine council, sat down hard on the Archbishop of Canterbury's lap and was dragged off and jumped on by the clerks present, the papal legate did report it, but only on a technical infringement, not on account of strange behaviour. The absence of half-tones cried out visually in dress, furnishing, caparisoning, in love of show, clamour, fanfares and in the magnificence of the Church's ritual.

The awareness of the ever-present struggle for survival manifested by this emotionalism involved absolute self-interest. In the lay world social consciousness did not exist; and while there might be emotion, with here and there islands of recognizable affection, there were few signs even of family interest except for some material gain. In the latter half of the middle ages good laws introduced were not necessarily effective since the people were still astonishingly savage.

To the present century the middle ages appear romantic or horrifying or both, but it is impossible to gauge the happiness of people living at a time so totally different from the present. There are aspects of to-day which would numb a 12th-century man with horror and nausea, and our bigoted nationalism would seem to him as much out of order as his individual selfishness seems to us. The acceptance of signs and wonders, relics and miracles, by the most highly developed men of their age may seem to us incredible; but they might think it no less strange that the greater part of mankind to-day accepts, just as ignorantly, the manifestations of science. There is of course one cardinal difference. The mediaeval pilgrim set out with the intent to worship, firm in the belief that knowledge and enlightenment could be found only in and through God. In his search to-day man sees in each discovery one more step, not heavenward but in extending the frontiers of knowledge accomplished by his own unassisted will. But even this is not altogether new, since it has much in common with the heresy of Pelagius in the early 5th century who declared 'If I ought, I can.' It was known as the British heresy and in whatever guise has always been popular in England.

It is as misleading to overrate the contrasts as to underrate them. The climate of behaviour, though exotic and violent, resulted from the same human passions as are working to-day. But the expression, the explosively emotional quality of the

middle ages, came from circumstances which are to us almost inconceivable. To understand the integration of pilgrimage in this we must on the one hand learn to feel at ease in the mediaeval atmosphere, and on the other recognize that the impulse to pilgrimage has always been and is the same, namely to discover something that transcends the known yet is within the possibility of experience. The pilgrim should be judged neither by the standards of our own age nor even too much by what is known of his own: rather should he be viewed *sub specie aeternitatis*. He ceases then to be a remote figure wandering on the screen of history.

The first obvious fact about pilgrimage is that it required a focal point. The point being established, and the power of its sanctity proved by miracles, the pilgrims flocked to it. The more pilgrims, the greater the reputation of the shrine and its consequent wealth. It followed that the monastic house in charge of the shrine, often with its accompanying cathedral, grew also in wealth and importance. The greater the house the greater its influence, not only over its dependent parishes and widespread farms, but even through representation at Westminster.

This summary is a simplification but shows what opportunities there were for exploitation. The gullibility of an illiterate and superstitious people, which included the highest in the land, must have been difficult to resist for men who could see how to take advantage of it. So there arose the monkish frauds, the collections of absurd relics, false miracles and indulgences, even mechanical contrivances that brought statues to life. The virtues of saints and the miracles at their shrines were greatly increased, particularly in the 14th century, by a spate of hagiological fictions. Politics, too, played a part; the bones of the ignoble Edward II acquired sanctity through his murder and brought in money enough for the monks to rebuild Gloucester: Thomas earl of Lancaster, a brutal scamp whom the king had executed, was made into a cult in opposition. There was no limit to chicanery.

The conversion of holy places, many of them truly so, to the purpose of money-making may seem to the reader blasphemous. There were churchmen such as the great Odo of Cluny in the 10th century who saw in the multiplication of relics and miracles a great danger to religion. But little was done to stop it. Pilgrimage grew out of a great need of the time. In a world where every man's hand was against another's, and where the chance of material prosperity was limited to a very few, the shrine was a focus of belief. Whatever the special object of the shrine, Our Lady, a saint, or a relic in itself unworthy of veneration, each was only an intercessor. There at the shrine was where God made His power especially manifest. Apart from the spiritual satisfaction, and often the physical healing of the pilgrim, a certain sense of unity with others arose which fulfilled a social need.

It fulfilled this need also in contributing offerings which went into the monasteries' funds. The responsibilities of a monastic house were considerable for they were bound to keep long stretches of road and the neighbouring bridges in repair. This work was always regarded as charitable inasmuch as some of the greatest sufferers in the middle ages were travellers. It was considered a pious work undertaken for the public weal, the continuation of an obligation to which all freeholders had been subject in Anglo-Saxon times. Pilgrims were therefore helping the hosts of other people who were continually on the move. Inclined to think of mediaeval England as a place in which each part was isolated by lack of communications, one is surprised at the speed with which news actually travelled, such as that of the murder of Becket which produced a miracle within twenty-four hours as far away as Berkshire. There was a ceaseless flow of travellers along the main highways: whether it was the Court, which had to move from place to place so that, at the least, it could eat, or, at the other end of the scale, escaped serfs posing as pilgrims, there were wayfarers in plenty.

These people had to be lodged and fed, and here again the monasteries supplied all society. One reads mainly of sumptuous banquets given to visiting royalty and prelates, but the monks cared for the poor, the distressed, the persecuted and the sick. It might be said that they were the only people who did. It is true that with the passage of centuries, when many of the monasteries grew far too rich, their sense of responsibility weakened sometimes to vanishing point. But, as in the case of most aspects of social evolution, their disappearance at the

Dissolution corresponded with their having outlived the need that had brought them into existence. Only in the north, where life was more backward, was there strong feeling among the people over the loss suffered. Not that anything can condone the abominable vandalism with which the Dissolution was carried out, robbing England and the world of some of its finest architecture. Architectural vandalism was rife in the middle ages as well, but then it was indulged in usually to replace the archaic with what was considered more worthy and more beautiful. The Dissolution just destroyed.

It is extraordinary how little attention has been paid to pilgrimage in relation to the rise and fall of monasticism. From the references to the shrines and the pilgrims one might think that they were merely incidental instead of one of the vital factors in the whole religious and social movement of the middle ages. As a rule a shrine was the main reason for a monastery's existence and growth. With increase of wealth from endowments, indults from Rome for appropriations of lands and churches, and gifts of wealthy benefactors, the larger monasteries became less and less dependent on the oblations of pilgrims. Though modern writers may lose sight of the shrines to which these pilgrims came, the religious houses certainly never did. That the shrine was all-important is illustrated by the immensely wealthy Glastonbury showing competitive jealousy in the last years of its glory when abbot Bere constructed a Holy House on the model of Loreto as a counter-attraction to the Holy House of Walsingham.

The 7th General Council, of Nicaea, in 787 forbade under pain of excommunication the consecration of any church without a relic, a regulation that still prevails in the Roman Catholic Church. With a relic a necessity to the very existence of a church, whether or not monastic, it is clear how much dependence was put upon its power to draw people to its shrine. In the first place, unless a church or monastery was well endowed, the offerings of pilgrims might be its main support. There is an outstanding example as late as the early 13th century when Bromholm in Norfolk, a poor Cluniac dependency of seven or eight monks, acquired a piece of the True Cross: within a few years its fame brought Henry III on pilgrimage, and for the 300 years until the Dissolution it remained one of the most popular shrines in England.

The value set upon relics explains the great amount of fraud, forgery of records, inter-monastic feuds and ecclesiastical controversy that runs all through the middle ages. No relic was too incredible, no reduplication of the same relic too impossible. Boccaccio's story of Gabriel's feather left behind in the house after the Annunciation is no more absurd than the stone from which Our Lord ascended and the coals of St Lawrence actually treasured at Durham. There were countless girdles of the Blessed Virgin Mary and at least ten heads of John the Baptist; pieces from the True Cross and its Nails would have sufficed to build a ship; the bones of the saints were distributed in their thousands all over Europe. Added to these were the copies of holy objects presented by pilgrims which in a generation became accepted as the originals.

The superstition of relic-worship, belief in miracles and the material exploitation of pilgrimage have been ridiculed and condemned as good enough reasons for the Dissolution which put an end to the whole business. A large part of the modern attitude has been due to the 17th- and 18th-century writers who, while there was certainly not available the material there is to-day, were clearly not interested in finding anything admirable about the mediaeval church. The legacy of Puritanism is powerful and its prejudice hard to overcome. With the great store of mediaeval literature now easily to hand there is no excuse for continued misunderstanding.

The most important thing to emerge from the writings of the middle ages is the prevailing sense of struggle against circumstance, relief in which could come only from God. The glorification of God was the corollary of this and the glorification might be for the purpose of ensuring survival at the hands of God or in gratitude for His mercies. Anything that contributed to this end was justifiable since there could not conceivably be a higher cause than God's glory which was ultimately for the benefit of all mankind.

A relic, however false, drew pilgrims; the greater the number of pilgrims the more praise to God and the greater the contributions to the shrine: the more beautiful the shrine the more pilgrims still were attracted, bringing even more riches to beautify the monastic church which housed the shrine, and so on, all to the glory of God. The theft of a relic from one religious house by another, as that of Bede's bones from Jarrow by the sacrist of Durham in the early 11th century, could be justified by the greater fitness of the place to which it was being taken to contain it. In the case of Jarrow there was surprisingly no protest, but usually a long wrangle ensued such as that between Ely and St Albans. Sometimes it was found necessary to supply documents that would prove the validity of a relic but there was nothing about the forgery that was considered criminal.

Forgery was a widespread practise in the middle ages. Professor Coulton quotes as an outstanding example the 12th-century lawsuit between the abbeys of Chertsey and Gloucester for the possession of Cardigan priory which was 'important enough to engage the attention of two popes, two princes and a king'. The fabrications were outrageous, particularly on the part of Gloucester. But the notion of literary morality as we know it did not exist, moreover forgers had benefit of clergy and it seems that church courts never took cognizance of forgery. There was the same attitude to forged deeds as to relics; if they were to the good end of enriching the religious house then it was for God's purpose, just as much as the miracle-working properties of a well-advertised shrine redounded to His Glory. It may be said that most mediaeval forgers were absurdly clumsy.

The genuine fear inspired by relics of a saint is shown by the common custom of making litigants swear on such bones rather than on the Gospels. Records of occurrences at the shrines of saints make it clear that the saints were often vindictive, as when St Thomas of Canterbury refused to heal a poor boy who fell asleep at his shrine. Giraldus Cambrensis, who was a very shrewd observer in the 12th century, said there was no doubt that saints were prone to punish those who despised them. There had been too many examples of this for an oath on a relic to be taken lightly. A complementary aspect of relic-worship, the traffic in indulgences for those who went on such pilgrimages, will be dealt with separately.

But in all this what mattered was the objective: if the end was good all means were justified. The strong contemporary criticism in the Church itself of the credulity over miracles and of the proliferation of relics is often overlooked. Even making allowances for the exaggeration and over-statement which were so expressive of the middle ages, the strictures were more to the point than those of modern critics, who often miss it. The point was that there was nothing wrong in itself in the veneration of relics: the relics were of holy men, who, respected when alive, should also be so when dead. If miracles occurred at their shrines and pilgrimage increased, that also was to be approved. But the extent to which all this should be encouraged had been hotly debated in the Church ever since Jerome had replied to the criticisms of Vigilantius in the early 5th century. The middle ages could sustain an argument of this sort in a way which we cannot, very largely because of their fundamental belief. The anxiety of the mediaeval critic was that the pilgrim in his laudable reverence for relics would associate the shrine with material things such as its social or popular reputation, wealth and bodily miracles, rather than realize its spiritual significance.

An incident in 1199 when Bishop Hugh of Lincoln visited Fécamp shows how involved was the attitude towards relics. Hugh, who was later canonized, was not only genuinely holy but highly developed in intellect, practical business sense, courage and ability to deal successfully with men from the king downwards. The monastery of Fécamp had a bone of Mary Magdalene, and the bishop, cutting the wrappings with a penknife borrowed from his chaplain, tried to break a piece off. When he failed in this he bit off two pieces and gave them to the chaplain to keep for him. The monks cried out that they thought he had asked for the relics to worship them, 'and Lo! he has put them between his teeth to gnaw like a dog!' Hugh soothed them by pointing out that they had all only just partaken of the Host and had 'passed Him on into our inward parts'. Why therefore should not members of the saints, when opportunity was offered, be taken thus for honourable conservation?

There are times when the critical approach must be suspended if the sense of the middle ages is to traverse the centuries. St Hugh of Lincoln was by the standards of any period a very great man.

* * *

Indulgences played an important part in pilgrimage. Offered to pilgrims as reward for visiting a shrine, they proved also to be a source of income to the protecting monastery. There has always been some confusion over the meaning of an indulgence although the Church has often essayed a definition. The one usually accepted is that it is 'the remission of the temporal punishment which often remains due to sin after its guilt has been forgiven'. It is not a forgiveness of the guilt nor a permission to sin, nor release from any law or duty such as that of restitution, nor does it secure salvation. It simply remits part or all of a penance imposed for a sin for which absolution has already been received.

One of the strongest causes of misunderstanding was a phrase that arose about the 13th century and subsequently appeared in writs of indulgence: 'indulgentia a culpa et a poena'. For centuries canonists argued about its meaning, and the Church's explanation of it is that the penitent, after receiving absolution from guilt, is afterwards freed from temporal penalty by indulgence. But the origin of the phrase is obscure and it seems that the words took the popular fancy because they were taken to mean that an indulgence freed the sinner from sin as well as from penance. To-day, the uninformed idea is that an indulgence is a piece of paper which forgives all your past sins and saves you from purgatory or even gives licence to behave as you will for the next few weeks; much the same, in fact, as that held by a very large number of the faithful in the middle ages.

The basis for the Church's power to grant indulgences or pardons are the words of Jesus to Peter, 'And I will give unto thee the keys of the kingdom of heaven: and whatsoever thou shalt bind on earth shall be bound in heaven: and whatsoever thou shalt loose on earth shall be loosed in heaven.' By the 7th century, although no doctrine was formulated until much later, the long bodily mortifications were already being commuted. At first it was possible to exchange, say, a year's penance for 300 lashes, with a psalm at the end of each hundred: but, while this got it over quickly, a fine was clearly preferable. Once established, by the Church as acceptable, the custom grew. Alongside it grew the indulgence granted to pilgrims undertaking some specific pilgrimage. The first Plenary indulgence was given to

Pilgrimage and the Mediaeval Mind

those going on the First Crusade in 1095 and ordinary partial indulgences were granted for visiting a shrine. The pope alone grants a Plenary, namely the remission of the entire temporal punishment so that no further expiation is required in Purgatory; a Partial commutes only a certain portion. Pilgrimage became one of the most popular ways of achieving commutation.

A point came when it was realized that a few prayers, a journey, or a cash payment could not seriously compensate for years of Purgatory or worse. Who, after all, was in a position to measure Purgatory and assess its value in terms of psalms, discomfort or money? To overcome this unbalance of payment the theory of the Treasure of the Church was formulated. This appeared first about 1230 with Alexander of Hales, and was confirmed by pope Clement VI in a Bull of 1350 which explained it fully. It received a strong re-affirmation by Pius VI in 1794. The Treasure consists mainly of Christ's merits, which are infinite, and the superfluous merits of the Virgin and saints, superfluous because the saints had earned more than they needed for expiation of their own sins. So there is an accumulation of expiation in the Treasury, 'to be usefully distributed to the faithful through the blessed Peter, keeper of heaven's gate, and his successors'. There is no fear of this Treasure becoming diminished, because the more people there are saved by drawing on it, the more it, in its turn, is augmented by their merits.

With this doctrine a wide field was opened for contribution to the Church, and, to put it into official operation, quaestors, sometimes called pardoners, were sent out with official letters to sell this heavenly surplus to the faithful. Although this doctrine had arisen to fulfil what seemed a genuine religious need its very simplicity made it fair game for rascals. In less than no time there were hordes of false pardoners, sometimes monks or friars, sometimes just travelling salesmen with the gift of the gab. They wandered the country producing rolls of parchment with impressive seals and declaring they had come from Rome and were ready to provide their customers with a pardon for anything.

The late 14th century was ripe for this. Rome had lost a great deal of her prestige, the popes were at Avignon, religiosity was overcoming true religious feeling and superstition was increasing wildly. Pilgrimage had grown as though to satisfy a personal need to compensate for lack of a guiding hand. Although the middle ages were not to be given their official death warrant in England for another 150 years they were already breaking up. Chaucer's Canterbury Tales are generally regarded as the perfect picture of a pilgrimage, but, as will appear later, they are so only of this particular period when pilgrimage, though exceedingly popular, had lost a great deal of its devotional quality. It is significant that by far the most unpleasant character drawn by Chaucer is that of the Pardoner.

Pardoners also frequently carried relics as an added attraction, and the story of one who had 'the sound of King Solomon's bells in a vial' shows how fun was poked at them at the time. On a grave note, Chancellor Gascoigne of Oxford in the 15th century counted the abuse among the Seven Rivers of Babylon beside which the True Church sat down and wept. He deplored the carelessness of sinners to whom pardoners sold indulgences for 2d, for a drink, for a stake at tennis or the hire of a harlot.

But however much this licensed rascality was ridiculed by poets and attacked by many high-principled churchmen besides the famous Wycliff, Huss and Luther, it prospered. Although a great part of the money went into the pouches of charlatans a vast amount went also into the coffers of monasteries and of Rome. A pope might inveigh against the gross abuse of pardons, but they were too large and steady a source of income to be cut off. The most to be done was to warn the credulous and threaten false pardoners with awful punishments, but neither expedient was effective. The official office of pardoner was abolished in 1562 by the Council of Trent. The doctrine of Indulgences remains, and because payment for them is now only in good works and prayer they are easily obtained and there is less chance for the old abuses.

It should be always borne in mind that what applies to the understanding of indulgences applies to all aspects of the middle ages in that, apart from official records, the only information of real value lies in contemporary writings. In these a multiplication of abuses and the growing worldliness of religion is continually exposed. The question was widely asked why, if

Pilgrimage and the Mediaeval Mind

heaven could be bought as easily with money as by a life of devotion, one should trouble to be devout. Finally, when the Reformation came, every possible scandal which could be used against the monasteries was unearthed. But to accept all this as a picture of mediaeval religious life as a whole would be foolish. Then, as now, publicity was given to scandals and to attacks on misbehaviour, which might be justified or merely scurrilous, because they had news value. Piety, kindness, peace, generosity and virtue are not news, and never have been. Not only in the middle ages, but throughout all periods of history it is the seamy side of life that is mainly recorded. To-day, it would be far more difficult to discover from our writings the goodness in our contemporary world than the evil of which we write *ad nauseam*. It is essential to approach the study of life in the middle ages with an open mind and to appreciate that, whatever its backslidings, the Church was the one power for good and comfort for ordinary men.

The eight pilgrimages I have chosen vary in fame. Though all of them were drawing thousands of pilgrims over more or less the same period, each has a strongly individual character. Between them, because of this individuality, they seem able to answer a wide range of questions. The order in which they are placed is deliberate.

The first, St Winefrede of Holywell, is a prototype of pilgrimage. It was very simple in origin, a healing well and chapel dedicated to a Celtic maiden saved from rape and restored to life. For 1300 years it has remained simple, and it is the only shrine in the British Isles to have to this day a continuous record of pilgrimage which even the Reformation did not break.

Glastonbury is perhaps the most complex of all. Its beginnings were more legendary even than Holywell and were pagan in origin. It is placed here because it contained in itself almost every element that went to the creation of pilgrimages everywhere. After the romance and tragedy of Glastonbury, nothing can seem strange.

Durham emerges from Celtic twilight into reality as the shrine of the great northern saint, Cuthbert. The wealth brought by the fame of this strong and virtuous man, most gentle of saints, made his successors into princes palatine of the Church.

The Holy House of Walsingham was the shrine most beloved of Englishmen, the 11th-century vision of a Norfolk gentlewoman translated into wood and stone. There is less of mysticism here and more of fashion and poetry, and latterly of superstition. It marks a step towards the style of Canterbury which at one time it came near to rivalling.

The shrine of St Thomas of Canterbury, the most famous in England and among the greatest in Christendom, was semi-political. Its history shows more vividly than any other the interweaving of pilgrimage with the social and political development of the country.

Following these five, told with a good deal of detail, are three which, though they did not attract so many pilgrims, acquired great fame on account of special characteristics.

Westminster, the shrine of Edward the Confessor whose saintliness was largely invented, was, and has remained, wholly mystical with its god-king entombed at the heart of his people's capital.

St Albans' great fame was based on England's protomartyr put to death for protecting a Christian missionary whose name, Amphibalus, means in Greek a cloak and who may have been no more than that. Worldly rich, near to the Court, its history, however fascinating, does it little religious credit.

Finally Bromholm, emerging from obscurity to fantastic popularity because a rascal chaplain of Baldwin, first Latin Emperor of the East, stole his relic of the True Cross and fled across Europe to give it to the small Cluniac house there after failing to sell it elsewhere. Long in total ruin and remembered by few, Bromholm holds in its small compass the very essence of the mediaeval spirit. It also brings into question the critical comment: 'La vraie religion du moyen age, il ne faut pas s'y tromper, c'est le culte des reliques.'

There is one general question which will arise in the case of all English shrines. Why are there so few records of individual pilgrimages? There are countless brief references to them, collected volumes of miracles giving the names of the people to whom they occurred and feretory rolls of monastic houses showing the contributions at the shrine. The bibliography at

Pilgrimage and the Mediaeval Mind

the end of each of the following chapters shows what a great deal of this has survived the centuries, but no complete diary of a pilgrimage in England has yet come to light.

The answer to this puzzle, I believe, is twofold. First, by far the larger number of pilgrims could not write. Literacy until well into the 13th century was for the most part confined to the Church or learned through the schools of a monastic house. The comparative illiteracy of the lay upper class was due mainly to its members being able to summon a clerk if the need to read or write arose. The nickname of 'clerk' given to Henry I was no compliment. This form of snobbery has died hard. Secondly, those who could write, and in the later middle ages there were a great many educated pilgrims, saw no reason to do so. There was nothing out of the ordinary in going on a pilgrimage, it was a part of the everyday scene. To go to Jerusalem, to Rome, to Compostella, that was outstanding, it warranted a detailed diary; not so a journey to a native holy place. The holy places of England must therefore speak their own histories of pilgrimage.

11

SAINT WINEFREDE OF HOLYWELL

THE HILLS RISE SHARPLY from the strip of marsh bordering the west side of the Dee estuary; the railway from Chester to the north coast of Wales follows the edge of the marsh, and at intervals there are foundries and factories. But the tumbled highlands are all fields and woods and small farmsteads, remote and serene and with a vast view over the water to the Wirral peninsula and westward to the vale of Clwyd and Snowdon. Near the broadest part of the estuary, jumbling down a spur of a hill, is the little town of Holywell, hardly bigger than a village but with textile mills on the stream which has its spring in a small ravine to the side of one of the steep streets. The stream pours on down by the ruins of 12th-century Basingwerk Abbey on the edge of the marsh a mile below and so into the Dee.

It is 1300 years since the spring bubbling from the hillside became the holy well of Winefrede. Near-by Offa's Dyke was new when the saint lived here where the feet of pilgrims still wear the stones a little thinner every year. The way to it is marked by the stones of the pilgrims' road from the south, from the Roman way to Strata Florida and St David's, and from the border towns of Chester and Shrewsbury by which the English came.

So precipitous is the hillside that the entrances to the well

Saint Winefrede of Holywell

and to the 15th-century chapel built over it are on greatly different levels. Only the south wall of the chapel rests on the earth, the main body of it stands out on twenty-foot pillars, sheltering beneath it the well and its ambulatory. The weight is taken by two ranges of fan-vaulting; in the centre the fans spring from slender columns around the basin with their ribs meeting in a ring of leaves around a pendant over the well; outward from these columns the ribs fan towards bosses above the ambulatory where they meet the ribs curving from the pilasters on the outer wall. The bosses bear the arms of Stanleys, Pennants, the House of Aragon, of an unknown abbot and the Tudor rose: one bears the profiles of Margaret Beaufort and her husband, the earl of Derby, others are decorative or fantastic.

The spring of the well flows first into a small basin with steps leading down at either end. The pilgrim goes first to this before entering the long pool in the garden outside the ambulatory. Just submerged in the pool is the stone on which St Beuno stood when he gave his parting instructions to Winefrede. The pilgrims kneel on it to pray before coming out of the water. By the east side of the tall archway of the ambulatory opening on the pool is a niche with a statue of the saint, replacing the one that stood in the earlier building clothed in the gown of russet velvet brought by Isabel, countess of Warwick, in 1439. The well's basin has a stone inscribed 1683, when the chapel was restored by James II's queen, Mary of Modena. On the columns are countless *graffiti* made by pilgrims declaring their cures.

Along the north side of the chapel is a deep recess with windows overlooking the pool. The pentagonal apse at the east end has five tall and narrow windows, and the whole is beautifully proportioned. One of the charms of this simple, Perpendicular building is the sculpture: around the exterior, just below the roof-line, is a frieze depicting all kinds of little animals which appear, too, in the interstices of the arches or doorways and windows where they alternate with the Tudor rose, the Welsh dragon and heraldic devices. It is being restored now, and though all the damage done by 17th-century vandals cannot be made good, it appears a small jewel of the 15th century.

Saint Winefrede of Holywell

How was it that a spring bubbling from the wild north Welsh hills in the 7th century came to be so enclosed, and what extraordinary power of saintliness could have brought about more than a millennium of pilgrimage?

'I would not choose such a Saint as Wenefrede of whose very being, there is no Manner of Certainty left to us. I would not pray to one, of whom I find no Mention made for full 500 Years, after the Time wherein she is said to have lived. I would not go on a Pilgrimage to a Saint's Well, whose History is only told by a poor Monk, that lived so long after her as 500 Years . . .'

So, Dr William Fleetwood in 1713 writing his *Life and Miracles of St Wenefrede*[1] dismisses one of the most enduring of British saints. No one man has written at such length nor gone into such detail to confute earlier authorities. He was greatly provoked: as an English scholar of Eton and King's, a staunch Hanoverian, friend of Queen Anne and Bishop of St Asaph, he found most distasteful the pilgrimage to St Winefrede's well in his diocese. Not only was he learned, of high repute and thorough in his research, he was also a fascinating writer; his long polemic provided a store of material for anyone who might want to look further. No one at the time seems to have answered back, but the fact that so leading a divine of the 18th century should have taken all this trouble emphasizes the peculiarity of this place, which, unlike others more historically famous, is the only shrine with an unbroken record to this day of pilgrimage.

The bishop's assault was based on Robert of Shrewsbury's *Life of Winefrede*[2] and on the 12th-century manuscript[3] in the collection of the Elizabethan, Sir Robert Cotton, whose library had recently been given to the nation. He makes fun of the note which looks like 16th-century handwriting on this manuscript 'per Elerium Brittanum Monachum Ano 660 aut Robertum Salopientem ano 1140'. No one, he says, has ever heard of a monk called Elerius so he could not have written it. The whole thing is nonsense. John of Tinmouth abbreviated the story in 1366 and John Capgrave picked it up and was in turn abbreviated by a Carthusian, Surius, and again by a German monk: the story could also be found in *Old English Rhime* three or four hundred years old: then in 1635 a Jesuit, John Falconer[4], had made a new translation of Robert of

Saint Winefrede of Holywell

Shrewsbury which became the material for Father Metcalfe's version of 1712[5]. This last was the special cause of the bishop's annoyance since it had a large circulation.

But his observations on 'The Editor's Preface to the Devout Pilgrim' in this work do make some shrewd points: there is no mention, he says, of Holywell in Domesday Book, and it is odd that Giraldus Cambrensis[6] is silent on the subject though he was a great gossip and stayed at the neighbouring monastery of Basingwerk on his crusading circuit of Wales with Baldwin, archbishop of Canterbury in 1188; he also quotes a British Calendarium from the Cotton Library, probably of about 1153, in which there is no mention of the saints Winefrede, Beuno or Elerius. Bishop Fleetwood of course knew all about St Beuno, a leading figure of Celtic Christianity whose greatest work was done in what had become the bishop's diocese; he also did not dwell on Caxton's *Life*[7] of the saint, written for the countess of Richmond, Henry VII's mother, in 1485. But, read without knowledge of these and other omissions of which the bishop was very well aware, his treatise strongly supported the view that the cult of St Winefrede was a monkish post-Conquest fabrication.

To approach the source one must take a journey backwards in time to the Age of Saints, to a time of Welsh heroes, of warring princes, before Wales was first unified by Roderick the Great in the 9th century, was divided by his sons and became one again under the lordship of the house of Gwynedd in the north. It was in the north that Winefrede was born and to the north that the saint Beuno came in the 7th century, and their story, as written by an unknown monk of the 12th century and afterwards translated variously[8], is briefly as follows.

There was in Tegeingle near the mouth of the river Dee a man of some standing named Tewyth ap Eylud, whose wife, Wenlo, was Beuno's sister; and to him there came one day Beuno asking if he might build a church on near-by land. While the work on the church went forward, Beuno lodged with Tewyth who commended to his instruction his only daughter, Winefrede. Winefrede soon resolved to dedicate her virginity to Christ, and to this her devout parents readily agreed. One Sunday, when all in the house but Winefrede had gone to the church, the young prince, Caradoc, thirsty from hunting, came to the house intent on seducing her. She slipped away and ran

Saint Winefrede of Holywell

for the church; but the prince gave chase on his horse, 'and overtaketh the innocent lambe, and he renewing his filthie suite, but she denying him, affirming that she was ioyned unto Christ, wherefore she could not, neither would ever couple herself with man, the furious youth raging at her answer, with his sword cuttes of her head: which falling to the earth, deserued of god to haue a fountaine of water to spring in the place, which to this day continueth . . .'

The head rolled on down the hill to the church, and, all coming out, Beuno cursed Caradoc so that he fell dead, his body vanishing 'as though it had so slonck into hell with the soule thereof'. Beuno lifted the head, wrapped it in his cloak and returned to Mass, asking the people to help him with their prayers for Winefrede. He then joined the head to her body and she at once revived, ever afterwards bearing only a red threadlike mark around her throat. Where her head had fallen the stones surrounding the fountain were stained forever with her blood, and the blood falling in the water coloured also the moss that grows there and which has the perfume of frankincense, though some say of violets.

Winefrede lived on for fifteen years. When Beuno left to continue his work he told her that the stones would never lose the marks of her blood, and that those coming to her fountain or well to ask her aid should receive it at most by the third time of asking. For her part she must send to him each year a cloak of her own weaving, putting it in the stream and leaving to God's grace its safe journey to wherever he might be. When, after some eight years, he died, Winefrede went into the mountains to Gwytherin near the source of the river Elwy. Some say that Elerius gave his name to that river and founded a monastery at Clwyd of which his mother Theonia was abbess, and that Winefrede came there and eventually succeeded her. Others say that a council of bishops ordered that solitaries be joined in one body and a convent was founded at Holywell by Winefrede's fountain, and here she lived. All agree however that she died at Gwytherin, somewhere about the year 660. Countless miracles occurred through the centuries at her well. 'Explicit una sancta Wenefrede virgine martyris. Incipiunt miracula eidem.'

Attempts have been made to rationalize this legend. It has been suggested[9] that Caradoc merely stabbed Winefrede in the neck so that she bled but soon recovered, and that his disappearance was another way of saying that he made off at high speed when Beuno appeared, that alleged decapitation was popular with saints and bubbling springs frequent. Leland confirms the identity of Elerius, Montalembert supports the basic truth of the story. There is a theory that there were two Winefredes, one a real virgin-martyr, the other a nun who lived later and became associated with the first, a confusion of two persons not uncommon in the early middle ages.

The amount of truth in the legend is not very important. What matters is that at some time in the 7th century something of the kind occurred in a valley near the estuary of the Dee which made a lasting impression. Of the hundreds of thousands who have gone there as pilgrims in the last thirteen centuries how many have known more than the naïve story of the saint or thought to question it? Most have been content that there was a place where a miracle of great repute had happened: given faith in the power of the tutelary saint to intercede with God who had produced the first miracle, the curative quality of the well's water was sure. So Holywell appears to have been a place for pilgrims seeking physical help rather than a pilgrimage of penance or pure devotion, however much the hope of healing presupposes a state of spiritual grace in the pilgrim to be blessed with the miracle.

Though the work of Christianizing Britain had begun some

three centuries earlier, St Augustine and Gregory the Great share the title of Apostle of the English. They died in 604, at the beginning of the century when Beuno and Winefrede were born, and when pagan belief was far more widespread than the new faith. The reverence in the primitive mind for water is timeless: without water life cannot exist, fertility springs from it, its power to revive is visible and sure. Gregory, in his wisdom, instructed his missionaries not to root out the old beliefs but rather take what was in them adaptable to Christianity and turn them to good account.[10] Water had always been an emblem of purity, and the blessing of a well in the name of Christ gave it new and even greater virtue. So the well, of which the spring came mysteriously from the underworld and was guarded by a numinous woman with the power to heal, became a place of Christian pilgrimage. The story of Winefrede contains all the elements for the making of a saint and of a holy place in that misty borderland not only of England and Wales but of paganism and Christianity.

Some three miles from Holywell by the Llanasa road stands a monolithic slab-cross eleven feet high, the Maen Achwynfan. Its massive shaft tapers slightly to a ring head embossed with a cruciform device. Such a head is found only in Anglesey and Flint and marks the monument as Anglo-Viking;[11] the decoration elaborately carved on all four faces is related to some Northumbrian crosses and is of the 10th or 11th century, since only the late crosses showed this Scandinavian influence. Here again, on one of the great Christian monuments, is pagan symbolism. On the lowest quartering of the face of the shaft, surrounded by looped knotwork, is a figure with a phallus apparently like that carried in Bacchic processions. Vertically, on the left side of the shaft and at the head of a hunting scene is a similar figure. Unlike the Celtic Christian monuments of earlier centuries which were usually tombstones and widely distributed, the later crosses appear to have been set up close to some centre of religion. Very few of them are inscribed, and this one near Holywell has nothing on it to show why it was put there. There was no monastery near by until about 1130, but Holywell was there, the beginning and end of a road from north to south[12], linking it with St David's, the other great centre of pilgrimage. There is no more than this circumstantial evidence and the symbolic sculpture on the cross to associate the cross with the shrine, but after a thousand years no other reason has been found for the erection of this mute monolith.

Beuno had been dead more than two centuries before this cross appeared, gone to join the host of saintly men buried on Bardsey Island. No Welsh saint, not even St David, has inspired such pilgrimage as St Winefrede, and no one did a greater work of Christianizing his people than Beuno who led her to sainthood. In writing of these two the island of Bardsey cannot be passed by. It is the very core of Celtic-Christian mysticism, symbolizing the grave yet imaginative quality of Welsh Catholicism. It is also one of the many western isles associated with the idea of the Hesperides. The magic ring of the Lady of the Fountain[13], together with the rest of the thirteen Rarities of Kingly Regalia went with Merlin into the House of Glass on the island in the 5th or 6th century. The cult of St Winefrede, which became highly esteemed in Rome, had its roots in a world where men and spirits easily communed.

Seen from the point above Aberdaron at the northern tip of Cardigan Bay, this Ynys Enlli, called Isle of the Currents because of the race between itself and the mainland, has an air of absolute remoteness. Its isolation and its deep haven appealed to the imagination and the practical sense of the early fathers. At some time in the dark 5th century when the Roman legions left and the country was ravaged, Bardsey became a place of Christian refuge. In the next century, it seems that an abbey was founded by Cadfan, a Breton saint: the first abbot was Laudatus, to whom Beuno was 'by the motherside cosingerman'. From then its renown grew. St Dubritius, predecessor of St David, died there in 612, and the next year the monks who survived the massacre by Ethelfride after the battle of Chester fled to Bardsey. The island became the Road to Heaven; to be buried there was the wish of all men of religious life. A time came when all the great English abbeys were sending their venerated dead to this Gate of Paradise, and by the late middle ages it is said that 20,000 had been buried there. Nearly four acres of the small island were filled with close-set graves; for many people it had become equal to Rome with its catacombs of saints. The abbey remained till the Dissolution without apparently ever having been assimilated to the English black monks or canons.[14] To-day, but for a few farms and some small ruins, there remains only the cemetery of saints, the stones turned sometimes by a deep plough.

The most important of Beuno's communities, founded a century after Bardsey, was at Clynnog Fawr, the chief stopping-place for pilgrims to Bardsey in later years and ranking with the monastery of Bangor. The present church is pure early 16th-century Perpendicular, its body square in form, its stone unadorned and all filled with sea-light. It has the sense of space and serenity that pervades some remote Italian churches such as Benedictine Fossacesia on its Adriatic cliff.

Of Holywell, on the road through Tegeingel to the pilgrim's way into Caernarvon to Bardsey, it is hard to trace any written historical mention earlier than the 11th century. Wales then was unified in her struggle for independence of the Normans; though the jealousy of the princes continued they had learned wisdom and for this the centuries of Celtic monasticism, which had grown in strength after the Romans had left, was largely responsible. But in 1093 the countess of Chester granted the holy well and chapel to the Abbey of St Werburgh founded that year at Chester;[15] and a further Norman link came in 1115 when the countess's son, the earl of Chester, went on a pilgrimage to Holywell on his return from education in Normandy. On the way he was attacked by the Welsh and took refuge in Basingwerk. He prayed to the saint Winefrede who raised sands between Flint and Wirral in the Dee estuary, ever since called Constable's Sands, over which he passed to safety.

At this point history takes over. Basingwerk is only a mile or so from Holywell and the castle there was fortified by the Normans though founded no one knows how long before. It stood near the end of Wat's Dyke which is of the 8th century, so this fort of Bassa's people was very old. The prodigious adventurer-poet, Thomas Churchyard, 'grandmother to our grandiloquentist poets at this present', who was born midway in Henry VIII's reign and outlived Elizabeth, said of this,

> Within two myles, there is a famous thyng
> Cal'de *Offaes Dyke* that reacheth farre in length:
> All kind of ware the Danes might thether bring,
> It was free ground, and cal'de the Britaines strength,
> Wats Dyke likewise, about the same was set . . .[16]

St Winefrede's well was on this neutral ground, and what pilgrimage went on there must have been risky. Basingwerk castle was destroyed in Stephen's reign, but Henry II rebuilt it and also established a house of Templars to protect pilgrims to Holywell. Then, only eight years later, in 1165, the Welsh under Owain Gwynedd levelled the castle and it never rose again.

Meanwhile, some time in 1131 or a little after,[17] monks of Savigny came to Basingwerk, and like the eleven other abbeys of that congregation in England they amalgamated with the Cistercians in 1147 to become the White Monks. From the partly Saxon ruins of the abbey at the bottom of Holywell hill, there must have been an earlier monastic cell. The Welsh having reasserted themselves, David ap Llewelyn granted Holywell to Basingwerk in 1240, ignoring the countess of Chester's earlier grant to St Werburgh's. Thereafter Basingwerk held the well and the administration of the pilgrimage until 1538 when the monastery was dissolved. The wealth it attained during 300 years of close association with the shrine is evidence of the quantity of pilgrims. In 1427 pope Martin V furnished Basingwerk with indulgences which could be bought by pilgrims: these must have brought in a large income, for, in the time of Edward IV, abbot Thomas was being glorified by the bards Owain and Tudur Aled for the beauty of his works, his water- and wind-mills, and his vast hospitality. Records show that distinguished visitors were entertained on a scale comparable to the greatest monastic houses of England.

The 18th-century chronicler, Pennant, descendant of the last abbot, Nicholas, says that in his time the church was almost gone, though the refectory was little damaged; the chapel of the Knights Templar was a spacious building with long, narrow, pointed windows and slender, elegant pilasters.[18] To-day, the ruins barely suggest the outlines of this once splendid place.

It is remarkable that Holywell never had a relic of its patron saint. St Winefrede's remains were at Gwytherin in the mountains where she died, until they were translated to Shrewsbury in 1138 and she became that town's patron saint. For the original account of this translation one must turn to Robert of Shrewsbury in 1140.[19]

Saint Winefrede of Holywell

The rich abbey of St Peter and St Paul in Shrewsbury was founded by Roger de Montgomery at the end of the 11th century. It came about that some years later a monk of the abbey fell sick and was about to die. A vision came to the sub-prior that a mass should be offered in the chapel at St Winefrede's Well: the mass was accordingly celebrated and the monk recovered. So it was in the reign of Stephen that prior Robert and Richard, an eminent monk, were deputed by the abbot Herbert to acquire the relics. They sent word to the bishop of Bangor who referred them to the principal lord of the area of Gwytherin, and this lord said he was delighted that the body should be translated to a place where it would be more honoured. But when the mission left him it met a man near Gwytherin who said that the local inhabitants were resolved to stop their saint's body being carried off by strangers. They then said Matins after which the prior fell asleep and dreamed that a former abbot of Shrewsbury told him that with God's assistance they would defeat those who opposed them. So they set off again, and on being met at Gwytherin by the parish priest, they humbly asked him for the relics. He agreed easily, for he also had had a vision: the previous Easter a beautiful young man had come to tell him that he must assist those who came to take the saint's body. He now ordered all the people to come to the church and told them what he proposed to do. The prior addressed them and said that he had come by divine appointment; the Virgin, having manifested her wish, would be very much displeased if it were not carried out. One man did protest at the removal of the saint, but it turned out that he was only counting on a bribe.

Dr Fleetwood, of course, makes great game of this.[20] All this talk about visions, and the whole thing settled by bribery! But the story rings true and is wholly in accordance with the mediaeval mind. It has the characteristics of a great number of cases relating to relics, an intense and deeply felt religious fervour combined with absolute unscrupulousness in attaining the object of veneration. It cannot be dismissed simply on the grounds that the monks knew the relics would be a fine source of income for their abbey church. Their church had been raised to the glory of God, and they believed their visions were for the furtherance of this holy aim.

Saint Winefrede of Holywell

Notice was sent ahead to Shrewsbury of the prior's success, and on arrival at the town the saint's body was first placed in St Giles, while arrangements were made for a procession. The procession was by every account a superb one, accompanied by all the brilliant colour, emotion, display and immense clamour and disregard for order with which the 12th century celebrated a religious occasion. The body was laid at last in the Benedictine abbey, torrential rain having fallen everywhere but on the route of the procession. From the very moment of translation miracles occurred at the abbey shrine. The first seems to have been one referred to in a sermon delivered on the feast of St Winefrede in 1401.[21] A dumb man falling into a trance at the translation was told by St Winefrede to drink of the water her bones had been washed in: on his coming to, the water was brought 'and when he had dronke of the water, he was as whole as anie fishe.'

The fame of the saint was greatly increased by her establishment in a town of importance. It became the headquarters of Edward I, and in 1283 David, the last native prince of Wales, was condemned to death by parliament held there. Shrewsbury was then the most important town bordering north Wales and pilgrims were drawn to the shrine from all over England. The saint's reputation was confirmed in 1398 when archbishop Walden of Canterbury ordered her feast on November 3rd to be kept with Nine Lessons in the province of Canterbury.[22] Greater splendour was added by Henry Chichele who ordained that the feast should be a double one, *cum regimine chori*.

There is a curious coincidence in this action of Chichele and that of pope Martin V, who, it will be recalled, granted to Basingwerk the right to sell indulgences to pilgrims to Holywell. Though agreeing in honouring the saint, the two men quarrelled viciously with each other. Chichele, famous for his educational foundations, particularly that of All Souls College at Oxford, was more of a lawyer and a diplomatist than a great churchman, though he once showed his regard for pilgrimage to saints by causing an excommunicated priest to be burned for declaring that prayers should be addressed only to God. His clash with Martin V came soon after Henry V's death when he appointed a jubilee in 1420 at Canterbury to celebrate the 250th anniversary of St Thomas's murder, to be carried out on the same lines as jubilees held in Rome. The pope was furious and denounced it

Saint Winefrede of Holywell

as being in opposition to the Apostolic See 'to whom alone so great a faculty has been granted by God'.[23]

Here again is one of the sublime contradictions of the age. Martin V readily granted Basingwerk authority to sell indulgences, but was in a righteous rage when the archbishop of Canterbury announced a St Thomas jubilee. It is true that the practical implications are as obvious to-day as they were then: in the case of Basingwerk and the pilgrims to Holywell the influence of Rome was being extended together with a useful profit, in that of Canterbury it was being curtailed inasmuch as the archbishop was acting independently and would make a very good thing out of it for himself. But there was a far bigger issue, the questioning of papal supremacy and the effect of the Schism on the whole fabric of the western Church. Compared with the two preceding centuries, the 14th and 15th were an age of scepticism. While the Church with its immense wealth and holding most of the chief positions of State appeared never to have been so strong, its hold on the minds of men had weakened.

This violent quarrel over pilgrimage is simply one of the many pointers to the remarkable fact that pilgrimage increased as the spiritual influence of the Church declined.

Meanwhile, in the abbey church of Shrewsbury, every

honour was paid to St Winefrede. No detailed description of the shrine seems to exist, though from incidental references it must have been a rich one: for example William Beauchamp, earl of Warwick, commissioned by his will in 1437 a gold statuette of himself weighing 20 lbs to adorn it. All that remains of the shrine now is a piece of sculpture some 2½ feet high by 3 wide showing St Winefrede with St John the Baptist on her right and St Beuno on her left. It stands at the west end under one of the Norman arches separating the nave from the north aisle, tacked on to a shoddy reconstruction of the shrine unworthy of this rose-coloured yet sombre abbey. Across the road to the south – the main London road cut by Thomas Telford in 1836 having destroyed what remained of the dormitory, cloisters and chapter house – stands the huge stone pulpit of the vanished refectory. The dome roof supported by arches has on its centre boss a representation of the Crucifixion with the Virgin Mary and St John at the foot of the Cross; on two of the four panels on the sides of this pulpit are sculptured St Winefrede and St Beuno, the others picturing the Annunciation and the saints Peter and Paul.

In 1486 the Guild of St Winefrede presented the abbey with a new bell, and the occasion was conducted with elaborate ceremony. The bell, being brought to the abbey church, was first named and baptized in the name of the Father. Then fine garments were brought in which the bell was clothed and invited to a great feast at which the abbey received presents on behalf of the bell. All concluded, the bell was blessed, receiving the virtue that thereafter would divert thunderbolts and evil spirits. On it was inscribed:

> Sancta Wynefrida, Deo nos commendare memento
> Ut pietate sua, nos servet ab hoste cruente.

and:

> Protege pura pia quos convoco Virgo Maria.

The guild's seal is in the church; the centre piece is of Caradoc cutting off Winefrede's head with above a Greek cross between the initials of abbot Thomas Mynde, the founder. Below are the keys of St Peter and the sword of St Paul, crossed.

The abbey's wealth and position must have made it an

attractive rival to Holywell, particularly in the early years after the translation. But whether or no Holywell lost in attendance, its very survival is remarkable. Centuries before, in 787, the 7th General Council, of Nicaea, forbade under pain of excommunication the consecration of churches without relics, and Holywell had never had a relic of any kind and did not have one until the 19th century. At the Dissolution, all that was found after the desecration of St Winefrede's shrine at Shrewsbury was a part of one finger. This was given to the care of the Marchioness of Powis and remained at Powis Castle until the end of the 17th century when it was sent for greater safety to the English College in Rome. It was not brought back to England until 1852 when it was divided between Holywell and Shrewsbury cathedral. Yet a pope had no hesitation in granting the right to indulgences at the original chapel at Holywell, and no question was raised when the now existing chapel was built at the turn of the 15th century.

It was not only the common people who continued to go on pilgrimage to Holywell. Early in 1416, says Adam of Usk, 'the king with great reverence went on foot in pilgrimage from Shrewsbury to St Winifred's well in North Wales.'[24] Though this fascinating reporter, lawyer, politician, pluralist and one-time papal auditor under Boniface IX was inclined to 'skimble-skamble stuff' there is no reason why he should have invented Henry V's fifty-mile walk. The account follows that of the celebrations in London of the victories of Harfleur and Agincourt, the suggestion being that the pilgrimage to Holywell was to give thanks. In the same breath Adam refers to the recent death of the old adversary, Owen Glendower. Edward IV's subsequent visit to Holywell was sung by the bard Tudur Aled, and Richard III gave an annuity of ten marks to Basingwerk to maintain a priest at the Well. Aesthetically the finest contribution was made by the mother of Richard's successor, Henry VII, the first Tudor.

There seems to be no exact record of the date when Margaret Beaufort built the existing chapel over the Well. The antiquary Thomas Hearne notes in his diary of Friday, January 19th, 1733, that it was said that the workmen who built this chapel also built Henry VII's at Westminster which was begun in 1503.[25] Though the chapel at Westminster had been designed as a

Saint Winefrede of Holywell

shrine for the murdered Henry VI, whose cult had already begun though successive popes declined to canonize him, Henry VII arranged for his own entombment there. He invited Torrigiano from Florence[26] to make his tomb, which, though begun in his lifetime, was not finished until several years after his death. Among the figures looking down on it is one of St Winefrede, owing no doubt to Henry's respect for his mother's devotion to the saint.

While it is possible that the same workmen did build the two chapels, Pennant argues that the one at Holywell must have been completed before 1495 because among the bosses of the vaulting over the well are the arms of Sir William Stanley and of his wife Elizabeth Hopton. As Stanley was executed for treason in 1495, it was unlikely that they would have been put there after that. But the fact that his arms and others of the same house, stag's head, eagle's claw and the three legs of the Isle of Man, adorn the vaulting is due to Margaret Beaufort having married for the third time, and as his second wife, Thomas, Lord Stanley, William's brother, in 1482. Thomas was rewarded for his skilful time-serving by being created earl of Derby by Henry VII in 1485 after Bosworth. As husband of the king's mother, even his brother's later treason had no effect

on his career. The arms of Katharine of Aragon, three pomegranates on a shield surmounted by a crown, are also in the vaulting, suggesting that she too was a benefactor. Catherine was born in 1485 and did not come to England till 1501 to marry first Arthur, prince of Wales, and then Henry VIII. She went with Arthur almost at once to Wales where the poor young man died within a few months. They were both only sixteen. So the answer may be that the chapel was started sometime before 1495 and finished about 1502, a little before Henry's chapel at Westminster was begun. Margaret, the mother of the first Tudor, died in 1509, outliving him by three months. 'All England for her death had cause for weeping', said Bishop John Fisher of Rochester. Christ's and St John's colleges at Cambridge are her other monuments in stone.

AFTER THE REFORMATION

Since Margaret Beaufort's chapel came to replace the one of which, tantalizingly, no recorded description has been found, the history of the Well has not had the vivid colour of earlier years. The dramatic quality of the middle ages when men expressed their joy or sorrow with sudden and violent intensity, when the contrast between riches and wretchedness, health and incurable sickness, deep piety and appalling cruelty made Heaven and Hell real and immanent not imaginary concepts, passed. Passed, too, were Tudur Aled and still greater bards singing the glory of Basingwerk and the virtues of the Saint, the border conflicts, the pilgrim bringing rich gifts to the shrine that glowed in a galaxy of candles. Bards there were, such as Byrsinsia of the 17th century, still to sing though with less golden voices; yet, what followed the earlier brilliance was in some ways more significant of the hold which the cult of St Winefrede had established. In former years it had been a part of a wholly Catholic English religious life, and so taken for granted: from now on it was to survive, at times even to flourish, in spite of the forces of kings, parliaments and the new church to destroy it.

Margaret Beaufort died in 1509, the year her grandson Henry VIII ascended the throne: and within thirty years the Defender of the Faith had changed the religious face of England. With the Dissolution, the protector monastery of Basingwerk fell with all the rest into ruins: the last abbot, Nicholas Pennant, more fortunate than some, or perhaps more foreseeing, retired to found a family from which the 18th-century antiquary was descended. The shrine of St Winefrede at Shrewsbury Abbey was desecrated; pilgrimage there perforce ceased, iconoclasm swept through the monasteries, and severe penalties were imposed on those who followed the old ways. But pilgrimage to Holywell continued. There is no record of such persistence at any other shrine in England.

In the first place Henry VIII did not permit the destruction of his grandmother's chapel. That this had anything to do with sentiment seems unlikely; the offerings at the Well were too considerable for the place to be closed down if the contributions could be diverted. So the right to collect the revenue was leased to a William Holcroft, a staunch anti-papist who complained of the trouble he had.[27] 'Bold Catholics' would come along with collecting-boxes and tell the pilgrims not to give their alms to Holcroft as they would only go to the king and do their souls no good. During the brief and unhappy reign of Edward VI there is no direct evidence that the Well was affected by the move towards extreme Protestantism, though it seems probable that greater caution had to be shown.

Then, with the accession of Mary in 1553, pilgrimage received fresh impetus. Thomas Goldwell, who had gone into exile with Cardinal Pole as his chaplain in 1535, returned and two years later was nominated to the see of St Asaph, being the last survivor of the ancient hierarchy. He encouraged pilgrimage to Holywell and obtained from pope Paul IV renewal of the indulgence granted by Martin V. But with the accession of Elizabeth he was expelled from his see for refusal to take the Oath of Supremacy and fled abroad, was the only English bishop at the Council of Trent and ended his career as vicar-general to the famous archbishop of Milan, St Charles Borromeo.

The first years of Elizabeth, owing partly to her religious indifference and partly to the methods of compromise she used to undermine Catholicism, were comparatively tolerant. It was not until a check to her plan for gradual change came with the smuggling back into England of priests, largely from the seminary set up at Douai, that her policy changed. The remarkable influence of such men as Campion and Parsons, combined with the real fear of agents from the continent working to upset the realm, caused a savage reaction in which several hundred priests were tracked down and either executed or thrown into jails where they died.

On June 13th, 1579, the Council of the Marches was given a general commission to enquire into and punish recusants and priests and suppress all papist activities.[28] With regard to the pilgrimages to St Winefrede's Well, in view of the claim that the water was medicinal two men were to be appointed to test it. If the water was not medicinal the well was to be destroyed. Nothing can have been done about the well itself since no test has ever shown medicinal qualities, but the hunt for papists was pursued. Father John Bennet, born in the neighbourhood, was one of the first Douai-trained priests to return to England; he came straight to Holywell in 1574 where he served until he was arrested eight years later and committed to Flint jail. Owing to plague in Flint he was brought to Holywell for trial, the chapel being used for the Assize Court. The influence of some of the Welsh gentry saved his life but he was imprisoned in Ludlow Castle. It is said that while he was on the rack, a Protestant churchman's disputation so incensed him that he cried: 'I pray you hoist him up on another rack, that from like pulpits we may argue the matter on equal terms.' He was banished in 1585, but two years later returned to Holywell where, astonishingly, he worked again until on going to London to care for the sick he died of plague in 1625.

In spite of persecution, pilgrimage continued. The *Acta Sanctorum* of the Bollandists, begun in the 17th century and worked at with increasing care for historical method up till the present century, contain many records of miracles at Holywell. Whatever view may be taken of the validity of these miracles, the fact that they are referred to as having occurred on certain dates shows that on those dates pilgrimages took place. In 1574 it is stated that William Shone, a servant of John Williams who had gone devoutly to the well, made fun of it by jumping in to wash his boots, whereupon his hand on his sword withered and his body was benumbed and he was taken home on a drag. Afterwards, being persuaded to return to ask forgiveness, he was taken back twice a day to the Well until he was healed;

Saint Winefrede of Holywell

he then became a Catholic.[29] In 1583 John Grinsham and John Baslow made their devotions; in 1602 Elizabeth Roberts, nine or ten years old, was cured of a stroke, and in 1604 Catherine Moore was cured of blindness.

The best-known pilgrims at this period were perhaps the Jesuit Fathers Oldcorne and Garnet, and Gerard who wrote of them. Oldcorne had left England in 1582 and five years later was ordained in Rome, returning to work as a missionary mainly in Worcestershire where he sheltered for sixteen years at Hindlip Hall. The house had only recently been finished and was full of secret tricks of all kinds, trap-doors, sliding panels, staircases and escapes designed by another priest, Nicholas Owen. While Oldcorne had been in Italy he had dined one night at an inn near Naples with an Italian merchant and another English priest; the innkeeper, with a view to robbery, had given them poison and, though they escaped and his companions suffered no serious effects, Oldcorne developed a severe ulceration of the tongue and mouth. He was devoted to St Winefrede and in 1600 decided to go to her Well. Staying near by with a Catholic family he was shown by the chaplain a stone taken from the water; he bathed in the Well, putting the stone in his mouth and was cured. It seems that the miracle was well attested and made quite a sensation at the time.

His return to Hindlip was, however, to cause his tragic death and to earn him in 1929 the title of the Blessed Edward, Martyr. With the accession of James I things went smoothly for the Catholics provided they lived peaceably, and in 1603 recusant fines were remitted. But toleration encouraged a fresh influx of priests from abroad and a rising spirit of resistance. In alarm at the suspicion of plots, fines were reimposed and an order made banishing priests. It was then that the organization of the Gunpowder Plot began, the date for the blowing up the king and parliament being fixed, after several changes, for November 5th, 1605. Father Garnet, the Provincial of the English Jesuits and a friend of Oldcorne, had full knowledge of the plot. How much Garnet tried to dissuade the conspirators has been much argued, and his keeping silent on account of his knowledge having been acquired under the seal of confession is controversial. But for one who claimed from the first to have been horrified at the conspiracy his behaviour was certainly strange. In September, only a few weeks before the date fixed for the attempt, he organized a pilgrimage to St Winefrede's Well to pray for its success.[30]

Almost everything about this strange pilgrimage seems to contradict the picture of the times suggested by the severe penal laws which had recently ordered the banishment of priests and a close watch on all Catholics. In August Garnet writes to Father Parsons, S.J., telling him he proposes to go to St Winefrede's shrine for his health. Then, in September, Garnet and Owen, the Jesuit who had made the hide-outs at Hindlip, meet in London and proceed to Gothurst, Sir Everard Digby's house. From there they set out with Lady Digby, Anne Vaux, another priest, Fisher, and a number of other Catholic ladies and gentlemen and their servants. This party, about thirty strong, crosses England to Holywell: for the most part they stop at private houses, but at Shrewsbury and Holywell they stay at inns. Mass is said daily, and at Holywell the ladies go barefoot to the Well and stay there all night. They return by the same route, staying at Huddington Court, the house of Robert Winter, Catesby's cousin. It appears that in every way they were courting trouble; but they were hardly the people to have done so at that moment, nor is there anything to show that in fact they had any difficulty. It should all the same be observed that the saint did not intercede to further the conspirator's design.

When the plot was discovered, Garnet fled to Hindlip. There is no evidence that until then Oldcorne knew anything of the conspiracy, but when, after being shut up in the secret hiding-places of Hindlip, he and Garnet emerged for fear of suffocation, their being caught together implicated him. Both were executed.

Following the general alarm, the severity of the laws against Catholics was increased. Again, one is surprised at the pilgrimage to Holywell not being interrupted. The very next year, Sir Roger Bodenham, a Protestant and a Knight of the Bath, went there: he had been treated for a long time for some serious skin disease of the feet by the famous Dr Sion Rhys of Padua, Siena and doyen of the College of Physicians, who reported the whole case to the College. Having failed in all his treatments, the doctor, a Catholic, persuaded his patient to go to Holywell.

Saint Winefrede of Holywell

The knight did so and was immediately cured. With the eminence of the physician and the social position of his patient, the miracle did not pass unnoticed. The doctor's name crops up again in 1618 over the case of Anne Price who was 'utterly debilitated by witchcraft'. Dr Rhys after some time concluded that there was nothing whatever the matter with her. As this diagnosis did nothing whatever to cure her, she decided to confound whatever evil power was destroying her by invoking the power for good of the saint. Having bathed in the well, she recovered.

The Bollandist records then continue almost yearly throughout the century, and it is reasonable to assume that for every miracle noted in them there must have been, if not miracles, a good number of pilgrimages by ordinary people. Confirmation of this is easily found. John Gee reported in 1625 that papists came in crowds and even intruded themselves 'into ye Church or public chapel at Holywell and there said Mass without contradiction'.[31] The next year the Bishop of Bangor informed the Lords that there was a great concourse of people to St Winefrede's Well, and public Mass said continually in an old chapel near by. In 1629 a government spy reported that on St Winefrede's day between fourteen and fifteen hundred people assembled at the well together with a hundred and fifty priests.[32] This occurred after the Privy Council had reminded Sir John Bridgman of his duty to put an end to these pilgrimages. Eight years later, as Chief Justice of Chester, he ordered the image of St Winefrede to be disfigured, all but two of the inns of the town to be closed and reports given of the pilgrims who stayed in these. The image was whitewashed, but the inn-keepers refused to give the names of pilgrims and were accordingly fined. There were frequent complaints that the inns were used as chapels, and in fact the Star Inn was bought for this purpose in 1638, and the Cross Keys at some time in the same century. The Jesuits in 1687 even obtained a lease of the Chapel itself which had evidently been taken over for some quite different use.

It seems, indeed, that the great events of Charles I's reign, the Commonwealth, the power of Puritanism for good or ill, did not halt, though they may have diminished, the tread of footsteps on the stones of Holywell. From time to time there were raids in which holy vessels were seized and priests jailed, but pilgrimage did not cease. In 1686 came the last visit of a king to the Well. James II with his queen, Mary of Modena, went in August to pray that through St Winefrede's intercession they might have a son. Blindly stubborn though he was, James was by then aware that all his attempts to force Catholicism on his unwilling country would go for nothing if there was no Catholic prince to succeed him. On his pilgrimage this monarch 'who lost three kingdoms for a mass' took with him the shift worn by his great-grandmother Mary Queen of Scots at her execution and presented it at the shrine; he also gave as favours golden rings with his hair plaited beneath a crystal.

In the following year the queen wrote to Sir Roger Mostyn informing him that the king had bestowed on her the chapel, and requesting him to give possession to a Mr Thomas Roberts so that he might put the building into good repair.[33] The next year, 1688, on June 10th she had a son, James Francis Edward Stuart, who as James III of England and VIII of Scotland was to be the Old Pretender. So the king's prayer was answered, but too late. There seems a tragic innocence about this whole affair when compared with most other actions of this dangerous bigot and most unwise of kings. Within a few months of the birth, the chapel was sacked by a mob of supporters of William of Orange.

But this sacking, though it unfortunately did a lot of damage to the arches over the well and to parts of the chapel, was the last outbreak of the kind. The very next year Celia Fiennes, who rode there out of curiosity, tells of the pilgrims she saw at the well, though she regards them as deluded folk.[34] The Catholic diarist, Nicholas Blundell, has much more to say;[35] he and his wife and servants went frequently to Holywell from Crosby Hall in Lancashire. His wife was delicate and went often to Spaw, famous for its waters in the 17th and 18th centuries: but her visits to Holywell for a cure were prompted by her belief in the saint. Sometimes they went comfortably by Chester, sometimes by the dangerous crossing of the Sands of Dee at low tide. The first note in Blundell's diary, detailing his expenses, is in 1703; on one occasion he drove his wife only as far as Liverpool as she had declared her intention of going the rest of the way on foot, and so presumably she did,

Saint Winefrede of Holywell

crossing the Mersey, the Wirral peninsula and the Dee sands. Of an old recusant family, they were in an uncomfortable position during the Jacobite rising, and in 1716 went over to Flanders partly to arrange for the Catholic education of their two daughters, whom they were not to see again for six years. Almost their first action when they returned home in 1717 was to go on pilgrimage to Holywell to give thanks for their safety. The next year occurred what appears to have been the last official raid when a party of dragoons sent by the Commissioners of Inquiry at Preston seized some of the valuable plate from the two inns used as chapels.

It all makes very clear why Dr Fleetwood, Blundell's contemporary, was so irritated by the continuing pilgrimages in his diocese. It is interesting that his attack on the saint, in whose existence at any time he refused to believe, was almost entirely intellectual. He does not invoke the laws of the land nor the regulations of the English Church. Yet these pilgrimages ignored not only the proscriptions of Henry VIII but every penal law enacted against Roman Catholicism in England in the following two centuries. Again and again the question arises of how this could be, since there was obviously never any secrecy. Granted the inadequacy of communications and the power of central government, as well as the small scattered population of the 17th century, the implication remains that the individual had a greater scope for expression in an ambience of greater toleration than most histories suggest. Individual actions, hopes and fears, expressed in letters of the Paston family, the diary of a Blundell, the poems of Dafydd ap Gwilym or the correspondence of a mediaeval monk may refer to events of the time but are not primarily concerned with them. The personal life, and the intention to pursue it, is very strong: the effects of wars, revolutions and penal laws may be shocking, but they are rarely more than incidental. Nevertheless, there is no complete answer to why the pilgrimage to St Winefrede's Well continued when every other centre of pilgrimage in the country had been suppressed.

In the two hundred years since Blundell, references become fewer and more scattered, owing probably to persecution having weakened and pilgrimage to the well being taken for granted. Dr Johnson went there in 1774 and gives a description of the bath which he complained was indecently open: 'a woman bathed while we all looked on.'[36] Pennant, describing pilgrimages in 1798, adds a curious piece of information about the first Sunday after St James's day being also kept to celebrate St Winefrede and St Beuno. Not kept, however, with prayers and masses but with frolicks and orgies. He says it is supposed to have originated in the Roman Church but was now celebrated by all but Catholics, and for most unsaintly ends. It is called Dydd fyl y Sant or Sunday of Saints which to him suggests a Druidical past, Deisul or Deisi – Deas, right hand, sul, sun, a turning from east to west, following the course of the sun. There are a number of articles about the pilgrimages in 19th-century periodicals, and in 1910 a paper on 'Modern Miracles of Healing' was read to the North Wales branch of the British Medical Association at which several doctors testified to cases of healing at the well. The hospice for pilgrims was established in 1870, and in 1896 the Chairman of the Urban District Council, who was not a Catholic, pointing out the 'widespread reputation of St Winefrede's Well as a healing power', asked the Council to recognize its duty to give every assistance. One thousand seven hundred and ten sick people were housed that year in the hospice apart from the pilgrims in hotels and apartments. In the last few years it has been modernized and is still in the charge of the Sisters of Charity of St Paul.

One of the last notable figures to be associated with the well was the demonic genius Frederick Rolfe, or Baron Corvo. The personality of this intolerable man, whose brilliance was frustrated by his vanity and distrust, emerges from his own writings, though never so clearly as in A. J. A. Symons's biography.[37] Some time in 1895 Corvo appeared at Holywell in the guise of a poor artist, Fr Austin, and appealed to Fr Sidney de Vere Beauclerk, S.J., the priest in charge of the well, for employment. He was commissioned to paint a set of banners to decorate the Shrine, in return for his board and lodging. The banners were completed, though unpleasantness of which Corvo was a master grew daily. Corvo demanded a thousand pounds, a hundred pounds a banner on the basis of a pound for every head painted in – he had managed to cram in some background crowd scenes – but in the end he accepted £50 for the lot. Meanwhile, he had joined a local newspaper and begun a campaign of innuendo and invective which in a few months stirred the small town of Holywell to a ferment. Then, suddenly, it all ended. Corvo, having ruined the paper with his scandal, deliberately entered the local workhouse to expose his sufferings, then departed on foot with all he had in a bundle on a stick. Five of his banners are kept as curiosities in the vestry of the Catholic church. The figures are those of St George, St Augustine, St Gregory, St Ignatius and Caradoc about to cut off St Winefrede's head: the fingers of St Ignatius holding an orb are elongated to talons, and all the faces are the pink faces of boys and almost identical. It is hardly surprising that they are not displayed at the shrine, which, for all his passionately declared Catholicism, Corvo did his best to cloud.

On November 23rd, 1851, Pius IX granted indulgences to pilgrims, and these were confirmed by Leo XIII on May 18th 1887. Then, on Friday, January 5th, 1917, what seemed like disaster fell upon Holywell. The spring, which had been bubbling at the rate of twenty-one tons a minute, went suddenly dry. Fourteen years before, an act of Parliament had prohibited companies lead-mining in the hills above from draining away the underground water supplying the well; now, through an accident in tunnelling, this had happened and the water poured away into the Dee. In the mills below the shrine, hundreds were thrown out of work: for Catholics it was a trial of faith. But by the autumn, the companies had diverted another stream from a source in the same hills to restore the supply. The mills re-opened and the devout held that the trial had been to show the credulous that the water had in itself no miraculous quality, that, whatever water came from the well, its benefit came from the saint's response to the prayer and act of faith alone.

The Feast of the Martyrdom is celebrated on June 22nd, that of St Winefrede's natural death on November 3rd: but, apart from these days, there is still after thirteen centuries a steady flow of pilgrims to the well in which grows the red moss symbolic of the saint's hair stained with her blood. There are two kinds of moss, the one jungermannia asplenioides, the other a byssus common to Lapland which Linnaeus calls Byssus Jolithus, the violet-smelling. The water in which they grow is

Saint Winefrede of Holywell

still the 'breath of Heaven in the vale' that Tudur Aled sang in his cywydd to Saint Winefrede:

> and the breeze that comes from it
> Is as the honey-bees first swarming,
> A sweet odour over the turf
> Of musk or balm in the midst of the world . . .
>
> The drops of her blood are as the red shower
> Of the berries of the wild rose,
> The tears of Christ from the height of the Cross . . .

From three centuries earlier comes the voice of Robertus, echoing the voice of an unknown monk who in turn has echoed a vision from the very cradle of religion: 'and her blood fell upon the stones, which, like the flowers of Adonis, every year commemorate the day with a colour unknown at any other time.'

III

THE SHRINES OF GLASTONBURY

THE ORIGINS OF SANCTITY at Glastonbury, as at Holywell, are separated by hundreds of years from the written records. In both cases no consecutive account appears earlier than the 12th century. During those years, certainly as many as between the middle ages and to-day, traditions grew, were modified or changed for reasons which are sometimes only possible to guess. But if the origin of Holywell seems fanciful, the subject, St Winefrede, is simple and consistent. Far otherwise with Glastonbury, which of all English shrines is not only the most ancient but the most complex in its history. To be fully understood, Glastonbury must be seen and felt. It is not only the visual emptiness of ruins peopled with ghosts, and the silence of pressing voices, which is revealing; the whole countryside, its very geography, answers many of the questions posed by its strange story.

At the eastern end of the west Somerset flatlands, between Queen's and King's Sedge Moor, rises a five-hundred-foot tor, conical and precipitous. On its narrow top stands the tower of St Michael, all that remains of the original church that collapsed in the 13th century. From here, where the last abbot of Glastonbury was put to death, the view is immense. Looking westward, there is a smaller hill near by named Chalice, for reasons that presently appear, and to the south are some other

The Shrines of Glastonbury

hills like beehives. Immediately below is Glastonbury on an almost imperceptible rise, the roofs and streets of the little town close about the abbey that once dominated them. The rise is the Isle of Avalon, swelling above the once submerged marshes of the Vale that spreads out and away to the Bristol Channel some fifteen miles distant as the heron flies. North runs the high ridge of the Mendips with its faults, caves and dwellings of pre-history: far to the south-west are the Quantocks. In the Vale were the lake villages, marked still by mounds in the lush meadows, the long dykes lined with pollard willows; gashes in the brilliant green show black where the peat has been cut, here and there are isolated farms surrounded with apple orchards. It is a good deal like the Camargue in its sense of remoteness under a wide sky, its singular, contained life.

There is no place which shows history more clearly as the product of myth, namely that collection of beliefs, which, whether or not ill-founded, lead to actions and events which affect the lives of men for centuries afterwards. Without weighing this poetic inheritance the prose of history is meaningless. Glastonbury is before all associated with St Joseph of Arimathaea, and the Isle of Avalon on which it stands with King Arthur: each is an historical figure surrounded with legend, the former wholly religious but the latter only by virtue of myth. Through the Holy Grail their stories are so interwoven that history cannot separate them. With the Grail recognized as pagan, Arthur fades into the background, and Joseph's shrine as a centre of pilgrimage makes Glastonbury the greatest abbey in England; in the view of some of its later abbots, the first in western Christendom.

The theories about how the very names of Glastonbury and Avalon emerged are like marsh-fire in the Celtic twilight. The earliest known name for this settlement in the swamps under the Great Tor was Ynyswytrin, the Isle of Glass. The later Saxon Glaestyngabyrig may have derived from this; on the other hand it could have been some association of the Celtic with the Teutonic kingdom of the dead, Glasberg. In the Celtic tradition the ruler of the dead was Avalloc, his realm Ynys yr Afallon; from this has come the interpretation Isle of Apples, from the Welsh *afal*, not, as commonly supposed, because of its

The Shrines of Glastonbury

orchards but because *afal* was symbolic of feasting in Elysium. Whatever the argument, the significance is the same: Avalon was the Island of the Dead, of the Blest. That Avalon in Welsh mythology was in the Western Seas does not affect this, since many islands in the west had this sacred reputation. Though there was no written association of Avalon with Glastonbury until the 12th century,[1] there is no doubt that the tradition was of great antiquity. Wherever possible, the early Christian missionaries chose to plant the Cross on ground already hallowed by an older faith;[2] and it was this existing tradition that almost certainly drew them to Glastonbury.

The earliest reference to an abbey is in an 8th-century Life of St Boniface by his disciple St Willibald. In telling of the mission of Boniface to Ghent and his being given permission by King Ine of the West Saxons to come to England, the writer says that Beorwald, abbot of Glastonbury, was one of those who brought Boniface to the king. It appears that Ine was recognized as the founder of the Saxon monastery, of which Beorwald was the first abbot, about 708. In the life of St Dunstan, who was abbot from 946 to 957, written in the year 1000, is the first reference to the primitive wattle church reputedly dedicated by Our Lord Himself, though there is no mention yet of Joseph of Arimathaea having had anything to do with it. It had been for long a place of pilgrimage when Dunstan arrived, and the monastery was probably then like Iona, Bangor and others a collection of beehive cells, the church oblong and the whole surrounded by an earthen rampart.

The threads of the story were woven into a pattern for the first time by William of Malmesbury: this Benedictine monk, who was the best historian of his time, stayed at Glastonbury in 1125 to gather material for his great history of Glastonbury.[3] It seems that an impulse to undertake this was his annoyance at the jealous assertion made by Osbern of Canterbury that there was no abbot of Glastonbury until St Dunstan. Almost all he learned came from the monks, and it has been said that he must be read bearing in mind 'that huge system of monastic lying in which Glastonbury had a bad pre-eminence'.[4] The caution is right, but not its generalization which neglects a way of life and outlook wholly different from to-day's. William certainly accepted much that would be incredible now, and interpolations by later writers, who thought he had not made a good enough story, have also blurred his work.[5] But it is possible to discover the main lines of what he originally set down and what he himself was prepared to believe.

He says that there was standing then the small church of wattles dedicated to the Blessed Virgin which had been built by missionaries from Rome in 166. This had been covered with wood to preserve it by Paulinus, bishop of Rochester. William knew of the monks' claim to a still earlier date but apparently was not ready to take it as fact. Seeing for himself that the abbey was a centre of pilgrimage because of the many saints buried there, he traces the succession of abbots from St Patrick. St Patrick, he says, having finished his work in Ireland, spent his last years at Glastonbury, bringing together the hermits he found there into monastic life. The fame of the saint naturally attracted other Irish saints, such as St Bridget and St Indract. When he died he was succeeded by St Benignus. Not long after this St David came with seven bishops and intended to consecrate the church. But he was warned in a dream that Our Lord had already done this: he therefore built another church and consecrated that.

More factual was the ancient charter which the monks showed William. This was dated 601, written in archaic characters and was almost illegible; it described the grant to the Old Church of land in the Isle of Yneswytrin by a king of Domnonia, a realm covering a good part of the west country. The abbot mentioned was Worgret, and the king has been identified with Gwrgon Varvtrwch who was a lieutenant of King Arthur and may have succeeded him. The importance of this lies mainly in its establishment of the Celtic link. It seems that the Saxons did not break it. By the time they reached Glastonbury they were to some extent Christianized and the first fury to destroy had waned. An illustration of this is the confirmation of the monastery by King Ine only a hundred years from the date of this charter, and his acceptance as patron of the Saxon foundation.

William of Malmesbury had never heard of Arthur in connection with Glastonbury, although in his *Gesta Regum* he relates in detail the life and deeds of Arthur as an historical character who defended Britain against the Saxons. But the

The Shrines of Glastonbury

main value of his work came from his honest attempt to make clear why Glastonbury had become so important. Along with his reporting the stories of St Patrick and St David having been buried there, there are verifiable references to the relics of such celebrated saints as Aidan and Benedict Biscop and Paulinus having been brought from the far north for safety from the Danes, just as others unverifiable had been saved from the Saxons. In setting down both fact and legend he certainly provided the material for elaborations by less scrupulous writers; on the other hand he succeeded in showing what he may well have intended, that, whether or no a legend is in itself credible, the very existence of legend is a fact arising from a cause and having effects that cannot be ignored.

Meanwhile, Geoffrey of Monmouth in 1135 was writing his *History of the Kings of England* in which he wonderfully developed the Arthurian legend. His claim that it was the Latin translation of a book written by a British hand probably meant that he had gathered together the stories preserved by the Welsh bards and particularly by Bleheris, using the writings of 8th-century Nennius[6] as a basis. He antedated by a few years Chrétien de Troyes' poem 'Perceval', the story of the Grail, the development of the *Matière de Bretagne* in France and the vast amount of lore eventually paraphrased in Malory's 15th-century *Le Morte d'Arthur*. Though most of his History, quite apart from the three books devoted to Arthur, was fantastic, his rich inventions inspired Shakespeare – all Lear is there – Milton, Drayton and many others. But even Geoffrey, in telling of the Isle of Avalon, does not connect it with Glastonbury. In a later work, the Life of Merlin, of which, however, his authorship is disputed, the bard Taliesin is made to describe the dying Arthur's voyage to the Isle of Apples; but there is still no identification of the place with Glastonbury.

In the 12th-century biography of the 6th-century historian, Gildas,[7] occurs the story of Gwenevere's capture by Melwas, king of Aestiva Regio, the summer region or Somerset. He carried her off to Glastonia, Urbs Vitrea, a stronghold surrounded by marshes. Arthur laid siege to it, but Gildas and the abbot of Glastonbury managed to make peace between the two kings and Gwenevere was restored to Arthur. But here again no mention of the word Avalon for the area. Chrétien de Troyes' variation of the story makes Lancelot rescue the queen and kill her ravisher in a duel; the poet adds a description of the realm of Melwas as being a land from which no traveller returns, an abode of the dead. This has been likened to the myth of the rape of Persephone by Hades and to the attempt of Orpheus to recover Eurydice. So by implication Chrétien associates the distant land with Glastonbury. Gildas himself, who was born while the historic Arthur, one of the Comes Littoris Saxonici, was fighting the Saxons, and who wrote not long after Arthur was dead, describes his campaigns though without suggesting his being more famous than his predecessors in command. Arthur's fame, as later developed by Geoffrey of Monmouth, almost certainly arose from his identification with a Brythonic divinity of the same name, a Culture Hero who conquered the Power of Darkness. The difficulty posed by the historical fact that the real Arthur was killed was overcome by developing the legend that he was carried away to the Isle of Avalon to be healed of his wounds, and would return one day to rule again. Thus, the Culture Hero myth was properly rounded without the reality of the historic Arthur being diminished. How these exotic threads interweave to colour Glastonbury's claim to precedence among the shrines of western Christendom will appear after consideration of the Great Fire.

On St Urban's Day, May 25th, 1184, everything at Glastonbury was destroyed, excepting the Bell Tower built by Henry of Blois. The Old Church, the tombs of the Saints and of kings such as Edmund I, Edgar and Edmund Ironside all disappeared together with the venerated relics. The monks claimed indeed to have saved the relics of St Dunstan which they had brought there from Canterbury after its sacking by the Danes in 1101. The monks of Canterbury naturally denied that Glastonbury had ever had them, and there is nothing to show they were wrong. The argument went on until in 1508 the commission of Warham and Goldston established that the Canterbury shrine had all the proper bones. As Glastonbury refused to accept the verdict, retorting that in future only one of her monks would be allowed to know where the bones were kept, the secret passing on his deathbed to another, and as the Dissolution followed soon after, the question was never settled. It was one of

The Shrines of Glastonbury

those insoluble mediaeval contests, like that between Montecassino and St Benôit at Fleury over the bones of St Benedict which continues strongly to-day.

After so much destruction, Glastonbury had to redevelop her attractions. Within a century of the fire the necessary additions were made to William of Malmesbury's original history as new 'evidence' emerged to confirm the ancient traditions of sanctity. The most elaborate composition was 'The Charter of St Patrick the Bishop'. William had accepted the tradition of St Patrick being the first abbot, and in the circumstances of his time this was not so absurd as it might seem now: the saint's tomb was there, a focus of pilgrimage, and not far from the abbey, at Beckery, was St Bridget's chapel to which pilgrims came from Ireland to look with awe on her wallet and distaff. But William accepted St Patrick without comment and with no mention of a Charter. The Charter appeared early in the 13th century, a remarkable invention indeed, purporting to be written by St Patrick himself. In it the saint tells how in 430 he had been sent to Ireland by Pope Celestine, and how, after converting the Irish, he returned to Britain. There he chanced upon the Isle of 'Ynysgytrin' where he found certain hermits whom he brought to the monastic life. These successors of the disciples of SS. Phagan and Deruvian showed Patrick the whole story of the Old Church built by disciples of SS. Philip and James. He then speaks of the indulgences granted to pilgrims to this holy place, and the whole concludes with a commentator's note that the saint, becoming the first abbot in the Isle of Avalon, was buried to the right of the altar in the Old Church.

The late invention of this Charter is confirmed by the reference to indulgences. There were three of these: ten years obtained by SS. Phagan and Deruvian from Pope Eleutherius who had sent them, a further thirty years for all Christian folk who came there, and twelve years granted by pope Celestine to St Patrick. In addition the saint conceded a hundred days of pardon to all who with pious intent should cut down the woods covering the approach to the Tor on which stood St Michael's oratory. Now, the first indisputable evidence of a plenary indulgence occurred in 1095 when Urban II granted one for the First Crusade:[8] in the next year he granted a partial one of a month at the dedication of St Nicholas' at Angers: in 1132 Innocent II at his dedication of the great church at Cluny granted forty days. Though the practice spread quickly, a period of forty days remained a high figure for some time; it was not for another century that a period of years was given.

The only genuine indulgences at Glastonbury seem in fact to be those referred to in a document existing in 1247 called 'Days of Indulgence for Glastonbury, of which we have not the Charters, though we once had them'.[9] These were secured by confirmation in a privilege granted by Innocent III (1198–1216) and begin with a list headed by one of a hundred days conveyed by St Dunstan, almost certainly a forgery that had somehow been overlooked in Rome, then one of Lanfranc of thirty days, and another fifteen small ones. There is a further mixed list of forty, and then a hundred and thirteen days for veneration of relics. The three ancient indulgences in St Patrick's Charter are referred to separately 'in carta sine sigillo', and no papal confirmation is claimed for them.

But the production of St Patrick's Charter served a very useful purpose in restoring the saint to prominence at Glastonbury at a time when the abbey had suffered so many losses. Although the jealousy of other foundations did not hesitate to condemn the claim to St Patrick, the Charter was not seriously questioned until the 14th century. Then Ranulf Higden, a Benedictine monk of St Werburgh, Chester, wrote his famous *Polychronicon*,[10] a survey of general history which became a standard work in the 15th century. But by then Glastonbury had established her primacy among abbeys with the far earlier saint, Joseph of Arimathaea.

At the time of the Great Fire of 1184 no mention had yet been made of Joseph; William of Malmesbury half a century earlier had evidently never heard of his having come there. The antiquity of Glastonbury did, however, depend on the story of disciples having been sent by St Philip from Gaul at a time when Joseph could in fact have been still living. Geoffrey of Monmouth, in his development of the Arthurian legend, had introduced the story of the Holy Grail which had been brought to England by Joseph of Arimathaea, though he did not connect Avalon with Glastonbury. There must all the same have been a strongly founded legend in the countryside to have given the monks the idea of searching for Arthur's tomb, once they saw the possibilities in store if they found it.

They were fortunate in having as patron the king. Henry II, for all that his resistance to the claims of the Church had brought about the murder of Becket, had never ceased to resist papal demands whenever possible. In this, Glastonbury had always been useful, inasmuch as her claim to have been founded by a saint surviving from the time of Christ Himself undermined Rome's historical supremacy. He at once began rebuilding the abbey, and within two years, on June 11th, 1186, the reconstructed Old Church was consecrated. When the monks asked for his permission to search in the surrounding ruins for Arthur's tomb, he gladly consented, since, apart from adding prestige, its discovery at Glastonbury would be a blow to the troublesome Welsh who held that Arthur would one day return to lead them to victory. The monks searched and a grave was found which they claimed to be that of Arthur. Whether or not the monks faked the inscribed cross which they said they found with the skeleton, the quirk of the whole affair is that what began as one more scheme to add glory to the abbey resulted in what is now believed to be their discovery of Arthur's actual burial place.

The first to relate this event was Giraldus Cambrensis,[11] who was also the first to bring together Avalon, Arthur and Glastonbury. In his *Speculum Ecclesiae* he tells how only three years before, in 1191, the monks found Arthur's body lying in the hollowed trunk of an oak buried deep between two pyramids in the cemetery. With it was a leaden cross with the inscription: 'Hic jacet sepultus inclitus rex Arthurus cum Wenneveria uxore sua secunda in insula Avallonia.' He added his usual fancies, the crumbling of Guinevere's golden hair in the monk's hand as he touched it, which, even if she had been in the tomb, would not have occurred. Adam of Domerham, who in 1290 gave the official story of the exhumation in more sober terms, omits any mention of Guinevere on the inscribed cross, though he does say that the monks subsequently found her tomb.[12] Two hundred and fifty years later Leland said that with the cross in his hand he read the inscription as Adam had done, 'Hic jacet sepultus inclitus rex Arturius in insula Avalonia'. Yet even he records that, for all this, the country folk of near-by

Cadbury held to their belief that Arthur and his knights still slept beneath their hill, one day to wake – *rex quondam, rex futurus*. The belief still lingers. Leland's version of the inscription appears on the first picture of the cross in Camden's *Britannia* in 1607, and the historian Sharon Turner refers to the cross as having been in the possession of William Hughes, Chancellor of Wells early in the 18th century.[13] No one seems to know what happened to it later.

So was established in the 12th century that association of Arthur with Glastonbury which was to have such great significance in the abbey's history. It was not until the 14th century that John of Glastonbury, who agreed with the shorter inscription on the cross, traced Arthur's descent from Joseph of Arimathaea;[14] but in the meanwhile the way was open to the development side by side of two of the greatest legends in Christendom.

How well-rooted and carefully nurtured was the story of Joseph is revealed long after in Dugdale's 17th-century account of Glastonbury.[15] For he states at the beginning as an accepted fact that Joseph 'about sixty-three years after the Incarnation of Our Lord', coming as the leader of twelve disciples of the Apostle Philip, 'erected, to the honour of the Virgin Mary, of wreathed twigs, the first Christian Oratory in England'. There is no historical evidence of there having been Christians in Britain before some time in the second century,[16] and the lack of any reference to Joseph by William of Malmesbury implies that the monks had not then adopted the story. If they had, William, as a scrupulous recorder, would have reported it even if he had not believed it. All that he says about the claim to so early a foundation is that if St Philip preached in Gaul then it was possible he sent some disciples over to Britain.

But the story of Joseph must have begun to grow fairly soon after William because St Patrick's Charter mentioned it: then in the middle of the 13th century an unknown hand added a note to William's *de Antiquitate*, and another a reference to Joseph's coming and to the Quest of the Holy Grail. Geoffrey of Monmouth had already told it in his History, and Chrétien de Troyes in his poems, though neither of these linked Joseph with Glastonbury, and Walter Map, the wit and ecclesiastic at Henry II's court, had written his *Lancelot*. By the 14th century

The Shrines of Glastonbury

there was a great deal of material on which John of Glastonbury in his 14th-century Chronicle could draw in piecing together the story, which, in the hands of the abbey, became its highest claim to glory.

Here is a mediaeval tapestry *par excellence*. The first impression is almost overwhelming; the accumulation of detail is at once scattered so that the eye wanders to and fro, up and down, trying to find some incident that will give the key, provide some starting-point. When in despair one such is chosen at hazard, and the enchanted wood is entered, it is found that there is indeed no one starting-point better than another. One moves back and forth in time, confronting each incident as it appears; the sense of improbability and any urge to criticize fade before the anxiety not to lose one's way. Gradually it becomes clearer as the mind accustoms itself not just to moving backwards and forwards in time but to appreciating all that is occurring in a timeless world, where historic figures behave in a legendary manner and creatures of legend appear fleetingly in historic perspective, where there is hardly a dividing line between the material and the spiritual because the former to become real must be inspired, and the latter to become significant must be embodied. It is without beginning and without end, the very stuff of poetry, indestructible.

The eye is caught first by the representation of the earlier account of St Joseph's mission, added in the 13th century to William's *de Antiquitate*, which tells how St Philip sent Joseph and his companion over from Gaul, how a British king gave them the island of 'Yniswytrin', where, instructed by the angel Gabriel, they built the wattle church which was dedicated by the Lord Himself to His Mother, and how the missionaries were given each a portion of land known to this day as the Twelve Hides of Glastonbury. There looms then the strange prophecy of the 5th-century bard, Melkin,[17] of whom nothing is known but that he was before Merlin. In rhythmic, hypnotic prose it gives the riddle of the Isle of Avalon, long the resting place of noblest pagans, where Joseph falls asleep and there lies on a two-forked line at the south corner of a wattle oratory, and in his sarcophagus are two white and silver cruets filled with the blood and sweat of the prophet Jesu. Neither water nor the dew of heaven shall fail the people of that Isle when this is opened to the world, and long before the judgement day in Josaphat these things shall be declared.

However bemused, one is startled by this extraordinary non-Christian vision which has never been satisfactorily explained. For a moment there is a glimpse of Arthur, and then appears the portrayal from the apocryphal Gospel of Nicodemus of Joseph's imprisonment by the Jews, of his escape, of his explanation to the high priests that angels had lifted his cell into the air and the Lord had appeared to him, taking him back to the sepulchre and showing him the grave-clothes and then going with him to his home of Arimathaea where the Lord left him.

The long-known Gospel goes no further and the thread is drawn from other sources, showing how Joseph was appointed by the apostle Philip to care for Christ's Mother while he is in Ephesus, and is with Her at Her Assumption. After this he goes to Gaul with St Philip, taking with him his son, Josephe, and then is sent at the head of twelve disciples to preach in Britain. The picture is rounded by a paraphrase from a book 'called The Holy Grail', which, omitting much detail, shows how together with many other companions they crossed the sea on Josephe's shirt, followed the next day by others in a ship sent by the Lord and which had been built by Solomon to last until the time of Christ. Soon, Josephe is imprisoned by the pagan king of north Wales, but is saved by king Evalak of Sarres whom he had converted to Christianity in France. Joseph, and his son, Josephe, and ten disciples, then travel southward and are given 'Yniswytrin' by king Aviragus of

Britain. They build the chapel and when Joseph dies he is buried on the two-forked line by the oratory in fulfilment of Melkin's prophecy.

The tapestry is now interwoven with the deep Arthurian legends; Arthur's descent is traced from Joseph, and that of King Loth, the husband of Arthur's sister, from Joseph's cousin. The story of Evalak's shield, argent, a cross, gules, given him by Joseph to preserve his life, told in the 14th-century alliterative poem of Joseph and the Seint Graal,[18] merges with the riddles contained in the ageless store of Brythonic mythology. The Grail has arrived, brought by Joseph of Arimathaea. Yet the connection does not appear in John of Glastonbury; though much of his history is drawn from the book 'called The Holy Grail', the Grail itself remains still a part only of the romances developed from Celtic myths. King Arthur, wit-

The Shrines of Glastonbury

nessing the wondrous Mass in the hermit chapel of St Mary Magdalen at Beckery in the Isle of Avalon, sees the Mother come with her Son to serve the old priest. When, at the elevation of the Host, the priest elevates the Boy Himself, king Arthur stands at the Sacrament and sees how the priest at the reception of the Host did eat that Boy, yet after the communion was made He appeared unharmed, the spotless Lamb. Then Our Lady came to the king and gave him in commemoration a crystal cross. Afterwards Arthur caused his arms to be changed to contain this cross, with the Mother and Boy in one quarter. And this became the arms of Glastonbury Abbey – Vert, a cross botonnée arg., on a canton of the last the Virgin and Child. The story is parallelled with variations in the Perceval romance in which Arthur does not receive the cross. But the arms became real enough, and the foundations of 'the chapel right adventurous' at Beckery can be seen to-day within the foundations of St Bridget's a short way to the west of Glastonbury. Moreover, within half a mile is the bridge of Pomparles over the river Brue, the Pons Periculosus or point

perilous that leads from the 'chapell auntrous' by a 'faire causé'.

What is this bridge that, rebuilt to carry thundering lorries, still bears its strange name? Is it 'li Ponz de l'Espée' so called because it was the edge of a sword two lances in length that Lancelot crossed to rescue Guenevere from the ravishing Melwas? If so, and the realm of Melwas was indeed the abode of the dead, it would explain how the fable arose, quoted by Leland, that Arthur cast his sword from this Pontperlus when he was borne over it after his wounding. And what of Evalak's shield? And who is Evalak, reputed king of Sarras who saved Joseph? Evalak after his Christian baptism is renamed Mordrein. He would seem to be the Mordrain of the Grand St Graal, he has also been identified with Melwas, at once an historic figure and a dark god: under whatever name in the romances, he remains 'the Unknown'. Only emerging from the mists is his being son to Arthur's sister, Anna – who is also Morgen – who, though married to king Loth, the Celtic Zeus, associated too with Beli, the dark father of Evalak. So he is Avallach who gave his name to Avalon, the Celtic divinity of the Shades whose daughters tended Arthur when he was borne to the Isle to be healed of his wounds.

In seeking the origin of the Grail, it can be well understood why the monks of Glastonbury refrained from associating it with Joseph of Arimathaea. At first glance the story in its simplest form may seem unexceptional from the Church's point of view. It is the Dish used at the Last Supper; stolen by a servant of Pilate, Pilate washes his hands in it before the multitude, Joseph begs Pilate to give it to him, and in it he catches the drops of blood from the five Wounds of Christ. When Joseph is imprisoned by the Jews, he is miraculously fed from it. It becomes re-transformed to the Cup of the Last Supper when Christ, appearing in a vision to Joseph, signifies that it is the Holy Chalice, 'Calices apelez sara'. Joseph carries it with him on his travels, feeding his companions from this inexhaustible source. It passes to his descendants and then mysteriously vanishes, until the noblest descendant of all, Arthur, initiates the search for it, 'The Quest of the Holy Grail'. Was it buried in Chalice Hill under Glastonbury Tor where the inexhaustible chalybeate spring still draws pilgrims?

The Shrines of Glastonbury

The literature on this is vast, and there is some risk in trying to elucidate briefly. Most of the many Grail romances were written in the 12th and 13th centuries, when the sense of the Old Religion was strong, and, whether French, German or English, they were permeated with Celtic myths which were a part of the universal mythology of paganism. The stories are made the more confusing by the inconsistency of the Welsh Triads which again and again give one character triple personality under three different names. The word 'Grail', in its various European forms, is a corruption of the Latin which derived from the Greek *krater*, a mixing bowl: in Celtic it was the always filled cauldron and cup of healing.

One of the earliest tales of such a quest as was later developed is in a poem by Taliesin, reputedly of the 5th century, describing Arthur's invasion of Hades, the realm from which all culture derives and of which his father Uther Pendragon is king. He brings away the cauldron of the Head of Hades. This was the basis for a later account[19] of Arthur's invading Erin to find the cauldron of Diwrnach which alone could hold enough mead for the wedding of Kulkwch and Olwen, of which there is a variation in the bottles of Gwidolwyn which, filled in the east, kept warm till they arrived in the west. This leads to the bringing to the west by Bron, to whom Joseph of Arimathaea had given it, of the Holy Grail containing the Blood. The story of Bron has the same account as that by John of Glastonbury of the passage over the sea on the shirt of Joseph's son, Josephe, and on the other hand resembles the early story of Bran of Wales's voyage to Ireland and his inexhaustible banquet. One version says the Grail was in Bron's keeping on one of the isles. This could refer to any one of the isles of the west with mystical qualities, possibly Bardsey to which Merlin is said finally to have taken the Grail, or to the Isle of Avalon. The cauldron of the Head of Hades had in common with the Grail that it would not provide food for those who were unworthy.

In the *Queste du Saint Graal*, there is the vision of Lancelot when his lineage is revealed. The story of Joseph and the baptism of Evalak, when the secrets of the Grail are opened to him, is told, and Evalak learns in a dream that from his nephew comes a lake from which flow nine streams. The eighth is

Lancelot and the ninth Galahad, the greatest of all, predestined to achieve the Quest. There is a return always in these stories of the power of the god of the underworld, whether by the name of Melwas, Uther Pendragon, Mordrein or Evalak, the Avalloch of Avalon who, though a power of darkness, also exercised that of light. In the Perceval version, it is Perceval who is the hero. He is the grandson of Bron who brought the Grail, and after Merlin's warning of the Quest achieves it. The earliest Grail tradition is in the Gawain stories of Bleheris which range from the purely pagan idea of the resuscitated god, with incidents paralleling Adonis worship, to the Host from which once a year the king partakes of the Sacrament.

One could go on for ever assembling, rearranging, trying to put in order all this often self-contradictory mingling of primitive religion, folk-lore and Christian belief. While hazardous to point any conclusion, it is fair to say that the Grail legend was an inevitable blend. There were the immemorial pagan mysteries, and there had come into being as early as the 8th century, in particular at Fécamp and at Lucca, a legend of the Holy Blood associated with Nicodemus who had been with Joseph. With these interwoven the mysteries became Christianized.

But, though the legend of the Holy Grail had for centuries a strong popular appeal, it was never accepted in its romance form by the monks of Glastonbury nor by the Universal Church they served. They would borrow what they chose of the story of Joseph's coming to Avalon, bringing with him the Blood from the Cross, but not in a Graal which was too clearly a pagan thing. One of the earliest substitutes is that in the alliterative poem already referred to,[20] older probably than *Piers the Plowman* and written about 1350. In this the voice of Christ bids Joseph 'make a luytel whucche', a little box, for the Blood. The tradition developed by Glastonbury was, however, that Joseph had two silver cruets in which he caught the Blood and Sweat from the Cross; these he brought with him and they were buried in his tomb. Here appear at last after nearly a thousand years the cruets in the extraordinary prophecy of the bard, Melkin. In the verse *Lyfe of Joseph*[21] written about 1502, probably by a Glastonbury monk, the Blood falls on Joseph's shirt:

The Shrines of Glastonbury

> And whan our lorde / in the sendony was drest,
> Thys blode in two cruettes / Joseph dyd take,

The arms of St Joseph became a green cross raguly, namely with short stumps from which branches had been lopped close to the stems, and on the whole field drops of blood; in the lower quarters two cruets. It is not certain when this was first displayed, but it can be seen now in the 16th-century south window in the church of St John, and on the stone capitals of St Benignus, rechristened for some reason in the 17th century St Benedict, at Glastonbury. The cross raguly almost surely represents Joseph's flowering staff.

> Thre hawthornes also, that groweth in werall,
> Do burge and bere grene leaues at Christmas
> As fresshe as other in May, when the nightyngale
> Wrestes out her notes musycall as pure as glas.

The poem speaks of the thousands who flock to Joseph at Glastonbury from every land, and recounts in detail many of the miracles performed there; but

> All the myracles to shewe it were to longe,
> There is many mo full great that I do not reherse.

Of all the legends, that of the Holy Thorn, Joseph's staff that took root when he rested on Weary-all Hill, is the latest and best known to-day. People go to the ruins at Christmas to see the marvellous flowering of the trees grown from the planted staff. Yet, though there must have been an existing story due to someone having brought this not uncommon winter-flowering hawthorn, no one thought of writing about it until the eve of the Dissolution, 1500 years after the legendary event. Did a crusader bring the first tree from his travels? The exotic flowering would hardly have escaped notice. More likely it was the charming conceit of the poet, one of the last monks of Glastonbury.

It is strange that after all this, no claim was ever made to the finding of Joseph's tomb. The prophetic Melkin had said that he lay on a two-forked line next the south corner of the oratory. The site of this, the earliest church built by Joseph, was marked by a column to the north of the Lady Chapel built after the Great Fire. On this column was a bronze plate inscribed with

The Shrines of Glastonbury

the story of Joseph's coming there and his building the church. But although in 1345 a royal writ of Edward III gave permission to a John Blome 'ut cum sibi (sicut asserit) divinitus sit injunctum' for a search to be made for 'the venerable body of the noble decurion Joseph of Arimathaea'[22] no one knows if it ever took place. Possibly the abbot did not give the licence and assent required by the writ, since the result might not have been satisfactory.

William Good, born in 1527 at Glastonbury and dying after the Dissolution as a Jesuit in Naples in 1586, relates in his memories of boyhood at the abbey that St Joseph was believed to have lived there, 'and even perhaps to have been buried there'. But 'the monks never knew for certain the place of the saint's burial, or pointed it out. They said the body was hidden most carefully either there or at a hill near Montacute called Hamdon Hill.'[23] Good remembers the bronze plate on the stone cross which was overthrown in Elizabeth's reign. Beneath it was the crypt of St Joseph's chapel, and above, on the south side of the wall of the chapel to the Blessed Virgin was a stone carved with the words 'Jesus, Maria', in 'very ancient letters'. The words may be seen there to-day low to the right of the south doorway. He says there was also a long subterranean chapel, 'a most famous place of pilgrimage which was made to a stone image of the Saint there, and many miracles were wrought at it. When I was a boy of eight, for I was born there, I have served Mass in this chapel, and I saw it destroyed in the time of Henry VIII by a wicked man, one William Goals.' It is not clear if Good was repeating himself and if these chapels were one. To the very end, it seems, there was still no certainty of where St Joseph was buried.

For the instruction of the multitudes of pilgrims who came to the shrines, the history of Glastonbury, the saints buried there and the whole story of Joseph was displayed in a remarkable work called the Magna Tabula. The source of the material is mainly John of Glastonbury, a little from William of Malmesbury, and the final section not from either: it ends with a list of indulgences. This Magna Tabula consists of a folding wooden frame some three feet eight inches high by three feet six when opened, and inside it are two wooden leaves on both sides of which, and on the inside of the frame, are pasted two pieces of parchment telling the story in Latin manuscript. So constructed and fixed to a wall in the church, the leaves could be turned by all who wished to read. As its date is the end of the 14th century it assumes perhaps more literacy among pilgrims than might be supposed. In Ussher's time, Lord William Howard, 'Belted Will', had it at Naworth Castle in Cumberland:[24] in 1947 it was acquired by the Bodleian where it can now be seen.

The strongest evidence of the importance for Glastonbury of the Joseph tradition emerged from the use made of it in Councils of the Church. It has already been noted that even the undeveloped legend of Glastonbury's foundation had been prized by Henry II in his relations with Rome. With its full flowering, Glastonbury used it not only to claim precedence in England but at international Councils.[25] At Pisa in 1409, Constance in 1417 and Siena in 1424 this was announced, though at the first two the French had put in the Provençal claim to Mary Magdalene, Martha and Lazarus, a claim still celebrated in the Camargue. At the Council of Basle in 1434, Spain tried in vain to claim priority on the grounds of its conversion by St James. No wonder that, in her glory, Glastonbury was reputed 'Roma secunda'; indeed, Rome herself could not claim such antiquity, such close connection with the living Christ as through Joseph of Arimathaea.

The mysticism which inspires almost every aspect of Glastonbury's rise to greatness, however much it was put to practical use, can at times be almost overwhelming. In following the intricate story, it is easy to forget how much the abbey owed to the historical figure of Dunstan who made virtually a new foundation. When he was appointed abbot in 940, Glastonbury was neglected, its buildings crumbling, served by a few clerks and Irish scholar-pilgrims, and with monastic life almost non-existent. This, owing to continual wars and invasions, was a condition common to nearly all such establishments. It retained its lands, and, though the *Liber Terrarum* is lost, a manuscript of 1247[26] from the Glastonbury library contains a Calendar, probably of the 10th century, which gives the charters. The earliest, other than the one of 601 seen by William of Malmesbury, is dated 670, a grant of land by king Coenwalch to abbot Beorhtwald to whom Bede refers as becoming arch-

The Shrines of Glastonbury

bishop of Canterbury. The Calendar, prefixed to the Bosworth Psalter written for Dunstan's use at Canterbury, was taken from this Glastonbury Calendar and records the coming of St Patrick, St Patrick the bishop, and St Bridget, and the bringing of the relics of saints and abbots from the north. It says these relics were sent by king Edmund to Dunstan when he was abbot, but William of Malmesbury favours the earlier date of 754, when Tica, fleeing before the Danes, brought the relics of SS. Aidan, Ceolfrid, Benedict Biscop, Hilda, and of Bede himself, or so he said.

Dunstan's light shines between two clouds, the disintegration during Alfred's struggles with the Danes and the misrule and oppression that led to the Norman Conquest. Allowing for the usual arguments about dates in his early life, he was born near Glastonbury about 909, some ten years after Alfred's death, was commended to king Athelstan in 923, became a monk in 936, and in 939 was made abbot of Glastonbury by king Edmund. After fifteen years as abbot he was banished briefly by the wretched Edwy, reinstated by Edgar, became archbishop of Canterbury in 959 and soon after Edgar's death retired from high office, dying on May 19th, 988.

This bare chronology has been best illuminated by bishop Stubbs whose preface to the *Memorials of St Dunstan*[27] is the most scholarly and complete picture of the great man's life and work. The first 'Life' was written only twelve years after the saint's death by an anonymous Saxon monk who had known him, and within little over a century four other 'Lives' appeared. Piecing together the subjective and objective, the legend and history of which they are compounded, a clear picture appears.

As a very young man at Athelstan's court near Glastonbury, Dunstan had an early schooling in politics through the comings and goings of princes and dignitaries from the continent; but after a while his precocious learning, his mechanical skill, his love for the 'vain songs of heathendom' and his own musical ability aroused jealousy among his young kinsmen who accused him of sorcery, procured his banishment and tried to drown him in the marshes. It was after this that he became a monk, and soon a teacher. In essence he remained one all his life. It was always his pleasure to talk to his pupils and associates about his life and work, and one has the clear impression, particularly in the earliest 'Life', of his relating to the young Saxon his memories of childhood, his dreams, his sleep-walking to the church of Glastonbury and climbing the tower with the vision of the great abbey that would arise; his visitation by the devil in the form of different animals, the harp on the wall playing to him as he worked and the many other stories that grew into the Dunstan legend. It was Osbern, seventy years after his death, who first told the well-known story of Dunstan seizing the devil by the nose which, enlarged with the spite of the 16th century, gave Dunstan an oddly out-of-character reputation for harsh temper.

When Edmund succeeded Athelstan, Dunstan was recalled to court as counsellor, but jealousy again banished him, though briefly. The king, hunting near Cheddar, seeing the stag and hounds disappear into the gorge and with his horse out of control, remembered Dunstan and vowed that if his life was spared he would make amends. The horse stopped and Dunstan was made abbot of Glastonbury. In the next fifteen years he completed the reconstruction of the abbey which stood until abbot Thurstan began a major rebuilding: more important, he established a strict observance of St Benedict's Rule and made it a place of learning the effects of which spread far beyond its boundaries.

It is not certain when, after banishment during the short, futile reign of Edwy, he became counsellor to king Edgar; it was probably two years before he became archbishop of Canterbury. From then on, except in so far as Glastonbury was a prototype of the whole church and monastic system which he

The Shrines of Glastonbury

reformed, Dunstan became concerned with wider issues, his life a part of the history of England. The unification of the country which he and Edgar achieved was due to a rare co-operation between Church and State. When after sixteen years of harmony he took his king's body to be buried at Glastonbury, he found that with the new king the forces of misrule were too much for him and soon after retired from public life. He was nearly eighty at his death: Adelard, writing twenty years later, describes it.

'On the morning of the Sabbath, when the matin hymns were now finished, he bids the holy congregation of the brethren come to him. To whom again commending his spirit, he received from the heavenly table the viaticum of the sacraments of Christ which had been celebrated in his presence; and giving thanks to God for it he began to sing, "The merciful and gracious Lord hath so done his marvellous works that they ought to be had in remembrance. He hath given meat unto those that fear him . . ." And with these words in his mouth, rendering his spirit into his Maker's hands, he rested in peace. Oh, too happy whom the Lord found thus watching'.

Almost at once Dunstan was recognized as a saint, owing not, as in the case of many reputed saints, to the miracles in his life but to his essential greatness. The miracles followed later at his tomb. His piety was not the kind for sentimental tracts; his steadfast godliness, his reform of the Church which gave him a name for sternness, was balanced by a deep understanding of his fellows. Though a mediaeval figure, he was both of and ahead of his times; there was a breath of the Renaissance in his art of musical composition, his craft in metals, his enthusiasm for education and the fascination he held for his pupils. These, combined with his statesmanship, brought him nearer to the ideal of the whole man than any other of his age. Strangely, for one of such learning, no literary work attributed to him has been verified as being by his hand. There remains only, doubtfully, the Kyrie *Rex splendens*. Falling asleep while waiting for Edgar to return from hunting, the famous trope comes to him in a dream, and when he wakes he dictates the music. Sung at his festival according to the Salisbury use it would be fitting if it was indeed his work.

Small wonder that Glastonbury claimed the saint as her

very own, even to the possession of his body. Eadmer, one of his biographers, rebukes the monks for their claim and for actually boasting of the theft. He himself had witnessed the elevation of the body when Canterbury was being rebuilt, and he asks if they have forgotten the annual pilgrimage there from Glastonbury before the Conquest. How could this have been if the body was at Glastonbury? The question has never been answered. But it did not prevent more than another four centuries of pilgrims going to his reputed tomb in Avalon. With the rise to greater fame of the lesser man and saint, Thomas Becket, the decline in pilgrimage to St Dunstan's tomb at Canterbury was all gain to Glastonbury.

The independence of the monks, and their pride in the abbey's traditions, worked usually to advantage. But two incidents show not only how the violence of the age could invade the cloistered life, but also the strong nationalism persisting generally in monasteries despite the international character of the Orders to which they belonged. In 1083, after Thurstan had been appointed abbot, this first Norman to hold the post tried to impose a new style of chant on his English monks, perhaps the late variation of the original Gregorian established by Benedict Biscop. The *Anglo-Saxon Chronicle* gives a horrifying picture of the result of the monk's resistance. Set upon by French soldiers brought in by the abbot to subdue them, the monks fled into the Great Church. 'And some of these men of war went up to the upper floor and shot adownwards with arrows towards the holy place, so that many arrows stuck in the Rood which stood upon the altar, and the wretched monks lay about around the altar, and some crept under and cried instantly unto God for His mercy ... and they smote some of the monks to death, and many they wounded therein, so that blood flowed from the altar upon the steps!'[28]

A more prolonged though less bloody disturbance occurred a hundred years later when the notorious bishop Savary of Bath, 'vir ambiciosus et prodigus', having failed to obtain the see of Canterbury, tried to make Glastonbury a cathedral monastery with himself as abbot. Related in some way to the emperor Henry VI, he persuaded his kinsman, in the course of negotiating for Richard Lionheart's release from prison, to get the king's consent to his scheme. But Richard, freed, shrugged

The Shrines of Glastonbury

off his consent as having been given under duress, though he was prepared tó accept the pope's view of the matter. The up and down at Glastonbury and Rome lasted twenty-six years. Savary in Rome procured the pope's order that the monks should not elect an abbot: when they did, the bishop excommunicated the appointee. After Richard's death, King John supported Savary, and the monks once more appealed to Rome. But the bishop had the doors of the Great Church broken open and 'having indecently arrayed the canons of Wells and other seculars in the vestments of the abbey' he had himself inducted as abbot. Soon there was a revolt and again the church was broken into and five of the monks jailed. Innocent III then heard the pleas of the monks' abbot, Pica, and of Savary in Rome, but decided for the bishop. To set the seal on this, Pica and three of the monks with him died strangely and at once of poison. But the bishop got nothing out of all the disruption he had caused, as he himself died in Italy within three months of the papal confirmation in 1205. Eventually, after the king, several bishops and monasteries had appealed to the pope to bring back the abbey to its ancient state, and even Savary's supporters had admitted the regrettable failure of the whole affair, the case for making Glastonbury a cathedral under Bath waned. It dragged on through the Interdict, and not until May 17th, 1219, when bishop Jocelin abandoned the double title, was Glastonbury restored to full independence.[29]

There is a sadly ironical footnote to this tale of intrigue and corruption. If Savary had succeeded in making Glastonbury a monastic cathedral, the Great Church of the abbey destroyed by the vandals of the Dissolution three hundred years later might be standing to-day, a masterpiece of mediaeval art. Instead, there are only the mutilated remains of a few once soaring arches that gaze eyelessly across the green lawns to the Lady Chapel, grass covering the crypt where pilgrims came to the shrine of Joseph.

Still, through all, came the stream of pilgrims without interruption. Already rich in Domesday, the abbey grew always richer, outstanding for the splendour of her buildings, her treasure and her vestments: her lands increased with royal grants and the gathering in of dependent benefices. Churches were even appropriated to contribute to the monks' own table, or for that pocket money which was strictly forbidden by St Benedict's Rule. Feudal dues, trading, masses, tithes, and even at times banking all added to the income. One of the least reputable, and financially unsound, ways of raising money was through corrodies, the sale of annuities for a lump sum contributed to the abbey.[30] Royal corrodies were of course not sold, but were granted at the request of the king and were an unrequited burden. But the others were burden enough, since they often arose not from a need to get the abbey out of financial difficulty but to meet an abbot's own extravagance. During Edward II's reign there were annual corrodies to be paid amounting to some £6,000 in present-day money. There were ways of avoiding too great embarrassments: in 1280, abbot John procured a papal charter 'that the abbey is not bound to pay its debts unless it have been proved that they had been turned to the profit of the monastery'. No means of furthering the abbey's interests were overlooked.

Always there was the steady income from the pilgrims to the shrines of Glastonbury's saints. On one occasion at least the covetousness to increase the number of relics to be viewed rebounded horridly. In 1052 abbot Aylward 'irreverently dug open the grave of king Edgar'.[31] Though dead for seventy-seven years, it seems that the great king's body had not wholly decomposed and was too big to be forced into the niche prepared for it. So with some difficulty it was placed on an altar with other relics. The sight of what he had done drove the desecrator mad, and as he rushed from the church the abbot fell over and broke his neck. There were, however, relics enough. By the end of the 13th century their veneration brought in at least £120 annually, say £8,000 in present value though this is difficult to assess. A yet greater sum came from the sale of indulgences granted not only to the abbey but to its dependent cells.

These enormous contributions should be seen in proper perspective. The deplorable is always more entertaining than the admirable, and in Glastonbury as elsewhere there were periods of laxity and corruption: but for the greater part of her history the abbey was well-conducted, and the interaction of piety and wealth well-observed. The modern mind, used to accepting secular fraud as natural and inevitable, finds it easy to regard the 'pious frauds' of the middle ages with contempt

The Shrines of Glastonbury

and distaste. Yet there is plenty of evidence that these 'frauds', even when designed to increase the wealth of church or abbey, were rarely for individual gain and were usually accompanied by a higher purpose. The extraordinary aura of sanctity, the mystical quality nurtured through centuries and inescapable to-day among those ruins in Avalon, brought valuable results. The capacity of the abbey to perform her mission to educate as well as to inspire religious faith grew as the faith of the religious with their alms gave her the power and independence to carry out her work.

This civilizing was notable: Leland who went there speaks of it, the probing antiquarian Hearne describes the free school where not only the sons of gentlemen but of the poor were brought up and fitted for the university. With wealth greater than any ecclesiastical seat in England, its state was one of great dignity, and latterly of simplicity. Hospitality on an astonishing scale was provided not only for the distinguished visitors but for thousands of the needy. At the time of abbot Bere the abbey was 'a well-disciplined court' and the descriptions sometimes remind one of the Montefeltri at Urbino, though without the emphasis on the courtier. It was this that was inherited by Richard Whyting, last abbot of Glastonbury.

The gaze is held fascinated here, drawn to the most brilliant star in the firmament the moment before it is extinguished. Even now, after more than four hundred years, and with more than a millennium of history to frame the view, the tragedy still strikes hard and suddenly, clutching the heart with pity and terror.

Richard Whyting was in his sixties when he succeeded the grave, discreet administrator, abbot Bere, friend of the diplomatist Richard Pace and acquaintance of Erasmus. He had been educated at Cambridge where he took his M.A. in 1483, and, after further years at Glastonbury when he was ordained priest, returned in 1505 to receive his Doctorate in Theology. From then until he was appointed abbot in 1525 he lived in the cloister, holding latterly the office of Chamberlain. He was a man of high character, and though not one to seek high office he accepted the abbacy and ruled with dignity but without losing his simplicity, even austerity, in his personal life. This was the opinion of all his contemporaries except the hired detractors brought in at the end to destroy him.

It is likely enough, though he seems to have retained his poise throughout, that Whyting perceived, certainly not the whole nature of the change that was imminent, but that the wind blew cold. The abbots of Glastonbury, peers representative in parliament, were in touch with affairs of State. They could not fail to see the results of the Wars of the Roses, the destruction of the old families, the rise of new men avaricious of power and wealth, toadying to the new monarch. Within a few years of Whyting's succession, for all his disinclination to leave his abbey and attend court or parliament, he knew the significance of Henry VIII's elevation of Sir Thomas Boleyn, the subsequent fall of Wolsey and the advancement of Thomas Cromwell. With the Act of Supremacy in 1534, and with a second statute making it treason to deny it, the slide to the end began.

The abbot and his community signed the Declaration acknowledging the supremacy of the king, as indeed did almost all other churchmen. It could be argued privately that acknowledging the king as head of the church of England did not derogate from the Pope his wider supremacy. Though the oath was shortly stiffened by another to the effect that the Bishop of Rome had no greater authority than any other bishop, this also was generally taken. There was no alternative but the loss of everything including probably life. It was difficult to apprehend that the king would deliberately destroy the religious, cultural and artistic heritage of centuries.

Hope vanished, apprehension was swiftly fulfilled. Within a year of the oath-taking, Cromwell devised the Visitation of all religious houses, its object being ostensibly reform, the means of reform so impossible to carry out that 'voluntary' dissolution was the only answer. He chose Dr Richard Layton to visit Glastonbury, but even the execrable doctor could find nothing evil to report. The regulations imposed nevertheless weakened the abbot's jurisdiction, not only over his own community but over the courts for the poor in the town; he appealed without success. Then came the rising in the north, the savage suppression of the Pilgrimage of Grace. In 1538, Cromwell circulated a letter of transparent hypocrisy to the monasteries to the

The Shrines of Glastonbury

effect that dissolution was far from the royal mind, and that if certain monasteries had not been voluntarily surrendered the king would never have received them: *proviso*, however, that should any house in fear of being dissolved start disposing of its assets, this would incur loss of all possessions and life itself.

With Glastonbury alone remaining in Somerset, and the sight of desecration, dismantling and homeless monks in all the country round, Whyting knew the end was near. By an act of April 1539 the king was empowered to take over any monastery by reason of attainder of treason. This was needed to give legal colour, for, in the case of a great abbey such as Glastonbury refusing to surrender, no law empowered its seizure. Already, though, the abbey had been relieved of its 'superfluous plate', including the great sapphire of Glastonbury, a superaltar garnished with silver and part gold. That year the abbot did not attend parliament, awaiting the inevitable at home.

In September the Visitors returned, this time with no pretence but that of confirming the abbot's 'cankered and traitorous mind'. This done, the eighty-year-old abbot, 'a very weak man and sickly', was sent forthwith to the Tower. Nothing shows more clearly the king's and Cromwell's preoccupation than the letters sent by the Visitors which speak of little but the items of money, gold and plate which they are collecting. Soon Cromwell could list 'The plate of Glastonbury, 11,000 ounces and over, besides golden. The furniture of the house of Glaston. In ready money from Glaston, £1,100 and over. The rich copes from Glaston. The whole years revenue of Glaston. The debts of [to] Glaston, £2,000 and above.'[32] With the monks cleared out and the abbey empty, it was as though the abbot was already condemned.

This was in fact so. There was no trial, only a secret inquisition in the Tower. The reasons for condemnation have never been clear: past views 'treasonably' expressed about the king's divorce, making away with the abbey's assets, the 'Robbing of Glastonbury Church', it mattered little. 'Item: The Abbot of Glaston to be tryed at Glaston, and also executyd there with his complycys', wrote Cromwell.[33]

An example was to be made, one which no Englishman could ignore. On Friday, November 14th, 1539, Whyting was brought to Wells. The farce had been well-prepared, the jury packed so that he would appear condemned by those closest to him, witnesses produced with framed accusations and no chance given to inquire their truth. There is nothing to show that anything happened beyond this and the reading to the jury of a sentence already passed. What strikes home to-day, making the horror vivid, is the likeness in procedure to that in the modern authoritarian state. The next morning, Saturday, Whyting was taken to Glastonbury. At the entrance of the town, the last abbot was bound on a hurdle and dragged through the streets, past his now desolate abbey, on and up to the summit of Glastonbury Tor with all Avalon below him. There, with the two monks, John Thorne and Roger James, who were to be executed with him, he was put to death. His quartered body was divided between Wells, Bath, Ilchester and Bridgwater, his head set up over the gateway of his abbey. In a reign begun with high promise and declining to a monster's progress, there was no act more foul, nor a man more noble who suffered it.

There is no palpable sequel, no reliable evidence of contemporary opinion. There was too much fear abroad for men to record their true thoughts: the silence that fell was broken only by the sound of the wreckers. In 1559, twenty years later, the estate of the abbey was granted by Elizabeth I to Sir Peter Carew, and in various private hands it stayed until 1908.

Four centuries of English weather and masons wanting good stone have worked thoroughly. The only building remaining almost whole is the abbot's kitchen, square outside, the interior octagonal, and crowned with a double lantern. But other parts still stand among the lawns, fragmentary, but showing as in the three walls and two doorways of the Transitional Lady Chapel the exquisite character of the sculpture. Called sometime the chapel of St Joseph, it stands partly on the foundations of the Old Church and once held the relics of a multitude of saints: 'the heavenly sanctuary on earth' William of Malmesbury called it. Adjoining is an Early English ruin, almost certainly a Galilee which linked the chapel with the Great Church. The nave of the Great Church is a greensward flanked on the south by three of the once ten bays; the choir had six, but none remain. The windows of the bays have pointed arches without and semicircular within. A tower surmounted the

The Shrines of Glastonbury

intersection of the transepts with the nave and choir, and two of its piers are there to mark its grandeur. With the Edgar Chapel built by abbot Bere, the Great Church is longer than any cathedral or monastic church in England, nearly two hundred yards; the nave has a width of eighty feet.

That is all the eye sees: the mind and the imagination travel on, drawn deeper by the numinous quality of the place, the sense of loneliness in a place once populous, and which, even when peopled, had its roots in a legendary past.

> And this I knowe well, both in prose, ryme and verse,
> Men loue nat to rede an ouer longe thyng;
> Therefore I entende this mater to short and sease,
> I pray you all to marke well the endynge.
>
> Ye pylgrymes all, gyue your attendaunce
> Saynt Ioseph there to serue with humble affectyon,
> At Glastenbury for to do hym reverence
> Lyft up your hertes with goostly deuocyn.
>
> Lo, Lordes, what Ihesu doeth in Ianuary,
> Whan the great colde cometh to grounde;
> He maketh the hauthorne to sprynge full freshely.
> Where as it pleaseth hym, his grace is founde;
> He may loose all thing that is bounde.
> Thankes be gyuen to hym that in heuen sytteth,
> That floryssaeth his werkes so on the grounde,
> And in Glastenbury, Quia mirabilia fecit.
>
> Sothely Glastenbury is the holyest erth of england.[34]

IV

ST CUTHBERT OF LINDISFARNE AND DURHAM

THE BEAUTY of the Northumbrian coasts where the hills rise in folds to the Cheviots is austere; often, even in summer, it is suddenly hidden by sea mists sweeping in over grey water. There is nothing to be seen then but puffs of spray from the breakers on the offshore islands of Farne. The islands are sanctuaries, especially for eider-duck, St Cuthbert's bird, and colonies of seals live there. The cry of gulls, the chorus of wild geese on the saltings of the mainland and the call of curlew wheeling in the mist are the overture to the curtain rising on Lindisfarne, Ynys Medicante, Holy Island.

Nearly halfway between the once royal Saxon capital of Bamburgh with its castle on a cliff and the border town of Berwick, a lane runs down from the coast road to the shore where a table of the tides points the danger of trying to cross the two miles or so of watery flats to the island except at certain hours. For some seven hours between high tides the way is safe, but the tides come in swiftly. A part of the track has been made into a causeway with a bridge midway over the Lindis that at all times flows fast through the sands, and there is a refuge box on stilts for anyone caught by the rising water. Unwise travellers are sometimes drowned. This modern way leads to hard sands under the dunes which curve towards the mainland: the old track, the Pilgrims' Way, goes at an angle

Saint Cuthbert of Lindisfarne and Durham

south-east for three miles over the flats to where the limestone rocks of the island join the dunes. This way is marked by tall poles, their tips showing when the tide is high.

The crouching village of Northumbrian stone is hardly visible among the windswept trees, but across the further flats on the other side of the island the castle of Beblowe stands high on a mass of basalt, commanding the sea from Berwick to Bamburgh and from Northumbria to the Cheviots. It was built in the 16th century with stones from the now ruined priory that had been built in 1093 on the site of the monastery destroyed by the Danes. This monastery had contained since the 7th century the cathedral of St Aidan, and above all of St Cuthbert, from which Christianity spread through the north country. It was from the time of the later priory that Lindisfarne became known as Holy Island, though the people there still hold to its old name.

At Durham, seventy miles to the south, the great new cathedral had already been begun by bishop Carilef. There might seem no greater contrast than that between the desolate beauty and simplicity of Lindisfarne and this vast monastic church raised in the saint's honour on a cliff in a loop of the river Wear. Yet the building represents the man remarkably: both in their separate ways are more than life-size, each has an austere simplicity, both disarm the doubter and critic with their warmth and holiness. The proportions here are perfect, the aesthetic balancing the ascetic, the work of mind and body inspired. The immense pillars, geometrically incised, give no sense of overpowering weight, the relation between the round arches they support and the triforium, and the clerestory from which the light pours down, is such that they seem to soar with the slimmer pillars to the vaulting. Wherever the eye falls there is light and strength and symmetry. The building admits the world, and its great space contains and orders it. Shuffle of footsteps, raised, inquiring voices, the hard tap of heels on stone or pattering boys, no crowded sounds can interrupt its vast tranquillity. It stands as did St Cuthbert for divine regulation in a world of chaos.

There is the physical background of Cuthbert, the isolation of Lindisfarne and the glory of Durham. In pursuing the train of events which he set in motion, you find yourself continually

Saint Cuthbert of Lindisfarne and Durham

moving backwards and forwards in time. Of all English saints he has the strange quality of never having seemed to die. Whether it is miracles after his death, grants of land to Durham, request to the king, advice to pilgrims, rebukes to transgressors, granting of sanctuary to fugitives, and the countless other matters, spiritual or economic, connected with his name and shrine, they are almost always referred to as though he himself was dealing with them. St Cuthbert has been pleased to bless, St Cuthbert demands, refuses, grants, accepts, is made sad by . . . Only rarely do the abbots or Prince Bishops who followed him speak in their own names or in that of the monastic see.

This is not due to hagiolatry: it arises and continues almost certainly from a combination of the man's qualities and the age in which he lived, together with the astonishing journeying of his body after death, which, in itself a pilgrimage, begat centuries of pilgrimage to come, giving a sense of vivid and continuous movement. The paradox of his life is that, though he always kept clear of any sort of politics, and sought seclusion, the fame of his physical and spiritual power never let him rest.

Cuthbert was born in 635 into an age of enormous confusion. It was only two hundred years since the Romans had left their settlers to fend for themselves; the incoming Anglo-Saxons had not yet final supremacy over the native Britons. England was not England until nearly two centuries after Cuthbert's death, when king Alfred, hiding in the marshes of Glastonbury from later invaders, the Danes, had his vision of the saint promising him victory at Ethandune.[1] There is a ticklish irony about this king, descendant of the annihilators of Britons, being inspired by a British saint to a victory that has made him one of our national heroes. The confusion in religion was as great. Only some thirty years before Cuthbert's birth, the kingdom that held Augustine's see of Canterbury reverted to paganism;[2] much later still the north, its king converted by Paulinus, went back to the old gods as soon as the powerful Edwin was defeated.[3] God, or the gods, were judged by a standard of success, understandable in people whose view of the one God or the gods of nature was anthropomorphic.

The required success soon came to Northumbria with St Oswald, who, returning as king from exile in Scotland, called

Saint Cuthbert of Lindisfarne and Durham

in Aidan from Iona to help him re-Christianize the north. 'The king appointed him his episcopal see in the isle of Lindisfarne as he desired. Which place, as the tide flows and ebbs twice a day, is enclosed by the waves of the sea as an island; and again, twice in the day, when the shore is left dry, becomes contiguous to the land.'[4] It seems to-day a strange place for a bishop's seat, but islands then were not only comparatively safe but possessed from long pre-Christian times a mystical significance as a part and yet not a part of this world. Also, Lindisfarne was only seven miles along the coast from the royal capital of Bamburgh.

Like the infant Samuel, Cuthbert, born in the very same year as the foundation of his future see, seems always to have had about him an aura of the co-incidental or the miraculous. He was born near the abbey of Melrose, nothing is known of his parents and he was brought up by a foster-mother named Kenswith. His strong body was to serve him well, and it was while playing hockey in which he excelled that he had his first revelation. A younger player stops suddenly and cries bitterly. When they gather round, he turns to Cuthbert who is trying to comfort him and tells him he should not be playing 'when the Lord has appointed you to be a teacher of virtue even to those who are older than yourself'. He becomes more serious; when he injures his knee it is cured by a man in white on a horse,

Saint Cuthbert of Lindisfarne and Durham

like the angels on horseback who came to the aid of Judas Maccabaeus. Then comes his vision of the door of heaven being opened and the spirit of some holy man being led there by angels. It was this vision, coming at the moment of Aidan's death, that decided Cuthbert on his vocation. He was sixteen.

There was an interval of soldiering against the pagans between the vision and his entry into Melrose, but once there he was exemplary, except that he would fast only on special occasions because he wanted to keep his strength. After a few years he was moved to the new monastery of Ripon, but, holding to the customs of the Celtic Church, he soon returned to Melrose when Ripon submitted to Roman usage over the date of Easter. Later, when his prior, Boisil, died, Cuthbert took his place. A great part of his time was spent travelling through the wildest parts of the country where few would venture and where many of the people were little more than savages. The yellow plague which had taken off Boisil and many of the monks had come from the south and was poisoning the whole land. The terrified people were going back to their charms and amulets, and Cuthbert went out not only to help but to revive the Faith. He seems to have had St Francis's way with birds and animals, and one of the happiest events was when he was visiting the abbess Ebba of Coldingham. Seeing that each night he went out and did not return till morning prayer, a monk

Saint Cuthbert of Lindisfarne and Durham

followed and watched him walk into the sea up to his neck and stay there praising God till dawn, when, to the monk's astonishment, two seals came after him, and, as he knelt to pray, breathed upon him and wiped his feet with their hair. After receiving his blessing they departed.

Bede, who was fourteen when Cuthbert died, in his *Life* of the saint from which all later biographers borrowed,[5] tells this and a great deal more of the healings he performed on his journeys. He says in his preface that he has written only what he had verified from talking with people who could give him first-hand accounts, and that even when he had finished he submitted it for correction to men 'who for a long time had well known the life and conversation of that man of God'. Bede was a scrupulous writer, and though there may have been over-enthusiasm in some of his informants the corroborative details he gives of many of the saint's miracles make it clear that Cuthbert possessed the gift of healing and prophecy.

In 664 occurred the Synod of Whitby to settle the long controversy over Easter, since the passionate convictions of the Celtic and Roman Churches respectively as to its date threatened the spread of Christianity.[6] Colman, bishop of Lindisfarne, spoke for the British, Wilfrid of Ripon for the Roman: Wilfrid's arguments, though arrogant, won. The king, summing up with good sense, declared that since St Peter held the keys of Heaven he would not contradict since otherwise the gates might not be opened to him. Colman, much regretted, retired to Iona, and Cuthbert was called to help his old abbot, Eata, taught as a boy by Aidan, who had been appointed to Lindisfarne.

There were still monks there who would not give way to the Whitby decision, and Cuthbert's qualities were needed 'to teach the rules of monastic perfection';[7] for although he had always held to Celtic usage he put the unity of the Church first. When spared from duty at the abbey, he travelled far over the mainland; it was taxing to his mind as well as to his body, and after twelve years he obtained his abbot's permission to retire to a contemplative life. First, he went to an islet just off Lindisfarne – a cross marks the place of the altar which Bede says he used – but it was too accessible. A few miles off Bamburgh are the Farne Islands; on the nearest of these, the Inner Farne, Cuthbert lived for nine years.[8] The monks helped him to excavate a dwelling out of the rock, and when they had brought him the tools for husbandry he asked to be left to look after himself. But though isolated often by weather, he could not escape his fame; people came from all over Britain to seek advice, consolation or healing.

In the Norman church on Lindisfarne a pre-Raphaelite picture shows king Egfrid and archbishop Theodore of Canterbury pressing the crozier on Cuthbert who is hanging on to his spade, while a pair of crows he had earlier rebuked for stealing look primly at a bunch of onions. Cuthbert could never refuse a duty, so he left his storm-beaten island of birds to become bishop of Lindisfarne.

This was in 685, and he was only about fifty. But he had led a hard life; now, as bishop, he at once began again his journeyings all over the north country. On a Saturday afternoon in May of that year, the 20th of the month, he was in Carlisle being shown round the Roman ruins by the town reeve; but he was disturbed and kept on stopping with a distracted air. Presently, leaning on his stick, he exclaimed: 'A-ah! I believe the war is over and judgement given against our people.' Excusing himself, he went off to the queen who was staying in the town while her husband was fighting the Scots, and told her to hurry back to Bamburgh. The next day being Sunday, it was unlawful to travel by chariot, but on Monday came the news of the defeat and death of Egfrid and she left. Cuthbert had prophesied a year earlier that his most Christian king would be killed if he went on ravaging other Christians.

Shortly after he foretold his own death to an old hermit friend near Derwentwater, and, when he had been bishop hardly two years, he left Lindisfarne for the last time. The monks crowded around him as he stepped on to the ship that was to take him to his retreat on Farne. 'Tell us, my lord bishop, when we may hope for your return.' 'When you shall bring my body back here.'[9] It was just after Christmas 696, and on March 20th of the next year he died. The story of his last days is told by Herefrid, abbot of Lindisfarne, who with other monks went to look after him and related it afterwards to Bede.

He had been ill for some time and for five days storms had prevented anyone reaching the Inner Farne; when Herefrid

Saint Cuthbert of Lindisfarne and Durham

came he found Cuthbert only just alive though with a clear mind. He declared that he wished to be buried there where he was. 'I think it better for you, also,' he said, 'that I should remain here, on account of the fugitives and criminals who may flee to my corpse for refuge; and when they have thus obtained an asylum, inasmuch as I have enjoyed the fame, humble though I am, of being a servant of Christ, you may think it necessary to intercede for such before the secular rulers, and so you may have trouble on my account.'[10] However, when they had assured him that whatever the trouble they would find it agreeable, Cuthbert gave way, but advised them that if they took his body they should 'bury it in the inmost parts of the church, that you may be able to visit my tomb yourselves, and to control the visits of all other persons'. Within a few hundred years, his shrine at Durham was to be one of the most famous places of 'sanctuary' in all England.

He died at vespers. A monk climbed a hill and signalled with torches over the dark sea to the watchman on Lindisfarne. They were singing then the 59th Psalm: 'O Lord, thou hast rejected us and destroyed us; thou hast been angry, and hast pitied us.'[11] In death, as in life, his passing was illuminated by prophecy. The end was near of an age when, for more than half a century, Lindisfarne had been supreme, and the torch of Christianity had shone from Lindisfarne rather than from Durham.

But though Northumbria fell into chaos, and the influence of Lindisfarne was temporarily diminished, the light did not go out. It was the north that kept culture alive and laid the foundations of English literature and learning. From Caedmon, the cowherd of Whitby, came the poetry of reflectiveness, the striving to interpret the mystery of life and of experience in place of the crude if vivid songs of war. And now there was Bede, the polymath, encyclopaedic in knowledge as he was simple and good-humoured, working all his life in Benedict Biscop's monastery of Jarrow. Biscop had already built Wearmouth in Roman style, using French masons and glass-makers to glaze the windows, and from Rome brought pictures, vestments and books.[12] 'The learning and civilization of the 8th century,' says Stubbs, 'rested on the monastery which he founded, which produced Bede, and through him the school of

York, Alcuin and the Carolingian school on which the culture of the Middle Ages was built.'

It is strange that among all the writings of Bede, who outlived Cuthbert by forty-eight years, there is no mention of Biscop and Cuthbert having met. They were both famous, were contemporaries, were great travellers, and Jarrow and Wearmouth were only sixty miles from Lindisfarne. Yet no record exists of their having come together. It seems inexplicable. Could it have been that they were so different in temperament that it never occurred to them to see one another? Biscop, the intellectual, the builder, the priest devoted to Rome and scholarship, may have been preoccupied by a busy and often material life, while Cuthbert, altogether a man of God, by nature a recluse and by calling a missionary, and who, moreover, still followed the old British way of Christianizing, may have held back from meeting a man who looked to Rome for guidance.

For nine years the body of the Great Thaumaturge lay undisturbed at Lindisfarne. Then the monks on the anniversary of his burial opened his tomb with the intention of putting his dry bones in a small coffer in a shrine above ground to be venerated by pilgrims. To their astonishment they found his body uncorrupted and the clothes in which he had been wrapped undecayed.[13] This piece of popular hagiology cannot in Cuthbert's case be wholly dismissed. After 1200 years, and two intervening openings of his coffin, there were still traces of mummification, and the exquisite quality of the wrappings can be seen at Durham to this day.

In 787 came the first warning of the coming terror, with the appearance of three ships of Northmen. Six years later they returned, and 'on 8 January the harrying of the heathen miserably destroyed God's church in Lindisfarne by rapine and slaughter'.[14] But when the monks who had escaped returned they found that the tomb of Cuthbert had not been discovered. Though they rebuilt the church and monastery, they lived in constant fear; year by year the Danish incursions became more savage, until in 875 the monks decided to abandon Lindisfarne. Taking with them the body of their saint they set out on their travels which were to last until one hundred and twenty years later they came to rest at Durham.

Saint Cuthbert of Lindisfarne and Durham

The first seven years were the most dramatic as they wandered, hunted from place to place, over the whole of Northumbria and Galloway. To-day, there are fifty or more churches to mark some of the countless rests taken by the saint's body. The destruction of monasteries by the Danes was complete: not only Lindisfarne, but Jarrow and Wearmouth and all others disappeared; all material evidence of Christianity was extinguished. There was only this extraordinary journey of Cuthbert's body to draw together the hopes of Christians and bring about finally a revival.

One of the strangest incidents occurred when in despair the monks decided to take ship for Ireland. Together with the coffin they had brought away a book of the four gospels in old-Irish calligraphy, illuminated with interlacings and arabesques, and decorated with gems and metalwork; a noble work given by Bishop Eadfrith as an offering to St Cuthbert's shrine. Soon after the monks set sail a storm hit them and they had to turn back; they reached land with the coffin but the book was swept overboard. Three days later it was found washed up at Whithorn unharmed but for brine stains.[15] Subsequently in the inventories of Durham and of Lindisfarne to which it returned it was known as 'Liber S. Cuthberti qui demersus erat in mare'. In the 10th century the priest Aldred wrote an interlinear gloss in Northumbrian Anglo-Saxon so that it might be more easily read, and made a short note of how the book had been made. It is now in the British Museum, *The Lindisfarne Gospels,* one of the most splendid manuscripts in Europe.

Cuthbert's years of travel after death were so like his wandering when alive that they must have seemed like a new manifestation of him. They were certainly so of his spirit, and were a strong reason for the continuing vividness of his personality. Wherever he passed, a network of legends went on growing for centuries afterwards, and remains firmly established. An example is at Crayke, where Symeon of Durham writes in the 12th century that Cuthbert's body rested four months in the monastery.[16] This is possible, but Crayke rises like an Italian hill town out of the plain only ten miles north of York which was then occupied by Danes. Not long ago, climbing the hill to St Cuthbert's church rebuilt in the 15th century, I met a woman who told me St Cuthbert had been born in Crayke and played on the village green. She stared in hurt disbelief, almost crying, at my doubt, and I said no more. One must be tender with such legends.

The legend that dies hardest, but deserves to die, is that of Cuthbert's dislike of women. The first reference to this is again from Symeon who says that in none of the churches where the saint's body rested were women allowed to enter, this rule arising from Cuthbert's horror at the disorders in the double monastery of Coldingham whose abbess, Ebba, was his close friend. He repeats Bede's story that a good monk of that place had a heavenly visitor who told him he had long watched how the monks and nuns 'either indulge themselves in slothful sleep, or are awake in order to commit sin . . . for which reason a heavy judgement from heaven is deservedly ready to fall on the place, and its devouring fire'. The monk hastened to Ebba who rebuked her flock; but soon after, when the abbess died, 'they returned to their former wickedness, nay, they became more wicked; and when they thought themselves in peace and security, they soon felt the effects of the aforesaid judgement'.[17]

Another reason is given by Reginald of Durham,[18] taking it from the Irish history which claimed Cuthbert as an Irishman.[19] Cuthbert, having crossed to Scotland, was a hermit near the king's court; the king, discovering his daughter to be with child, was told by her that the young hermit had seduced her. Thereon, the king with men at arms sought out Cuthbert, taking with him his daughter, who, made bold by her father's rage, repeated the accusation. Cuthbert called on God to prove his innocence; there was a hissing noise and the earth swallowed up the girl. The king was so frightened that he told Cuthbert to forget all about it. Although this is a fairly common sort of tale, often secularized, as by Boccaccio, it gained currency in Cuthbert's case by being perpetuated in the *Nova Legenda*.[20]

In any event, the result was a strict rule either prohibiting women or confining them to certain parts of the church. In Durham cathedral there is a blue stone cross let into the floor, the long arm of which stretches between the pillars of the nave just west of the north door. Beyond this no woman could pass. In the 12th century king David of Scotland came to Durham with his bride who had a woman of the bedchamber named Helisand.[21] At that time there was no blue cross and the limit

Saint Cuthbert of Lindisfarne and Durham

was somewhere in the churchyard; when the queen reached it they turned back, but Helisand returned dressed as a monk and entered the church. St Cuthbert saw her and told the Sacrist to turn her out, which he did in the most disgusting language. The poor girl afterwards became a nun and the saint forgave her. A little later, about 1175, Hugh de Puiset started to build a chapel for women at the east end of the cathedral, but it began to collapse because it was too near to the shrine of St Cuthbert who disapproved. So the bishop moved as far away as possible and built on to the west end the graceful Galilee chapel of slender columns and dog-toothed arches. In 1333 St Cuthbert discovered queen Philippa sleeping with her husband Edward III in the priory – now the Dean's house. He informed the monks who rapped on the door and told her to leave at once, which she did in her underclothes, according to the narrator, who adds with relish that it was a very cold night. In the 15th century, two women from Newcastle dressed up as men, and, being caught, were made to parade in the same clothes under a shower of abuse from the public.

These are only a few of the countless occasions when Cuthbert's dislike of women was demonstrated. Yet there is no contemporary evidence to show that he ever breathed a word against women, and indeed he had many close friends among them: nor is there anything near-contemporary about his having had a building on Lindisfarne called the Church on the Green – Grene Cyrici – for women only. It was not until after the Conquest that the legend appeared, and it was probably a Norman invention when the Cuthbertine community was replaced by Benedictine monks in 1083 by bishop Carilef. Cuthbert, although persuaded by the Synod of Whitby to adopt Roman usage over Easter, had remained in many ways faithful to the British manner of conducting his church which permitted marriage in religious communities. To make sure that so eminent a saint was in full accord with the new rule, a fresh revelation had to be given of his views on women.

But another 113 years were to pass before this happened. From Crayke the Community bore Cuthbert's body to Chester-le-Street. The victories of Alfred, aided by his vision of the saint, had brought a sort of peace. Though the Danes had not been driven out, they had for the moment stopped tormenting

Christians, and a measure of the awe surrounding Cuthbert showed itself when the abbot informed the Danes that the saint required Guthred to be king of Northumbria and they agreed. Moreover, they acceded to the saint's demand for all the land between the Tyne and the Wear. This gift, confirmed by Alfred the suzerain, was the foundation of the mediaeval patrimony of St Cuthbert and the cradle of the palatine princedom of Durham. So Eardulf, the 16th and last bishop from Lindisfarne, became bishop of Chester-le-Street. When one considers the wildness of that north country, the dense forests, mountains and hard climate, the famine caused by the Danish devastation, the distrust and terror which turned men to beasts fighting for survival, the survival of the bishop, abbot and the monks who for seven years bore the coffin seems as remarkable as the incorruption of the saint's body.

Undisturbed at last, the Community set up the shrine of St Cuthbert at Chester-le-Street where for more than a century it was a focus of pilgrimage. The royal injunction to honour the saint had been passed down by Alfred to his son, Edward, and in turn to Athelstan and Edmund. The first royal pilgrim was the magnificent Athelstan on his way to subdue Constantine of Scotland in 934. Among his many costly gifts were the stole, maniple, girdle and two golden bracelets found nine hundred years later in St Cuthbert's coffin and now in Durham.[22] Ten years later, when the Scots were again giving trouble, his brother Edmund came on pilgrimage with many more handsome gifts. Victory resulted, as the king had made 'some use of that opinion which his soldiers had conceived of St Cuthbert's being a tutelary Deitie against the Scotts; in conceit of whose protection, the English much were encouraged to the grave disadvantage of their enemies'.[23]

But in 995 the Community was on the move again. The Danes made a sudden incursion and St Cuthbert went with his men to Ripon further inland. It was the spring of the year and they stayed at Ripon until the autumn, when the danger was over. Then, when they set off on the way back to Chester-le-Street, a decisive miracle occurred, the miracle of the Dun Cow.

It is impossible to know what really happened. The first account is Symeon's in which he says that at a place called

Saint Cuthbert of Lindisfarne and Durham

Wardelawe St Cuthbert's coffin became immovable. Every effort to shift it having failed, the bishop declared three days of fasting, during which there was a revelation that St Cuthbert wished to go to Dunholm and stay there. They at once set off, and, having arrived at this cliff in the loop of the Wear, built a wattle church. No mention of the cow; no mention of it either by Reginald of Durham more than a hundred years later. In fact the first mention seems to have been in a manuscript of 1620 which tells that the monks heard a woman whose cow had strayed asking a milkmaid if she had seen it. When the milkmaid replied that it was down in Dunholme, the monks took it as a sign from heaven, since, though their saint had said Dunholme he had not said where it was. Guided by the woman, they soon found it. The manuscript says it was bishop Ranulf Flambard who died in the 'dies caniculares' in 1189 who put up the monument of a milkmaid milking her cow on the north-west turret of the nine altars to commemorate this event.[24] Flambard's sculpture[25] crumbled and was replaced in 1775 by the one that is there now of two women standing by the cow. The famous legend is probably a bit of local folklore which may have arisen from Flambard's fancy in sculpture or may have pre-dated it. The bishop cannot have been commemorating a well-known miracle or the early writers would certainly have told of it. Like the flowering hawthorn of Joseph of Arimathaea it seems to have been a late-flowering legend at a time when the Age of Faith had waned.

St Cuthbert was at last at rest. He did have one other journey in 1069 when William the Conqueror, enraged at the continued defiance of the north, decided to subdue it in person. The Community fled with the body to Lindisfarne, the waters opening like the Red Sea to let them pass; but in a few months St Cuthbert returned to Durham, safety and perpetual veneration. But for this short affair, the story from the building of the first wattle church in 995 is one of rapid growth in fame and splendour. For 'after that Aldhunus and his wandering mates had reposed the reliques of their great patron Cuthbert and buylded somewhat at Durham, then begged they hard not for cantels of chese, as other poor men doe, but for large corners of good counties, as all there profession used'.[26]

The wattle church lasted only three years and was replaced

by a stone building known as the White Church, which, according to Reginald, had two towers with brazen pinnacles, and stood for nearly a hundred years. It was during this time that many of the important relics were brought to Durham by Ealfred the Sacrist, who, even allowing for his burning faith, was wholly unscrupulous. As a guardian of the shrine of St Cuthbert, he 'attained to such a degree of cordiality with the saint that it was his custom to cut the evergrowing hair of his venerable head, to adjust it by dividing it and smoothing with an ivory comb and to cut the nails of his fingers, tastefully reducing them to roundness'.[27] While this evidence of incorruptibility can be discounted, the ivory comb taken from the saint's coffin now in Durham is from its description probably the one Ealfred used. In his relic-collecting he was guided by a vision ordering him to disinter the bones of a number of important saints. In the course of this he removed among others those of Boisil who had taught Cuthbert at Melrose, of Cuthbert's friend, Ebba, of Bilfrid who had illuminated the Lindisfarne Gospels, and, most important, of Bede. In Bede's case, he had to be patient; year after year he visited Jarrow on Bede's anniversary of May 29th when the bones were exhibited. At last, no one knows how, he seized some chance, and the bones, or some of them, were removed and placed in St Cuthbert's tomb. It is queer that no record exists of anyone making a fuss. Some 140 years later de Puiset enshrined Bede's bones in a gold and silver casket placed on a blue marble tomb in the Galilee Chapel he had built.

Meanwhile, the Normans had recognized Durham's importance. In 1072, the Conqueror, stopping on his way back from Scotland to see that a castle was begun there, decided to make sure he was not being fooled. He demanded to see Cuthbert's body and threatened to put the Community to the sword if they did not produce it. In their fear they prayed Cuthbert to intercede with God to help them, whereupon the king who was attending Mass was seized with an awful choler and rushed out of the church. Ignoring the banquet prepared for him, he leaped on his horse and did not draw rein till he had crossed the Tees.[28] 'Thus St Cuthbert had the victory over the Conqueror ... for after this the king had a reverend opinion of St Cuthbert.'[29] A good deal of fun has been poked at this story,

Saint Cuthbert of Lindisfarne and Durham

but the Conqueror may well have been suddenly struck by the enormity of his ordering the exposure of the saint's body for his inspection. One must bear in mind always when judging the 'miracles' and the behaviour of men in face of them that emotions were then more violent as well as more susceptible to religious awe.

Ten years later with pope Gregory VII's approval, the king also giving his assent, Benedictine monks of Jarrow and Wearmouth were brought to Durham and the Rule established. According to the Charter this was done because of the incorrigible life of the clergy.[30] It seems more likely that with the growing importance of Durham, the Community, many members of which were married, was not suitable to the new discipline being established in other great monasteries. So there passed away the last remnant of Lindisfarne Celtic custom established by St Aidan and inherited by St Cuthbert.

In 1091 bishop Carilef began to dismantle the Saxon Church, and two years later to build the cathedral, which, except for the late 12th-century Galilee, was completed in forty years. With the further addition of the 13th-century chapel of the Nine Altars at the east end it stands magnificent to-day as it did then, virtually unchanged. But before he made a start the bishop had built a splendid tomb above ground in the cloister garth to hold St Cuthbert's coffin until a place was ready for it in the new building. When he died in 1099, Ranulf, nicknamed Flambard for his capacity for mischief in helping William Rufus oppress his subjects, obtained the see. This witty rascal continued building until his general unpopularity caused Henry I to put him in the Tower, from which he was allowed to escape to France although Henry disliked him intensely. There he became bishop of Lisieux and eventually made his peace with the king. It would seem unlikely that he returned to England before Tinchebray, yet accounts of the Translation of St Cuthbert in 1104 refer to him as being present. The contemporary Symeon speaks only of 'the bishop': one more nice historical point.

The memorable Translation of 1104 came about when the cathedral, though not completed, was ready to receive its saint.[31] The monks were much worried by doubts spread of St Cuthbert's incorruption, and, since the Translation was to be attended by a throng of bishops from all over the country, they felt they must make sure in case of awkward questions. So the prior and nine monks, of whom Symeon was one, were appointed to investigate. Symeon had come from the south, first to Jarrow and then transferred to Durham; a man of exemplary life, he was probably included now because he was a writer and would give a good account of what he saw.

The monks waited in the cathedral until night before opening the coffin. To their astonishment, they found it contained two more coffins one within the other, and the carving on the innermost tallied with Bede's description of it. Overcoming their fear at this revelation after 400 years, they raised the lid and found first a shelf on which was a copy of the gospels and the saint's little silver altar. Beneath lay the body on its side and surrounded by a crowd of saintly bones placed there by the relic hunter, Aelfred, a century earlier. Removing the linen covering, they found the body entire and flexible. So much so that there was nearly an accident when they lifted it from the coffin to lay it on the pavement while they cleared the coffin of the bones. Dawn being near, they replaced the body. The next night, laying it on a carpet in the choir, they examined it more closely. Its outward covering was a pallium, then a purple dalmatic with flowers and animals worked into it and interwoven with gold, and then a linen sheet. Making sure once more that their eyes and sense of touch had not deceived them, they wrapped it, in addition to its existing robes, in the richest robe they possessed, covered it with fine linen and replaced their saint in his coffin, putting back with him the head of king Oswald, the founder of Lindisfarne.

But then their troubles began. Unable to contain their joy, it became known at once. Among the prelates assembled was one abbot, either from York or Selby, who objected strongly to what they had done. He even suggested that their secret action showed they feared an independent witness and might well be lying about the whole affair. This set everyone by the ears and divided the visitors into two camps. Fortunately there was a man of great tact, Ralph, abbot of Seez, later archbishop of Canterbury, who without taking sides declared in all humility that the stronger the evidence of the miracle the

Saint Cuthbert of Lindisfarne and Durham

wider would be spread the glory of God in the blessed Cuthbert.

A number of abbots and eminent persons, and certain of the clergy, were invited into the choir, the Prior making it a condition that no one but Ralph de Seez should touch the body, the others seeing the truth only with their eyes. Ralph approached, raised the body, tested its flexibility, and declared it incorrupt. The voices rose in 'Te Deum laudamus', the coffin was raised shoulder high and borne into the open air to be greeted with tremendous enthusiasm by the vast and expectant crowd. Then, after a long sermon during which a storm broke without spoiling anything, the saint was carried back to the place prepared for him in the feretory behind the High Altar and solemn Mass celebrated. After which 'all returned homewards with joy, glorifying and praising God for all those things that they had seen and heard.'

It was one of the greatest events ever to occur in the long history of the shrine of Durham. It illuminated the sanctity of a man already revered for four centuries, ensured it, indeed, for ever. Moreover, the riches it brought increased the power and independence of the Princes Palatine which were to last for another seven hundred and fifty years. The account is Symeon's, he touched the body and wrote of it in a simple and straightforward way. Later writers embellished it with some incredible and irrelevant miracles. What makes Symeon valuable is the confirmation of all his findings when the coffin was re-opened 723 years later in 1827 by Dr Raine: all, that is, but the state of the body itself. But even the 'incorruption', after the anatomical study of 1899, cannot be dismissed as myth. For the periosteal skin still on the bones showed that the body had long been in a mummified state as a result either of embalming or of its interment in a stone coffin in the sandy soil of Lindisfarne.

Dr Raine makes too much game of it. His book on St Cuthbert, all that relates to him at Durham and his own opening of the tomb,[32] is written in much the same vein as Dr Fleetwood's attack on the cult of St Winefrede a hundred years earlier. Both can be said to be authoritative works, the authors have taken immense pains to unearth material; but they exemplify the paradox of so much post-Reformation criticism. Anxious to prove the blasphemous absurdity of the old Faith, they present so much detailed information that they end with a wholly understandable picture of the very beliefs they condemn, and engage the sympathy of the reader for these far more than do their opponents who overstate their case by taking for granted a credulity in the face of miracles that makes little sense. The worst that can be said of Dr Raine is that he would never have been Principal Surrogate of the Consistory Court of Durham and Librarian of Durham Cathedral, and enjoyed his golden emoluments, if it had not been for the cult of St Cuthbert which he ridicules; the best, that he wrote a most valuable book. He must have been a tedious man.

The great cathedral grew, successive bishops glorified it from the wealth that flowed in from the far-spreading lands and the thousands of pilgrims to the shrine. No shrine in England surpassed it: 'exalted with most curious workmanship of fine and costly marble all limned and guilted with gold, having four seats or places under the shrine for the pilgrims or lame and sick men sitting on there knees to lean and rest on in time of their devout offerings and fervent prayers to God and holy St Cuthbert for his miraculous relief and succour, which being never wanting made the shrine to be so richly invested

that it was estimated to be one of the most sumptuous monuments in all England, so great were the offerings and jewels that were bestowed upon it, and no less the miracles that were done by it even in these latter days . . .'[33]

Also in the feretory, the whole raised enclosure at the back of the High Altar where the precious relics were kept, and in the centre of which stood the shrine, there were 'accounted to be the most sumptuous and richest Jewells in all the land, with the beautifulness of the fine little images that did stand in the french pier within the feretory, for great was the gifts and godly devotion of kings and queens and other estates at that time towards God and St Cuthbert in that church'.

The 'french pier' is the Neville Screen, made of franche peer or free stone. It stands behind the High Altar which it separates from the feretory, Gothic-sculptured from Caen stone, worked in London and given by John, Lord Neville, about 1380. 'A splendid piece of decorated work, though now but the skeleton of what it was before it was plundered of the 107 figures that graced its niches', writes the Catholic archbishop Eyre in 1887.[34] 'Not the less beautiful, perhaps, for its having been deprived of the various images which darkened its niches,' says Dr Raine in 1827.[35]

The solid basis of Durham's wealth can be seen from the *Bolden Book* of 1183 which deals mainly with its vast properties: but it is no more than a compilation of information to meet the administrative needs of a great estate. The 'patrimonium Sancti Cuthberti' was soundly organized, with nothing to bring in question the prince bishops' rights. Durham was a realm within a realm. On the other hand, what one longs most to know is difficult to find. The personal offerings to the shrine itself which contributed to the great wealth, the kind of people who gave them, and why, are referred to only in scattered records.

The monastic accounts give the impression that the monks only dotted down notes when they felt like it; and the fact that in 1340, in spite of repeated demands by the bishop to see them, they were not forthcoming, suggests that the monks knew how slipshod they were.[36] In any year, there are never more than about a dozen haphazard entries; for example, in 1399 out of only seven there were payments to the laundress for the altar cloth, for a jewel bought for the shrine, for six capons to the

Lord Prior for eating with the Lord Bishop, and for redeeming a gown of cloth of gold in pawn. In 1401 there was the cost of a belt for carrying St Cuthbert's banner and the general expenses on the march when Henry IV took it with him on his invasion of Scotland, the cost of coffers to hold relics given to the king, the earl of Rutland and the countess of Nevill, and fourpence for drink for the men who made a new cord for elevating the cover of the shrine. As a general indication of how the money went, these jottings are quite amusing and sometimes enlightening, but nothing of any import was ever entered.

There are also some feretrar's accounts, those kept by the keeper of the shrine and relics, which run, with a good many gaps, from 1378 to 1489, but these are only of the amount of coins put as offerings by pilgrims into a box at the shrine called the pix of St Cuthbert. There is no comment on what sort of people these were or what brought them on their pilgrimage. The average takings for these years was about £24, to-day worth forty, perhaps fifty, times that sum; our money depreciates so fast that the relative prices of corn would be more accurate. There was little money about in those days, and offerings came more often in the form of gifts.

So one has to build up a picture from an accumulation of detail scattered through the centuries. There, in the heart of Durham, stands the shrine, its gold, its jewels and silver ornaments, the gifts of kings and nobles scintillating in the candles' hundred flames. Around it in the feretory are lesser offerings: the lance of wax given by one in representation of the lance that wounded him, the waxen figures of those who would be cured; put in the feretrar's keeping are a girdle of green silk ornamented with silver, a pewter dish, two pairs of pillows, 'one of Cuthbert downe, his eider duck', a mare for the saint's use, and countless poor men's gifts of little value to the monastery but in their hope evoking the saint's blessing.

Second to the shrine, but famous, are the stores of relics kept on shelves around the walls of the feretory.[37] Bought, given, stolen, fabricated, they make a fabulous collection: 'for from hence at the Resurrection St Stephen will fetch his tooth, Zachary a leg, Simeon an arm, St Christopher an elbow, St Lawrence a finger, St Ambrose some of his hair, St Ebbe her

Saint Cuthbert of Lindisfarne and Durham

foote, with many more . . .' There were too a number of griffin's eggs, a piece of John the Baptist's shirt, a pix containing some of the Blessed Virgin's milk, some of St Andrew's cross, of the rock from which Christ ascended and of His manger, a thorn from His Crown, and countless garments of the saints. Item: some hair from several saints, in some cases with skin attached, not named. Besides these were rich gifts, cups, crosses, plates and caskets of silver, ivory and gold, and precious stones. Hundreds and hundreds of offerings from the wealthy, the poor, the gullible and the faithful.

But of the pilgrims individually there are few records. One in 1171 has a double interest in that it was the year after Becket's death and shows the immediate rise of his cult.[38] An ailing young Norwegian is advised to cast lots thrice to find if he should go to the shrine of St Cuthbert, St Edward or St Thomas; the lot falls to St Cuthbert and he goes to Durham and is cured. The casting of lots seems to have provided a popular competition. Soon after, a boy from Berwick with dysentery is intercepted on his way to Becket's tomb by St Cuthbert and is cured. There is little more to be found but general references to the saving of the halt, the lame and the blind.

If, for so great a shrine as Durham, these references seem scanty, we must try to imagine the conditions of the place and time. The vision of great wealth, pomp and beauty that enshrined St Cuthbert glowed before the eyes of men whose lives were ordinarily spent in struggle with want, disease and fear. If the relics listed seem to us horrible and idiotic, they must be seen as a part of the rich Gothic fantasy which for the upper orders meant chivalry and romance, for the majority some comfort from the evils that surrounded them, and for all an escape from the evident fallibility of man and worldly reward through faith in the miraculous.

Add to this general sense the particular conditions of the north from Reginald's time clear through to the early 16th century and it is easy to see why there should be so little noted of regular day-to-day events. Unlike the south, life in these border lands remained very grim indeed right up to the Dissolution. Even then, when in 1541 Durham was refounded as the Cathedral Church of Christ and Blessed Mary the Virgin, there are hardly any records of what happened in the final scenes of the take-over. For three years plague had been rampant, and the city was almost deserted. The state of the countryside was appalling, with every man's hand against another in a desperate struggle for survival, while in isolated valleys where farming communities might have lived self-contained, all went in fear of the Scottish robbers who added to the general wretchedness. It is significant that the most careful records of the time are those of Sanctuary, and that in the years from 1477 to 1524 out of two hundred and forty-seven seeking Sanctuary one hundred and ninety-five are homicides.

The right of Sanctuary was of great consequence for everyone in the middle ages. Though through canon law and papal decretals it became abused, it was one of the real benefits brought by the Church, protecting the innocent and saving the culprit from the vengeance of persons taking the law into their own hands. Kings rarely violated it, and then by guile; for lesser men the fear of God and the awful penalties were a restraint. Though the privilege arising from the universal belief in the contagion of holiness had existed from ancient times, it was only given the sanction of law in the Christian Church by Boniface V in the 7th century. St Cuthbert's dying words were the first known reference to it in the north, and the very fulfilment of his prophecy made the saint's own Sanctuary one of the most renowned in England.

The area within which a fugitive was safe varied. At Durham it was the whole church and churchyard and its circuit, the penalties for a pursuer infringing it increasing as he advanced towards the shrine itself, where it was death. But no fugitive if he had time would take his chance of safety till he had reached the great sanctuary knocker on the cathedral's north door and hammered for admittance. The knocker hangs there still. Reproduced in ten thousand little ornaments, its face has travelled over all the world. How many people ponder its dread significance when they take it from a shelf or meet it on a bathroom door?

A monstrous face with flaring nostrils glares from black eye-sockets, surrounded by a sunburst mane of bronze, an image of the mediaeval mind to strike terror in pursuer and pursued. From its jaws hangs the heavy ring with which the fugitive

Saint Cuthbert of Lindisfarne and Durham

frantically knocked. Above his head, until James Wyatt's 'improvements' destroyed them in the 18th century, were the watchmen's rooms. Here always day and night two monks did duty to preserve the right of sanctuary according to the rules. The rules at Durham were strict. At the sound of rapping one monk ran straightway to let in the fugitive, while the other went to toll the Galilee bell to give notice that a man had taken sanctuary. The man was then taken to the prior and questioned on oath before witnesses about what he had done, the name of his victim if there was one, and what weapon he had used. Then he was given a black gown with the yellow cloth cross of St Cuthbert on the shoulder of his left arm. Near the door of the Galilee chapel on the south side was a place where the refugee was allowed to stay and given bedding and food for thirty-seven days, after which he had to come before a coroner, confess his crime and abjure the realm.

The *Sanctuarium Dunelmense*[39] gives a detailed case of a man from Wokingham imprisoned for theft who escaped and found sanctuary. After the ritual of admittance he takes his stand before the shrine of the saint and, refusing to be moved, begs for the coroner at once. The coroner of the Chester Ward comes and hears his confession; then in the presence of the sacrist, the under-sheriff and others the culprit swears to renounce the kingdom. He strips and gives his clothes as fee to the sacrist who hands him the cloak of St Cuthbert and a white cross of wood into his hand. His journey to the coast begins; consigned to the under-sheriff, he is then committed to the nearest constable who hands him on to the next and so on to the next until the last sees him on to a ship and he bids eternal farewell to his country.

That criminal was perhaps more fortunate than many. An abjurer had to keep to the king's highway and was not allowed to stop more than two nights in one place. At the port he could wait only one tide, and if there was no ship he had to go into the sea each day up to his knees and cry 'Passage for the love of God and the king his sake' until one came to take him. Moreover, although his dress and cross ostensibly protected him, both because of the severe penalties incurred by anyone breaking the law under which he moved and of the superstitious fear of harming one reprieved by sanctuary, he moved in terror. If his enemies were men of blood with no scruples there were ways enough of seeing he never reached the coast.

But such men of blood could not always escape the penalty of breaking sanctuary. In the 12th century a youth in the service of the bishop of Durham was slain and the murderer took sanctuary. While the monks were at supper friends of the dead man broke in and attacked the murderer at the very shrine. This appalled the bishop who the next day, after reconsecrating the violated church, pardoned the wounded murderer and jailed the sacrilegious friends of his slain servant, reserving them to be 'tortured with a horrible kind of death'.[40]

The best-known of all such records of St Cuthbert's Sanctuary is of the hunted stag. It was in September of 1155, the Festival of Translation in a church in Lothian. The stag takes refuge in the churchyard, the hunters pause, the crowds swarm out of the church and watch, until a man tells his son to tease the exhausted beast. The stag rounds on the boy and gores him to death, then leaps the churchyard wall and is killed in flight. But because it is a murderer it is left to lie, uneaten. There is a double moral of the times; no man would break St Cuthbert's peace, it was the hunted stag that became the criminal for killing in his sanctuary. But it is the first part which has become legendary, showing how men revered the saint's love of animals.

When the gale of the Dissolution reached Durham, its effect compared with that on other monasteries was small. In the first blast of 1536 it had swept away the nine dependent cells including Lindisfarne; with the smaller monasteries this was inevitable. But later, when the great monastic houses were attacked, the new foundation charter of 1541 shows that Hugh Whitehead, the prior, was made dean, and among many other members even the feretrar, of all people, remained to be made canon of the twelfth stall. The behaviour of Cromwell's Visitors, Dr Legh, Dr Henley and Mr Blythman was certainly remarkable in that time of wholesale plunder and iconoclasm.[41] They began, of course, by stripping the feretory of all its precious ornaments and the jewels which embellished the shrine, including the great emerald estimated by the valuer they always took with them to be 'worth a prince's ransom'. When the saint's marble tomb had been smashed they told the smith

Saint Cuthbert of Lindisfarne and Durham

employed to break open the coffin inside. The smith, having aimed a blow, cried out that he had broken one of the saint's legs. Henley told him to throw out the bones, but the man said they were held together with sinews. Legh took a look and called to Henley, but Henley only shouted to have the bones cast down. Whereupon Legh told him he really must come to see what he saw. The result was that the Visitors commanded the saint to be carried into the Revestry till the King's pleasure was further known. Then the prior and monks, by order of the bishop, buried Cuthbert again under the very place in the feretory where his shrine had stood. All contemporary accounts confirm this astonishing event, so that it may well be that it was not just opportunism so much as what must have seemed an evident miracle that made many of the Durham clergy outwardly conform and stay with their saint.

There arose in the 17th century a tradition that the body was later secretly removed and buried in another part of the cathedral, the exact place being known only by three Benedictines, each as he dies passing it on to one other until the present day.[42] Similar to the Glastonbury tradition, it seems to have no more foundation though it has been more hotly argued. One part of the tradition says the body was removed in the time of queen Mary, but if this had been so it would have been recorded; moreover, there was no reason for disturbing the body. Finally, the exhumation by Dr Raine showed that it was most improbable that the grave had ever been touched.

On May 19th, 1827 the *Durham Advertiser* reported: 'a very curious discovery was made in the cathedral here yesterday, which has occasioned a great sensation in the town ... believed to be no other than the Patron Saint, St Cuthbert "whose restless body in the 309th year after his first buriall was with all funeral pompe enshrin'd" in the White Church at Durham in the year 995 or 832 years ago! We hope to obtain further information before our next, and, should we succeed, we shall most certainly communicate the same to our readers.' The Haliwerfolc of Durham were excited, and with good reason. Everything about their saint, except his continuing incorruptibility which could hardly have been expected, was confirmed.

The coffin in which the skeleton lay was recognized by its carvings as that in which he had been laid in 698; the stole and maniple were those given to the shrine by Athelstan in 934; the wrappings of the body were the same as at the Translation of 1104; and there, too, were the portable silver-covered altar and ivory comb, and the head of king Oswald recognizable by the cleft in the skull. Moreover, when the wrappings were removed there was found concealed a small gold cross encrusted with garnets, unmentioned by any earlier writers. The workmanship showed it to be contemporary with the saint, and from its appearance it had been worn for some time and so was most likely of the middle 7th century.[43]

The fragments of the wrappings on the body have been carefully re-examined in the last few years. Some have been established as of the Lindisfarne burial, the outer ones being of the Translation in 1104 which Reginald described. The one known as the Duck Silk, or Nature, Goddess is almost certainly of Cuthbert's time,[44] but Raine's suggestion that it had been specially interwoven with representations of St Cuthbert's favourite eider ducks seems to have been disproved by the assurance that it is Byzantine work showing the influence of Sassanian design which was then displacing the traditional Hellenistic. This Byzantine figured-twill is one of the most important in existence; and the Peacock Silk, probably 12th-century and one of the 1104 wrappings, is unique in that the peacock has two heads. Standing before these relics in the cathedral library, one tries to envisage the origins of these precious silks reserved only for great royal or ecclesiastical occasions, their journeyings: the first perhaps from Antinoë, passing through many hands and years to the storm-swept island of Lindisfarne to wrap a British saint; the second, it may be, from orientalized Sicily to enrich his coffin at his Translation. On one is embroidered 'There is no God but Allah.'

In the three centuries that passed, from the Visitors of the Dissolution to Dr Raine and the further conclusive examination of St Cuthbert's remains in 1899, there is silence over the tomb. Only the fortunes of the saint's cathedral are recorded; the bigoted vandalism of the late 16th and early 17th centuries, partial restoration in the Laudian reaction, further destruction in 1650 when the Protector's unhappy Scots prisoners after the battle of Dunbar were shut up in the building and made fires of the choir stalls to warm themselves. At the end of the century

Saint Cuthbert of Lindisfarne and Durham

Dean Sunbury began his library in the walls of the old refectory, where, as in the sometime dormitory, are housed the splendid collection of mediaeval manuscripts which fortunately had suffered hardly at all. Though in later centuries some 'improvements' were made to the cathedral it has absorbed them. The battlements of Nicholson, the screen of Sir Gilbert Scott, the stained glass of Easton: nothing, whatever its incongruity, seems to have disturbed the all-embracing power of this vast and tranquil place.

Where once there was the feretory is a grey stone slab in the place of St Cuthbert's shrine, at each corner a tall candlestick. Beneath it the saint still lies. Pilgrims come there again, though not in such numbers as they go to Lindisfarne. On one summer's day of 1962, twelve hundred and seventy-five years after the saint's death, a procession at low-tide to that island of seabirds stretched unbroken from shore to shore. It may be that many such pilgrims know little of Cuthbert, their interest often no more than curiosity or an excuse to go on a jolly excursion by the sea. The black terrors, extravagant fancies and passionate hopes of the mediaeval mind may not be there, but the reasons for setting out have not greatly changed.

Still, to many of the north country and the border lands, there is an extraordinary feeling for the man who journeyed there both when alive and dead. Cuthbert's great quality, outstanding in his tumultuous times and no less vital to-day, was his serenity. Calm in spirit, yet restless in body, he strove always against odds to pursue his belief that: 'It is good for a man, when he hath borne the yoke from his youth; he shall sit alone, and shall be silent, because he shall raise himself above himself.'[45]

V

THE SHRINE OF OUR LADY OF WALSINGHAM

> As ye came from the holy land
> Of Walsinghame,
> Met you not with my true love
> By the way as you came?
>
> How should I know your true love,
> That have met many a one
> As I came from the holy land,
> That have come, that have gone?[1]

NINE HUNDRED YEARS AGO at Walsingham in Norfolk a widowed gentlewoman named Rychold petitioned Our Lady to say in what work she could best honour her. Our Lady took Rychold in a dream to Nazareth and showed her the place where Gabriel had greeted her. She told Rychold to observe its measurements carefully because she wished her to build a house like it at Walsingham. In this house all should find succour, and it was to be a memorial to the joy of Gabriel's salutation and the root of mankind's redemption. To make sure that Rychold made no mistake over the building, she was given the vision three times.

Having taken careful note, Rychold called her builders and explained what she wanted. But when they went to the place where the Holy House was to be built they found two pieces of ground of the same measurements as the Holy House, each of

The Shrine of Our Lady of Walsingham

which was dry while the surrounding meadow was wet with dew. This miracle of the holy maid, Mary, though like the fleece of Gideon, was confusing. By one piece of land there were two wells, and these seemed to Rychold to make this place the more suitable; but when the carpenters began to set out the foundations they could make no timber agree with another in geometry. They were full of agony that they could not join together their work. Their mistress told them to lay all aside and go to rest, for she thought Our Lady would manage the work in her own way. So, having sent her household to bed, Rychold remained all night in prayer. When the builders went early in the morning to their work they found that their materials had been carried to the other site two hundred paces off, and joined better than they could have done. So, homeward they did wind, and the holy matron thanked Our Lady for her great grace . . .

The *Pynson Ballad*[2] which tells this story in twenty-one verses is the earliest known written account of the shrine's origin, and takes its name from Richard Pynson who printed it about 1496. It was composed only a little before then, since it speaks of four hundred years having passed from the foundation of the House in 1061. Walsingham's fame was at its peak just before the Dissolution, and the Ballad was almost certainly inspired by a mixture of verbal tradition and history which had been sung for centuries.

The whole aura of Walsingham must from the beginning have been remarkable to have drawn people from all parts to so distant a place. Even to-day this north East Anglian world seems remote. The road from Cambridge which Erasmus took on his seventy-odd miles' pilgrimage is joined near Newmarket by others from the south and midlands and from there on is still named the Palmers' Way. By Barton Mills, Brandon and Swaffham the miles run almost straight through the Breckland, sandy flats, scrub and forest as empty as the Landes, the sense of isolation deepened by the great sweep of sky and cool light. Beyond Fakenham there are small billows, hardly hills, and then in farming country is Walsingham, five miles from the sea.

A mile before the town, to the left across a ford from Houghton-le-dale, is the Slipper Chapel where traditionally

The Shrine of Our Lady of Walsingham

pilgrims stopped to pray before going barefoot on to Walsingham. Built in the 14th century of flint and stone and with an elegant decorated west window, it now contains the Roman Catholic shrine of Our Lady which pilgrims honour on their way to the site of the Holy House. The chapel is only a few paces in length and width and disproportionately high; there is so little room to stand where the eyes can be shaded from the candles before the shrine on the north wall that the beamed roof is almost invisible.

The entry to Walsingham from there is by the narrow High Street; on the right side runs the priory wall with here and there houses that were built into it centuries ago. Here is the priory gateway, with a grotesque stone head and shoulders still staring up the road to see who comes. The door is not large, and with it closed behind you there is the feeling of being in a ringed park; the light is a little green from the high trees by the wall, and to the right is an 18th-century mansion built on to the ruins of the refectory. But what draws your eye directly is the high pointed arch rising at the east end of the long lawn that was the floor of the church. The tracery of its great window is gone, though the stonework still remains in the circular window above, and this, the chancel end, is all that remains to suggest past magnificence, except for two massive ruined piers that once supported the western tower.

It is below ground that the vision of Rychold acquires substance. About half-way along and outside the north foundations of the church the grass-covered ground rises to an almost square platform. Though evidence is scarce, all that there is agrees on this being the site of Rychold's Holy House. How or why it was moved here from the ground by the wells,

The Shrine of Our Lady of Walsingham

if it was, is unknown: the wells are there at the proper distance of the Ballad in a small enclosure behind the eastern arch, and the stone tank in which pilgrims bathed. Not far beyond is the shallow Stiffkey river and a stone bridge over it that leads to thin, tall woods still within the priory precincts. Near by there was once a Norman manor; though unhistorical it is possible that Rychold lived there. Everything of the Ballad is contained within the encircling walls of the domain.

It is natural to suspect written descriptions that first appear hundreds of years after the event celebrated: the Glastonbury Thorn, the Dun Cow of Durham, the story of St Winefrede are examples of the sort connected with most places of pilgrimage, and range from the impossible to those acceptable through interpretation. The *Pynson Ballad* belongs to the last group. But though arguments about when the Holy House was founded seem futile, they must not be left out. Modern controversies of this kind perpetuate the mediaeval obsession with splitting hairs and serve to show how traditions grew from the simple urge to prove a point, however irrelevant. The arguments about the date of the Holy House circle mainly around a Pipe Roll entry of 1130/1[3] and an undated charter in the Walsingham Cartulary.[4]

The Pipe Roll records that a William of Hocton rendered account of 10 marks gold to have as wife the widow of Geoffrey de Favarches with her land and custody of her son till he becomes knight and holds land of him. The Charter declares a gift of alms by a Geoffrey de Favarches for the foundation of a religious body to take care of the chapel his mother had built at Walsingham in honour of the ever Virgin Mary, attaching to it the church of All Saints in the village and its lands, tithes and so forth possessed by his chaplain when he, Geoffrey, went to Jerusalem. *Post hoc, propter hoc*: this widow to be married in 1131 becomes Rychold, and the Geoffrey of the Charter is not her late husband but the minor in the Pipe Roll who afterwards provided for the care of his mother's chapel, the Holy House. The Ballad, therefore, from which the name Rychold has been taken, is quite wrong about its date of 1061, since the lady could not have founded her chapel before the 12th century. But why, argues the other side, should this 1130/1 widow be Rychold? The old documents never mention the name, and she could just as well be the 1061 widow of the Ballad whose son Geoffrey, after going on the First Crusade, gave the undated Charter; and it was his widow who married William de Hocton in 1130/1. There is nothing to show that this widow's son was named Geoffrey, indeed from a Feet of Fines in 1199 it seems to have been Richard.[5] Back and forth it goes: there is no de Favarches in Domesday Book so the foundation must have been 12th-century. On the other hand Domesday Book is not infallible, as Holywell shows. With so little to go on one could devise interminably. The fact remains that the *Pynson Ballad* alone gives the date, 1061, and it might as well be accepted.

The real interest of the early charter is that it shows the widow's Holy House to have already attained such importance that it needs a religious foundation to take care of it. The first undated charter was probably made between 1120 and 1130, and refers only to an *ordinem religionis*;[6] a second undated one, presumably after Geoffrey's death since it is by a Robert de Brucurt, refers to *canonicis de Walsingham*, and a third by Roger de Clare to *ordinem canonicale regularii*. The picture of local ties and family association persists, the families of Robert and Geoffrey had come to this part of Norfolk from Brucurt and Fervaches not far from one another in Normandy, and the earl of Clare's mother had some years before confirmed Geoffrey's gift of land to the priory of Castle Acre. Roger de Clare's charter must have been made about 1153 as he refers to his clerk Ralph who was in fact the first prior of Walsingham,[7] and the Order was of Augustinian Canons.

Compared with the great monastic orders, of which the Benedictines had taken the lead up to the 12th century, these Canons have made little popular impression. But they were to care for the Walsingham shrine for the next four hundred years and had a peculiar importance. Organized religious bodies had always existed to serve as staff for large churches though they had twice practically disappeared in decadent periods before the 10th century.[8] When they were finally revived by the Gregorian reforms of the 11th century, their Rule was the same as that on which they had been earlier based, St Benedict's, and they were called the Black Canons. They adopted, however, the Rule of St Augustine, the 5th-century Augustine of Hippo, author of *The City of God*, and from this they were known as

The Shrine of Our Lady of Walsingham

the Augustinian or Austin Canons. Though introduced into England at the end of the 11th century, it was during the first half of the 12th that they established the greatest number of foundations, usually attached to churches, and nearly always priories acknowledging no outside control and having few links with other houses. They kept themselves to themselves, their not very large properties were concentrated near home and their concerns and loyalties were mainly local. In the case of Walsingham they fitted perfectly with the parochial, family atmosphere.

Except for the early charters there is nothing to tell of what happened at the chapel in the first hundred years. It is a mistake to expect anything at all obvious in a mediaeval document, since what was obvious to the writer usually seemed to him needless to record. So what set the chapel on the road to fame has to be imagined. Though the lady Rychold's building was surely an act of private devotion, the strange story of this chapel being a copy of the House in Nazareth must have aroused awe and curiosity. Nothing like it existed: in Nazareth itself the only place claimed for the Annunciation was a cave; so the creation of Rychold's dream had even less relation to a reality than our picture of the chapel she built.

Our picture relies mainly on a rather sketchy description by Erasmus in the 16th century.[9] 'A small chapel, made of boards, and admitting the devotees on each side by a narrow little door. The light is small, indeed scarcely any but from the wax-lights. A most grateful fragrance meets the nostrils ... You would say it was the mansion of the saints, so much does it glitter on all sides with jewels, gold and silver.' At 'the shrine of the holy Virgin, one canon attends the altar, that he may receive and take charge of what is given. She [the Virgin] stood in the dark at the right side of the altar ... a small image ... of no extraordinary size, material or workmanship, but in virtue most efficacious'.

No one else has described the shrine except William of Worcester in 1479, who gives the measurements of the chapel of the blessed Mary as 23 feet 6 inches by 12 feet 10.[10] Yet by the time of its end in 1538 it had been for nearly three centuries by far the most notable shrine of Our Lady in England, and second only to Canterbury in general popularity as a centre of pilgrimage. In the words of the Ballad its fame had made England glad

> To be called in euery realme and regyon
> The holy lande, Our Ladyes dowre.

But, though it was the Holy House that first drew the pilgrims, devotion was by some time in the 12th century already centred on a statue of Our Lady in it. Reference to offerings, prayers or pilgrimages are always to Our Lady of Walsingham, the House enshrining her is not mentioned. Nevertheless, the House must have possessed extraordinary sanctity; otherwise, as happened in almost all other cases where an old building contained an outstandingly precious object, the old would have been quickly demolished to make room for something more splendid. At Walsingham the original wooden structure was carefully preserved, and Erasmus gives the impression that it had been enclosed in an outer shell of which the windows and doors were still empty. He describes its position on the north side of the priory church by saying that 'the Son . . . when He looks to the west has His Mother on His right hand'.

The measurements, the position and general description are similar to those of the Santa Casa at Loreto, and the legend in the Ballad of the miraculous moving of the House has been said to have been borrowed from the Loreto legend. The similarity is there, but any borrowing could only have been the other way round, since the Holy House at Walsingham existed 200 years before the one at Loreto is reputed to have appeared and 400 years before anything was written about it. There was a brief reference to Loreto thirty years earlier than the Ballad,[11] but the Loreto legend does not appear in full until eighty years later.[12] Curiously enough, though, the legend was given some status in England by the last but one abbot of Glastonbury: returning from Italy at the end of the 15th century he built a chapel of Our Lady of Loreto on the north side of the Great Church. It was in the tradition of Glastonbury not to be outshone in its collection of shrines, and the grave and scholarly abbot Bere was only following this in seeing in his visit to Loreto a chance to take some of the glory from Walsingham.

The Shrine of Our Lady of Walsingham

Very little is known of abbot Bere's chapel; time was short to the Dissolution, and Walsingham's Holy House remained the star. But one may perhaps to-day feel something of Walsingham's atmosphere in the Santa Casa at Loreto, the little hilltop town about the same distance from the Adriatic as Walsingham is from the North Sea. They are almost the same size, dark except for the glitter of candles on the jewelled statue of the Virgin and Child. A narrow doorway on one side admits, and on the other side lets out, the stream of pilgrims that passes steadily before the statue. Walsingham was of wood, Loreto is of small bricks, but both are enclosed: the one in the shell of an outer chapel, the other by a marble screen by Bramante and Sansovino. Each is part of a large church built to care for the shrine.

Loreto, now world-famous, was only beginning its career when Walsingham was at its height in the late 15th century. Its story seems the more fantastic for being so late in invention. The apostles converted Mary's house in Nazareth into a church, and in 336 the empress Helena enclosed it in a basilica which was used till the fall of Jerusalem. To save the House from the Turks it was carried by angels in 1291 to a place near Fiume where it remained for three years and after doing many miracles was flown over the Adriatic to come at last to rest in a grove of laurels. Though the floor fell out over the sea, the House is otherwise intact. The implausibility of every detail here makes the story of Walsingham's origin seem simple and straightforward. The stories are also representative of their respective times. Walsingham's is mediaeval and visionary but capable of interpretation, that of Loreto is Italian Renaissance, bursting with imagination, for a picture, a poem or a building, to be taken at its face value or not at all. Yet their appeal has been ultimately the same in strength. If men wish to believe, they believe. No one going to Loreto to-day after 500 years could doubt it. Galileo went there.

But all this was long after the time when the first pilgrims came to Walsingham, early in the 12th century. The humble ones are unchronicled; pilgrimage was too common to be noted unless linked with the movements of an important person. So the first record, besides that of members of the Clare family, is of Henry II's brother, William, who gave some land before he died in 1164. This made a good beginning: the priory was not a rich foundation, nor yet so poor as some historians suggest; it owned two churches, and, taking into consideration the loss of most of the priory deeds, probably several hundred acres. In any event, considerable building took place as the need grew. Though there is no mention of royalty until 1226, neither John nor Richard I being inclined to pilgrimage unless there was some earthly profit, the fact of Henry III's enthusiasm for the Holy House shows that its reputation must have remained strong in the intervening years. It was Henry III, in fact, who really brought Walsingham to the fore, and established it securely by setting a fashion.

The king came to it by way of Bromholm, the Cluniac priory famous for its relic of the Holy Cross, some forty miles east near the coast; it was founded by a cousin of the Paston family who owned much of the land there, and was a shrine to which Henry went several times. Having passed on to Walsingham in April 1226, the place seems to have exercised some charm on him, for after that he went there repeatedly in the next thirty years. The Calendars of Close, Patent and Liberate Rolls record some twenty visits, together with his benefactions. His gifts with one exception were not of the jewelled sort associated with kings; his earlier donations were of forty and twenty oak trees for use in constructing new buildings, and again and again he gave vast quantities of wax and tapers: in 1241, 3,000 tapers for the chapel on the feast of the Assumption. Then five years later he gave 20 marks for the golden crown to be made for the head of Our Lady.

It has been remarked as strange that, after 1256, Henry III does not seem to have gone to Walsingham again until September 1272, sixteen years later and not long before his death. But considering what was happening in those years it is hardly surprising. However strong Henry's piety, his extravagance, misgovernment and preferment of foreigners and papal nominees had aroused strong resentment. The great figure of the latter years was Simon de Montfort, earl of Leicester, a Frenchman by birth and married to the king's sister. Though his headship of the State ended after only a year in his tragic death at the battle of Evesham, his conqueror, Edward Prince of Wales, had learned the lesson that the king must follow the law.

The Shrine of Our Lady of Walsingham

But from these years of misrule and conflict sprang the stream that was to show its full force two and a half centuries later. It seems a paradox that Henry, to whom Walsingham owed most for establishing its fame, should have contributed to its eventual downfall. Partly to overcome the Church's opposition to his frivolity and partly from real veneration for Rome he put himself wholly in the Pope's hands, with the result that the Church was flooded with papal appointees. The king alone could have protected the clergy from papal exactions; instead he asked for a nuncio which made matters far worse. The antipapal current which began to swirl then was never afterwards to abate: it was given impetus by the intellectual awakening in the 13th century which would not accept papal dictation and analysed piercingly the decline of the spiritual qualities in the Church in England. The intellectual stimulus still came from churchmen, the religious or their pupils, led for a time by the newly-arrived Friars Minor. To recall their names – Edmund Rich, Adam Marsh, Bishop Grosseteste, Roger Bacon, Ockham, Duns Scotus – makes one realize that the conflicts around Henry III were only a manifestation of an awakening in the mediaeval mind, the budding in England of the Renaissance already flowering in Italy.

The continuation of royal pilgrimage to Walsingham by Edward I must have greatly confirmed its position, since he was as strong and intelligent a monarch as his father had been weak and futile. In the busy thirty-five years of his reign there are a dozen recorded visits, and it is possible there were more. He always stayed several days, sometimes with his queen Eleanor of Castile, and in 1296 on the Feast of the Purification, *le jour de la chandeleur*, a treaty with the count of Flanders was sworn to in the chapel of Our Lady.[13] So it goes on; king after king pays his respects, makes gifts, extends rights; only of Richard III there appears to be no mention. The example led nobility, both English and foreign, into the same path, the Walsingham Way, a title by which for some years even the Milky Way was known as pointing the road in the heavens.

Accordingly, the wealth of the Priory grew, and there is a revealing statement in 1346 when there was a proposal to found a Franciscan house in the town.[14] The canons were strongly opposed to this as to any possible competition, particularly as the proposal came from their own patron, Lady Elizabeth de Burgh of Clare. They pointed out that owing to the great value of the jewels and other offerings at the shrine the priory gates had to be closed at night, and pilgrims arriving late gave their offerings the next morning; but if they were entertained by the Franciscans they would probably not do so. In spite of the canons' displeasure Lady Clare founded the Franciscan house the following year. Eighteen years later the Black Death had struck down clerics and laymen alike and in this devastation pope Urban granted a faculty to the prior Thomas to dispense four canons to be ordained priests provided they were over twenty-two.

It seems remarkable how quickly Walsingham recovered from the pestilence, for the last quarter of the century marks the great period of rebuilding, including the exceedingly fine church of which the east window remains; there also arose trouble from what seems to have been a desire for aggrandisement. It is not entirely clear what Prior Snoring was after; he no doubt wanted to be independent of Visitation and certainly wanted to raise the priory's status to that of abbey for which he apparently procured papal consent. Richard II, guardian of the abbey's patron, young Roger Mortimer, at once intervened on the grounds that his leave had not been asked. The real point was that not only did the bishop of Norwich view with alarm a rich house passing from his control, but the king saw yet one more attempt by a religious house to go over his head to the pope. Snoring was defeated, though it took several years.

The continuous interest of royalty in Walsingham and the high birth of most of the recorded pilgrims is inclined to build up a picture of an essentially aristocratic shrine. The atmosphere of only the very best families, and the delicate refinement of the *Pynson Ballad* in its story of the charming vision three times enjoyed by the noble widow of Walsingham pervades history with a flavour of snobbery perceptible there even to-day. But, while it is true that no shrine had such consistently splendid patrons, the lack of documentary evidence about ordinary folk is common to most centres of pilgrimage, and one has to turn to a poet to balance the weighted impression.

In the latter half of the 14th century the writers who reflect their age are not, as a century earlier, scholarly intellectuals but

The Shrine of Our Lady of Walsingham

poets. Two remarkable men, Langland, with his *Vision of Piers the Plowman* and Chaucer with *The Canterbury Tales* were born, wrote and died within a few years of one another. Both had a penetrating eye but each a wholly different approach to the same subject, pilgrimage. Chaucer, the court poet, writes with brilliant readability of the real pilgrimage to Canterbury, a work of art as alive to-day as when it was written. In contrast, Langland, the poor provincial cleric wandering to London, seems strange and sometimes crude. He writes in Middle English alliterative verse and his whole poem is a vision; though there are references to real shrines, the main thread of his pilgrimage leads not to these but to Truth itself, a painful and tormenting and dangerous search, unrelieved by any of the humour of Chaucer's witty or just garrulous pilgrims. Yet, symbolic as are Langland's characters, the intensity of the poet conveys through them a picture of the age as strong as Chaucer's. Profoundly loyal to the Church itself, he attacks the dissipation of its hangers-on and exploiters, whether lowly or of high rank, and the running to waste of its spiritual leadership. His references to Walsingham are among the few that survive to show it as a place of popular as well as aristocratic pilgrimage.

The *Vision* begins, as two hundred years later Bunyan's *Pilgrim's Progress* was to begin, with: 'and I dreamed a dream'. The world is laid out as a great plain between the hill-top of Truth and the dreadful gulf of Falsehood. In this plain are all manner of men and women, and among them are false hermits with hooked staves on the way to Walsingham together with their wenches, a lazy lot who prefer to beg their way rather than work. Then, after a while, Piers the Plowman, who sometimes seems to be the dreamer and sometimes the hero, sees the seven deadly sins making a confession to Repentance under the influence of Reason. There is crafty, mean, dirty old Avarice confessing how he gave short weight, thinned beer, false measure; but now he swears no more to swindle, he will break

himself of sin by a pilgrimage to Walsingham with his huckstering wife and they will pray to the Rood of Bromholm, too. It is significant of Walsingham's standing that in this rough poetic masterpiece no other shrines but Rome and Compostella are mentioned.

But there is no further literary development: Langland, Chaucer, and then nothing worth while for nearly another century. Intellectually, John Wycliff is the great figure of the age, the man who first stood with unswerving courage for freedom of religious thought. He was contemporary with the poets and was so highly esteemed that in spite of denunciation by archbishops and bishops he died in retirement in 1384 two years after his being forced to leave Oxford. In the very year of his leaving, his followers the Lollards were crying out against 'the wyche of Walsingham'[15] since they felt particularly strongly about this pilgrimage. Nearly half a century later Bishop Pecock reports their declaring that 'it is vein waast and idil for to trotte to Wasingham rather than to ech other place in which an ymage of Marie is'.[16] By then Walsingham was near the point when it would outshine all other shrines, even that of Canterbury. While it is impossible to say with any certainty why this should have been, the circumstances of the time suggest explanations.

The 15th century was perhaps the most convulsive of any in English history, and was filled with fantastic contradictions. The Hundred Years War was in mid-swing when the century opened; indifferently handled at first, it swung against France with Agincourt and Henry V's brutish conquests: enter Joan of Arc, and treachery, confusion, patriotism caused the pendulum to dither hither and thither, swinging finally against England and driving her out of France. Almost at once the unoccupied soldiery were enlisted in the ranks of York or Lancaster to set on foot the most loathsome conflict, the more despicable for its having no impulse but lust for power. Yet, while the nobility was slaughtering itself to no evident purpose, the country was in general prospering, town commerce flourished, justice was well dispensed and the sense of Englishness that had grown steadily in the preceding century was established.

The two main impulses to this Englishness were language and the low prestige of the papacy. The Church had always provided culture and moral leadership; now the one-time illiterate laity was thinking for itself, writing letters, seeking for information in the written word. All through the 15th century the written stuff grew to meet the demand, which was a good deal like to-day's, for popular digests, semi-scientific or historical, half-baked facts: in a century after Chaucer almost the only memorable book is Malory's *Morte d'Arthur*, itself not an original work. But the demand led to the encouragement of printing, and to the book-collecting that went to the building of superb private libraries.

This vulgar interlude was an inevitable part of the cultural evolution. The Church had lost its real leadership, although its material wealth and in some cases even its power was greater than ever. Because the king wanted its support it could get the Act *de heretico comburendo* passed, and the Lollards inveighing against the superstitions of Walsingham could be burned. It could even have bishop Pecock, who had attacked the Lollards, found guilty of heresy because he questioned the Church's infallibility and wished 'bi clear witte [to] drawe men into consente of trewe faith otherwise than bi fire and swerd or hangement', and the great theologian saved himself only by publicly renouncing his views. With the suppression of all religious criticism, intellectual life almost flickered out: the Church could do nothing constructive, it was incapable even of reforming itself.

It was incapable because it was simply a Church in, and not of, England, a part of a complex international organization with headquarters in Rome, rich, powerful and resisting all change. Even if a bishop wanted to reform he could do nothing; nearly all the monasteries were subject to the pope, ecclesiastical law was Roman Canon Law and appeal was only to Rome. At the same time the papacy inspired no respect; its sojourn in Avignon made it appear hand in glove with the enemy and now there was the schism to expose its lack of spiritual force. With all this, how was it that the Church could not attempt to save itself by some more intelligent way than by persecuting its critics? Almost surely because persecution was in the very nature of the intertwining roots of Church and State, an integral part of the mediaeval spirit. What is obvious to us, but was not to the men of the 15th century, is that the middle ages

The Shrine of Our Lady of Walsingham

were ending, if not already done. In Italy the Renaissance was already in full flower.

How was it, then, that in this convulsive yet dismal century pilgrimage not only continued but in the case of Walsingham reached its peak of popularity? It may be that it was the very decadence of the Church that caused men to seek even more than before an individual way to salvation: on the other hand, the widespread revival of magic and witchcraft following loss of faith in the Church may have sent some, as the Lollards had said, to 'the wyche of Walsingham'. Was it that the age of faith had finally abdicated to one of gross superstition? It is not possible to know; but it is fascinating to read of the pilgrimages to Walsingham during the bestial Wars of the Roses. The Duke of York before the first battle of St Alban's in 1455, Warwick the Kingmaker in the year of York's capture and execution, Edward IV in the midst of the chaos and again after he had defeated and killed Warwick,[17] then Buckingham, presently beheaded by Richard III: all these and more came to Our Lady in Her Holy House. The pious Henry VI, king or fugitive, sane or mad, was more understandably often there. There are letters of 1454 from both York and Warwick to John Paston, the landowner from near Bromholm, respectfully asking him to see that the Kingmaker enjoys peaceably the conveyance by purchase to him of two manors in Little Snoring belonging to the priory of Walsingham.[18]

John Paston, for all the interminable difficulties and lawsuits in which he became involved, came of a family that had long been of great influence in that part of Norfolk. Eleven years earlier, when he was very ill at the Inner Temple, his young and determined wife had written that not only was she going on a pilgrimage to Walsingham to pray for him, but 'my moder be hestyd a nodyr ymmage of wax of the weytte of yow to oyer Lady of Walsyngham'.[19] Though it may be difficult to equate the undoubted faith of the Pastons in Walsingham with the impulses that brought there the bloody and treacherous warlords, that image of wax the weight of a man, though not unique, seems symbolic of an age in which superstition had overlaid faith.

It is now, towards the end of the 15th century, that Richard Pynson prints his Ballad which brings together all the legend

The Shrine of Our Lady of Walsingham

and history of the shrine. This song of praise tells how Walsingham stood at that time, the original wooden House still there (as later confirmed by Erasmus) and a chapel of St Lawrence by two wells in the place where Rychold's builders had tried to start building the House. These wells had by then developed an importance of their own for pilgrims who came to be healed. In a service book inscribed 'Iste pertinet Ricd Vowell, Priori de Walsingham' there are detailed instructions for the conduct of the bath connected with these wells. The superintendent must see that no one went in alone, and that pilgrims whose condition would suffer from immersion be prevented unless under the orders of a physician. There is no written evidence of these wells earlier than the 15th century, but the Holy House may well have been built in the sacred place of an older religion.

'They say the spring is sacred to the holy Virgin', says Erasmus.[20] 'The water is wonderfully cold, and efficacious in curing pains of the head and stomach.' But he gets what was clearly the bath-house mixed up with parts of the original House. The famous Colloquy of Erasmus on a visit to Walsingham is indeed a curious piece of work. From a letter from Cambridge to a friend on May 8th, 1511 it seems that he probably went there that year though what he wrote of it was not published until 1526. The scene of the colloquy is Antwerp and the two characters are Ogygius (Erasmus) and his friend Menedemus who welcomes him from his travels. It follows the line of Erasmus' usual attack on clerical abuses and superstitions. But for a man of his intellectual attainments it is curiously ambivalent and at times silly. The form is that of a skit on his visit, bringing in a description of the buildings and the Holy House, the relics in St Lawrence's chapel, the story of the knight who escaped his pursuers by the Virgin's help in bringing him and his horse through a small wicket-gate,[21] and of course of the Milk of the Blessed Virgin. Erasmus spends more time making fun of the *lac sacrum beate Marie*, which was kept on the High Altar, than on anything else; yet by then it was generally acknowledged, except by the most simple, that this popular mediaeval relic was made from chalk scraped from the Grotto of Our Lady's Milk in Bethlehem.

Erasmus said in his letter of 1511 that he was going to visit the Virgin of Walsingham to hang up some votive Greek verses

The Shrine of Our Lady of Walsingham

to her. But when it comes to his later Colloquy he treats the whole thing as a joke, and ridicules the canons for thinking his verses are in Hebrew or Arabic. It is as though he was ashamed of the simple prayer he had made, which, after enumerating the rich gifts of others, ends:

> But the poor poet, for his well-meant song,
> Bringing these verses only – all he has –
> Asks in reward for his most humble gift
> That greatest blessing, piety of heart,
> And free remission of his many sins.

The canons were not very well-educated, but there was no reason to expect them to know Greek, very few people did. Erasmus' apparent indifference to facts appears too when he says that the place has no income except offerings to the Virgin, at a time when the larger part came from the estates it owned. He also makes Menedemus ask Ogygius if the prior and canons are of good reputation and gives the reply 'They are highly spoken of: richer in piety than in revenue', this at a time when they had never been so materially rich nor so morally decadent: it is strange that Erasmus should have missed a chance to be critical. Except for the description of the Holy House itself and the statue of the Virgin, the Colloquy for all its reputation is a crude but donnish joke, the kind of thing a classical Fellow might compose after too much port in the Combination Room, revealing all kinds of inhibitions and ending by being neither clever nor funny.

Erasmus apologized later to Wolsey, explaining that he had meant only to show that men ought not to go on these pilgrimages leaving behind wives and children and other responsibilities: a 'Reynard the Fox' sort of statement. The popular French cycle of animal stories in verse about Reynard and Isengrim the Wolf had by the 14th century already become satirical comment on man and society. In 1481 Caxton printed his *Historye of reynart the foxe* based on a Dutch version of the *Roman de Renart* which had greatly grown during the centuries. Erasmus was paraphrasing to Wolsey Reynard's declaration: 'There is in the world many a good man who has never been to Rome. Such an one has come back from the seven saints worse than ever he was. I mean to take my way home, and I

The Shrine of Our Lady of Walsingham

shall live by my labour and seek honest earnings, I shall be charitable to poor people.'[22]

The first evidence of internal conditions at Walsingham is in the records of a Visitation by bishop Goldwell of Norwich on September 1st, 1494.[23] Though the report is short the picture is unpleasant. The prior and canons are all together for the examination, and the prior is afraid to say all he knows of the state of the house because some of the canons might spread it abroad; he is also said to be partial, the servants are insolent and there is a lot of tale-telling; one of the brothers reports that the prior had refused to have him ordained priest and had imprisoned him, another that there was no schoolmaster in the house to teach them grammar. No remedy seems to have been applied, except that accounts were ordered to be regularly kept. This was during the years when Henry VII repeatedly came there, and, after defeating Lambert Simnel, the bogus earl of Warwick, had sent his standard to the shrine as a thank-offering.[24] In his will, this shrewd, pious and unintellectual monarch left instructions for silver statues of himself praying to be placed facing the shrines of Edward the Confessor, St Thomas Becket and Our Lady of Walsingham, the three greatest in England. His last visit seems to have been in 1506; three years later he died.

From Henry VIII's accession until 1515 there are regular entries in the King's Book of payments: for a priest to sing before Our Lady, for the King's Candle always burning there, for gold for Her little chain, for glazing the windows of the Holy House – a work carried out by Barnard Flower, notable for his windows in King's College Chapel, Cambridge. Erasmus had complained of the unfinished windows 'exposed to the ocean, the father of the winds'. The Norfolk antiquary, Sir Henry Spelman, writing nearly a century later, tells of Henry walking barefoot two miles from Barsham Manor where he was staying, to hang a gold circlet round Our Lady's neck.[25] It is possible that a good deal of this devotion to Our Lady of Walsingham shared by Henry's first unhappy queen, Katharine of Aragon, came from longing for a male heir. He was there immediately after the birth of the little prince Henry in 1511 and renewed his offerings after the infant's death. On September 16th, two years later, queen Katharine writes to the king who is with his army in France, telling him of Surrey's victory over the Scots at Flodden Field, concluding: 'and with this I make an ende, praying God to sende you home shortly, for without this no joye here can bee accomplished; and for the same I pray and now goo to Our Lady of Walsyngham that I promised soo long agoo to see'.[26] The queen's devotion brought no fulfilment of her longing. She went again and again, and the manors of Great and Little Walsingham were granted to her, and she died, providing in her will 'that some personage go to Our Lady of Walsingham on pilgrimage and distribute 20 nobles on the way'.[27]

In 1514, the year after Flodden, Admiral Sir Edward Howard wrote to the king telling him he had given leave of absence from his ship to Sir Arthur Plantagenet on account of a vow. Plantagenet, in a moment of great danger, had called upon Our Lady of Walsingham and had vowed that 'and it pleased God and her to deliver him owt of that peril, he would never eet fleshe nor fyche tyl he had seen heer'.[28] So to Walsingham continued to stream the humble and the great, among them Wolsey to correct the weakness in his stomach, presumably with the water from the wells. Yet, in the midst of all this noble pilgrimage, the splendour of royalty, the wealth of the shrine and the piety of pilgrims, we read the account of the Visitation of Bishop Nix on July 14th, 1514.[29]

There had been some trickery about William Lowthe's

The Shrine of Our Lady of Walsingham

election as prior in 1504, and with the Visitation due he threatened the brethren with frightful punishments if they revealed anything. But everything came out, largely owing to many of the brethren being as ill-behaved as their prior and hoping to save themselves by blaming him. The prior had been seen going alone to the Chapel of the Shrine and taking the offerings of money and jewels; he kept a fool whom he dressed up to receive Holy Communion; he had two favourite servants whom he enriched out of the monastery funds, and with the wife of one he was accustomed to sleep; this woman was given the prior's horse to go on a pilgrimage to Canterbury where she made a show of herself; the prior also sold land and kept the money, never paid anything into the common chest, nor presented accounts. William Houghton, the custodian of the chapel of the Blessed Virgin, the Holy House, went shares with the offerings. A number of the canons were named as riotous, others as sitting drinking and joking in the pimp servant's house till eleven at night, some till dawn; one would not come to the choir but sat drinking in the 'halibred hous', namely where the Communion bread was kept; some of the canons hunt and hawk. One of the brothers on being rebuked replied, 'As long as I doo noo wors than oure fader priour doithe he can not rebuke me.'

In view of all this the bishop's Injunction was astonishingly mild. The servants were to be sent away, but the prior was to remain in office under supervision of the prior of Westacre. As the prior of Westacre had himself rendered no account to his own brethren for the last two years the Injunction was not likely to do much good. However, the bishop soon had second thoughts and within a month obtained prior Lowthe's resignation and issued strict regulations covering the future conduct of the abbey.[30] But then, when Lowthe resigned, he was made prior of Westacre. What was at work behind the scenes is unknown, but, as may be imagined, the incredible second appointment of Lowthe had results as deplorable as the first.

His successor at Walsingham, Richard Vowell, was to last until the Dissolution. Records of the three remaining Visitations do not reveal any such goings on as in 1514.[31] On July 13th, 1520 there were certain insubordinate canons, and some dissensions: on August 11th, 1526 individual answers to questions vary from 'everything is well' to 'drink and bread badly served, rotten and dirty' and 'sub-prior partial': and on August 9th, 1532 everything seems to be well observed and conducted except that two of the brothers will not get up for matins. There is a wry taste to this progress in self-reform at a time when the Reformation from outside was about to sweep everything away. But there is also in this last half-century of mingled splendour and shame a significant comment on pilgrimage and its inspiration. Extraordinary though it may seem to-day, the moral corruption of the guardians of the shrine appears to have been wholly irrelevant. It is hardly possible that only the bishop of the Visitation discovered their behaviour; the canons misbehaved in houses of the town, so it must have been a fairly well-known scandal. Yet it was ignored. The temporary depravity of the Church's servants was of no account beside the eternal source of succour to mankind represented by the jewelled Mother in the Holy House.

The King's Book continued to record the cost of the King's Candle perpetually burning and the stipend of the Mass priest to sing before Our Lady. The end began on September 18th 1534 and prior Vowell, the sub-prior and the twenty canons subscribed their adherence to the Act of Supremacy accepting Henry as head of the English Church:[32] great Walsingham was among the first to submit. There followed the Valor Ecclesiasticus, undertaken to discover the wealth of the English Church, showing that of a grand total income of £707.7.10½ the offerings amounted to £260.12.4½.

In 1535 the particular Inquiry into Walsingham was made, the Articles of which are detailed.[33] They ask: is there a permanent inventory kept of jewels, ornaments, plate and so on? if so, the books must be produced; have any of these been sold or pledged, and when and where? what relics are most esteemed and what proof is there that they are true? do the keepers of the relics exact money by making people ashamed of not giving? what have been the highest, the average and the latest offerings to Our Lady? what is the greatest miracle done by Her and could not such miracle have happened by natural means or by the help of God? why should it be imputed to this image of Our Lady rather than to any other? what is the saying about how Our Lady's chapel was built, when the first image was there, and what of the house with the bear-skin and the story of the knight and any other wonders? has Our Lady done so many miracles lately as she did when there were more offerings? what precautions are taken as to proofs of reported miracles? is Our Lady's Milk liquid or no? if it is, then the man who was sexton ten years before must be examined to discover if he had renewed it; whether the house over the wells has been recently built or renewed?

Most interesting about these Articles of Inquiry is that they show how the Commissioners had been fooled by Erasmus. The questions about the canons shaming pilgrims into making offerings, the nonsense about the bearskin in the building over the well and whether the house was new, the story of the knight and the state of Our Lady's Milk were all obviously prompted by their having taken seriously Erasmus' Colloquy. Unfortunately there is no record of the replies. The undermining continued: in 1536 Cromwell's Visitors, Legh and Ap Rice, were appointed; there is no trace of a formal report, and in their so-called compert there is only scandal such as the confessed incontinency of six canons and the amount of superstition in feigned relics and miracles.

But steadily the work goes on. Richard Southwell, a Norfolk gentleman appointed a commissioner, writes to Cromwell on July 25th that Lestrange and Hoges, apparently delegated by the Visitors, had 'sequestered all suche monney, plate, juelles, and stuff, as ther wasse inventyd and founde'.[34] Further, they had found a 'secrete privye place' which was clearly a mint for counterfeiting coin. They also advise that offerings from Saturday night over the next Sunday were 33/4 'over and besyd wax'. So already Cromwell's hand is on the money; and to confirm the need to suppress, his men are fabricating evidence from the mint where pilgrims' emblems were cast. Yet there is 33/4 over and beside wax, a good sum for forty-eight hours. The pilgrims were not deterred. Ironically, this commissioner, Richard Southwell, whose wife was an ancestor of Shelley, was grandfather of the Jesuit poet Robert Southwell who, returning to England from Rome in 1586 when only twenty-three, was later caught, tortured and at length executed without having incriminated any of his friends.

In September 1536 prior Vowell wrote to Cromwell a rather mysterious letter which suggests that someone unauthorized had been writing on the canons' behalf; at the same time he sends Cromwell his 'fee'. It was pathetic how so many of the religious houses clung to the hope that somehow they could save themselves. North, in Lincolnshire and Yorkshire, the nobles were leading the people in revolt at the desecration of the monasteries. Some thought that if Norfolk and Suffolk had joined them the devastation could have been stopped. But with so brilliant, ruthless and treacherous a man serving the king, there could never have been any chance of success. The Pilgrimage of Grace was undermined by the duplicity of the King's creatures and then bloodily crushed. Yet the King's Candle continued to burn before the shrine at Walsingham, and his priest sang daily in the Holy House. The Calendar records the arrival of some Cornish soldiers coming from the north on a pilgrimage to Walsingham.[35]

But the fears of the king's men made them alert to any sign of a plot, and one was uncovered in April 1537, though the evidence was only hearsay. The plot seems to have consisted of little more than a certain Ralph Rogerson saying to a George Gysborough that all the abbeys were going down and Walsingham with them, and that something ought to be done about it. A few local people seem to have got together with an idea of appealing to the king. When this was betrayed to Sir John Heydon, a Norfolk supporter of the government, Commissioner Southwell wrote to Cromwell that Heydon had told him that in fact there were no more than a dozen conspirators and all unimportant. But Southwell's attempt to save his countrymen, and one feels it was genuinely that, failed. He and his fellow commissioner, Sir Roger Townsend, were ordered to execute the conspirators 'without sparing'.[36] There was, as nearly always, no proper trial. Eleven were condemned, and to show a terrifying example their executions were spread over the countryside. On May 30th Gysborough and Nicholas Myleham, canon of Walsingham, were hanged, beheaded and quartered at Walsingham, two more pairs at Yarmouth and Lynn and five at Norwich.

Demoralization must have been complete by then, but the end did not come for a while yet. The ripe fruit of the Dissolution was dropping so freely into the laps of the king and his vicar-general that it is astonishing that they collected it as fast as they did. A little more than a year and Latimer wrote to Cromwell, 'Our gret Sibyll of Islington with her old syster of Walsyngham, hyr younge syster of Ipswych, with ther other two systers of Dongcaster and Penryesse wold make a jooly mustre in Smythfield. They wold not be all day in burnynge'.[37] All these figures of Our Lady were burned sometime in July at Chelsea, and it is believed with Cromwell watching.[38]

On the 14th of that month the prior had written to Cromwell reporting that he had done everything to follow his lordship's mind and pleasure in his attendance on the commissioners removing the Image and all gold and silver and such other things from the Holy House. 'And as to the gold as far as I do know they took it all with them at the departing the which I was right glad withal, with all my heart unfeignedly, and I beseech Almighty God to send our sovereign lord as much good of it as I would to myself of the other portion of silver which yet remaineth with me until our Sovereign Lord's pleasure be further known therein.'[39] He begs to be allowed to keep the silver, as otherwise the House will be unable to meet any of its debts and obligations; he beseeches some remedy for their poor condition, prays for his lordship's health and so on and so forth. The prior had hoped to save something by turning the priory into a college, and when he found Cromwell was uninterested wrote a month later asking to be given the parsonage of Walsingham with its three churches worth £30 a year.[40] This seems to have been in addition to an annuity allotted to him of £100, a very considerable sum, but he follows with a beseeching to help the poor brethren.

It is easy to say these subservient letters are despicable. But the prior was not a brave man, and although quite a good scholar and ruler of his house he must also have been naïve to have clung so long to the hope that all was not lost. His paying 'protection money' to Cromwell at a time when his sub-prior was being hanged for 'treason' has been held against him as a cowardly attempt to save his own skin. But all the houses were paying bribes to Cromwell, either forced or voluntary in an effort to save something. The alternative for the head of a house could be, and often was, a very horrible death. To die for a principle, when the cause is already lost whatever action is taken, may be admirable: but if a man is not of the stuff of martyrs then he must do what he can. Prior Vowell was at least able to obtain for most of his brethren pensions or livings as well as the comfortable vicarage of Creake for himself.

Between these two letters had occurred the final act. On August 4th, 1538 the prior and canons acknowledged the 'voluntary' surrender of Walsingham and all its possessions to the king.[41] In September there appears the last entry in the King's Book of Payments. There exists no sharper epitaph on the splendour, the learning, the spiritual leadership, corruption and tragic decline of the Church and the end of mediaeval pilgrimage: 'For the King's candle before Our Lady of Walsingham and to the priest there for his salary – Nil.'[42]

With the light extinguished, the priory was stripped, and the site and buildings sold the next year for £90 to one Thomas Sydney, governor of the hospital, and Agnes his wife, sister of Sir Francis Walsingham.[43] There is no record of how quickly it physically disintegrated, but by the end of the century there is some evidence in an anonymous Lament found with the papers of Philip, earl of Arundel, after his death while imprisoned by Elizabeth.

> Bitter, bitter, oh to behould the grasse to growe,
> Where the walles of Walsingham so stately did shew
> Levell, levell with the ground the towres doe lye
> Which with their golden glitteringe tops pearsed once to the skye.
> Where weare gates, no gates are nowe; the waies unknown,... [44]

Earlier, the scholar Roger Ascham, tutor to the princess Elizabeth and later Latin secretary to queen Mary, was with the travelling embassy to the Emperor Charles V, and his letters appeared in 1553 as a Report on Germany. In Cologne cathedral were the enshrined bones of The Three Wise Men, Kaspar, Melchior and Balthazar, brought there from Milan in the 12th century by Frederick Barbarossa, a focus of European pilgrimage and one of the richest shrines in Christendom. Yet Ascham writes, 'the Three Kings of Cologne be not so rich, I believe, as was the Lady of Walsingham'.

> ... the waies unknown,
> Where the press of peers did passe while her fame far was blowen.
> Oules do scrike where the sweetest himnes lately were songe,
> Toades and serpents hold their dennes where the palmers did thronge.

The Shrine of Our Lady of Walsingham

Weepe, weep O Walsingham, whose dayes are nightes,
Blessinge turned to blasphemies, holy deeds to dispites.
Sinne is wher our Ladie sate, heaven turned is to hell,
Sathan sittes wher our Lord did swaye, Walsingham oh farewell.

So for three centuries Walsingham disappeared from the English scene. Then, as times allowed, men began to return, not to Walsingham itself as there was nothing there but to King's Lynn where there had been a pilgrimage chapel, Our Lady of the Mount, and where in 1897 was built a Holy House. In 1934 the Slipper Chapel at Houghton-le-dale having been restored, the shrine there became the centre of devotion to Our Lady of Walsingham for Roman Catholics. Meanwhile, in 1931, members of the Church of England had built a Holy House according to the dimensions of William of Worcester on a site just outside the priory walls to the north. The mediaeval foundations and the well found there suggest that this was probably the site of the almonry and 'a certain fountain called Cabbokeswell' referred to in a deed in the tenth year of Richard II's reign.[45] Every year now tens of thousands of pilgrims go to Walsingham: the Roman Catholics to the Slipper Chapel and then to the site of Rychold's Holy House in the priory ruins, the Anglicans to their Holy House enclosed in the elaborate church that looks across to the Knight's Gate in the walls of the priory grounds.

No high drama attends the four and a half centuries of Walsingham. Immensely popular though the Shrine of Our Lady became, the feeling that its story leaves is of the steady development of a family chapel open to the public, well cared for and made increasingly attractive by its noble and regal patrons. When Henry VIII's candle at the shrine was put out, the noble family that had first opened the doors had long disappeared, the canons were sole custodians. The end was inevitable. For the 20th-century revival there remains only the delicate invocation of the Ballad:

> Therefore blissid Lady, graunt thou thy great grace
> To all that the deuoutly visyte in this place,
>   Amen.

VI

SAINT THOMAS BECKET OF CANTERBURY

> Pur ceo vus començai a traiter cest sermon
> Del martyr saint Thomas, cel glorius baron
> Ki tuit li munz requiert a la seinte maison
> De Seinte Ternité, u suffri passion,
> Par ceo que il maintint verité e raison . . .[1]

THE SENSE OF INEVITABILITY GROWS as the 12th century alexandrines pound on to the violent climax in the dusk of the great cathedral. The archbishop is standing at the foot of the steps that lead from the north-west transept up to the High Altar. He has come to Vespers on this late December afternoon, crossing the windy cloisters from the room where he has dined, and where already he has exchanged strong words with the four men who have come from Normandy to kill him. Ever since he returned in triumph from exile in the late autumn this proud and brilliant man has known that his end would come soon. He has known it more surely than his adversary the king, or even than the four knights who are now battering at the doors.

At the sound, and at the cries of the people in the nave being jostled by the knights as they clatter after their prey in the twilight, the monks try to drag the archbishop to the sanctuary of the High Altar. But sanctuary would frustrate his resolve to die. The monks retreat as he turns to face the knights. The

Saint Thomas Becket of Canterbury

knights try to carry him out of the building, but the archbishop is a powerful man and hurls the first knight away.

'Hic faciet, quod facere vultis', he shouts.

They all go at him with their swords, and after two blows he is still standing; the third drives him to his hands and knees, and at the fourth, a blow so terrible that the sword is shattered on the pavement, his crown is severed and he falls full length. Mauclerc stirs out his brains on the floor. As the murderers rush out to loot the palace, the darkness and the terrified silence are split by lightning and thunder. The archbishop lies on the steps, his body covered by the splendid cloak that had spread over him as he fell. His panoplied life has ended in a setting as dramatic as any he could have conceived, and in a manner as savage as the anathema he himself had uttered and the penances with which he had afflicted his own body. But not even he, for all his pride, could have imagined the surge of emotion that would sweep England at his death, still less the waves that spread out and out over Europe to make him England's greatest martyr-saint, and his shrine one of the richest in Christendom.

> Oh, mal eüré! Pur que l'avez ocis,
> Cel seintisme arceveske? N'i avez rien conquis.
> Il n'aveit rien mesfit; trop i avez mespris . . .

Oh, evil indeed! Why did he have to be killed? King Henry II, whose angry words had caused the deed, shut himself up for three days and wept ceaselessly, repeating to himself this maddening question.[2] The pope would see no one for eight days, and issued an edict that no Englishman should be admitted until he raised the ban.[3] Why, he cried, had his champion of the Church been slain? The people poured into the cathedral, prostrating themselves, groaning, howling the question of why their one protector should have died.

The terrified monks had crept back to the body; they had carried it to the crypt and laid it between the altars of St Augustine and St John the Baptist. They had closed the doors and set guards about the place. Every drop of the blood that oozed from the martyred body was caught. That very night a blind man was directed there from the church of St Nicholas, mysteriously since he had no knowledge of a saint's death. His sight was healed. The miracles had begun.[4]

Why? Why did Thomas Becket have to be murdered? Why, from the very instant of his death was he regarded as a martyr-saint and his cult spread like a fire through Europe? The questions have been asked and various answers given for eight hundred years. No life of a man living so long ago is more fully documented, and there can be few men of any time whose last two hours of life can be followed almost minute by minute.

Within a few months of the murder the story was put into verse by Guernes de Pont-Sainte-Maxence, named from the little town in the department of Oise. He was a *clerc vagant*, a wandering scholar-northern-troubadour, and, dissatisfied with his first verses, he crossed to Canterbury in 1172 less than two years after the murder, to learn the truth. He had not known Thomas personally, but says that he saw him in France when he was chancellor and conducting war against the king of France. The prior and the monks received Guernes kindly and he stayed for two years writing his poem, 6180 alexandrines, 1236 strophes of five rhyming lines, vivid, dramatic, moving with the sureness of fate to a conclusion that was evident from the first. To this he added a brief poem of thanks for all the help and kindness he had received from Becket's sister Marie, made abbess of Barking in April 1173, and Eudes, prior of St Trinité of Canterbury since 1167 and later abbot of Saint-Martin-de-la-Bataille at Hastings. The whole as we know it is put together from manuscripts transcribed by Anglo-Normans.[5]

Within a few years another ten biographies of Becket had been written in prose by contemporaries, some of whom had known him as intimately as was possible with such a man. Among these were William of Canterbury and John of Salisbury, pupil of Abelard, who were both certainly in the cathedral at the end; and Edward Grim, the Cambridge clerk, who alone had stood by the archbishop and caught the first blow on his arm. There is yet more circumstantial evidence in hundreds of letters from and to pope Alexander III, Henry II, Louis VII of France, cardinals, bishops, abbots, priors, cellarers, monks and Thomas Becket himself. Many of these letters were immensely long and little more than literary speech-making, the real tidbits of news that mattered probably being given ver-

Saint Thomas Becket of Canterbury

bally by the bearers. The main collection covers the years from 1155, when Becket became chancellor at thirty-six or -seven, to 1220, the date of the Translation of his body to his new and magnificent shrine.[6]

Why, then, with all this accumulation of recorded knowledge do people century after century continue to speculate about Becket? What is there that is so mysterious and fascinating? There are almost no material facts that are not well-documented, his political-religious career and his relations with the king can be traced step by step, so that assessment of the rights and wrongs can be reasonably made. The story is complicated, and made more so by the workings of the mediaeval mind; but on the whole it is no more difficult to disentangle than many other historical situations. It is when we recall what happened after his death, that he was a martyr, a saint, that all the West flocked to his tomb where miracles were legion, that the question rises and hovers over the whole scene, not just of his posthumous glory but of his life. The facts we know so well no longer seem a logical sequence of historical events, but pieces of a jigsaw puzzle of which one vital piece is missing. We have all we need of his actions, of his appearance, his chastity and devotion, his physical prowess and his intellectual strength, even of his apparent relationship with his contemporaries, high and low: but we have not the main piece, his personality.

This imponderable evades us. Becket never gave himself away. Of all the letters he wrote none is known that was not official. True, even in official letters a man can show himself; but not Becket. His mother, who died when he was twenty-one, was the only woman he ever loved, and of the men there was only Henry II and the young prince Henry for whom he seems to have had any real affection. A number of men who knew and worked with him admired him greatly, but tenderness did not enter into their relations. Becket's cloak of personal invisibility has been a continuing challenge to artists as well as historians. No English saint's life, death and miracles contributed so much to mediaeval religious art throughout Europe, and none has provoked more entertainment, wit and drama for later generations.

Thomas, the son of Gilbert and Matilda Becket, was born on

Saint Thomas Becket of Canterbury

December 21st, 1118 on the north side of Cheapside where the building of the Mercers Company stands. That same evening he was baptized in St Mary Colechurch, and as it was the feast of St Thomas he was given his name. Both parents were Norman, Gilbert being first-generation in England from Rouen, Matilda a native of Caen. These details are quite unimportant and are given only as examples of the kind of close information that can be given about Becket throughout his life. How unimportant are such facts is shown by the far more interesting story of his parenthood which grew up within a few years of his death.

This widely believed account asserts that Gilbert Becket, when on a pilgrimage to the Holy Land, was imprisoned by heathen men. His captor, the emir, took a fancy to him and allowed his daughter to visit him. She fell in love, was converted to Christianity, and swore to be christened so that they might be married. Gilbert agreed to all this, but evidently took advantage of the relaxed watch on him to plan escape on his own. When the princess found her lover fled, she trustingly resolved to follow him. 'O mirandum nimis hujus mulieris tam audaciam quam amorem tanta difficilia et ardua praesumentis!' rightly says the chronicler. She did not hesitate, she found a boat which took her to England. She had only two words of English, 'London' and 'Becket'. 'London, London', she repeated till she reached it: 'Becket, Becket!' she inquired in the city's streets. A crowd began to follow her, jeering, and by luck attracted the attention of Gilbert's manservant, Richard, whom she recognized and who ran in to tell his master. Gilbert, a respected and prosperous citizen, found it most embarrassing. He told Richard to take the princess, who had swooned with joy, to his mother's house while he took advice on the matter. At St Paul's he found six bishops at a meeting to whom he confessed his predicament. They had no doubt that the faithful princess should be at once baptized and married to Gilbert. This was done without delay, so that the very next night the future archbishop and martyr was conceived. Gilbert did not, however, see his son for three and a half years; not very long after his marriage he had a strong desire to revisit the Holy Land, his reasons though religious were not convincing, his wife was distressed as well she might be, left alone in an alien land. But Gilbert was firm and put her in charge of his servant Richard until he should return.

The story has been told many times: the earliest we possess is in a 13th-century hand, the latest in Pynson's unique 'Here begynneth the lyfe of the blessed martyr Saynte Thomas.'[7] But though little details differ it is substantially always the same. Why, if it was pure invention, was it invented? It has been suggested that it grew from the idea that Thomas Becket had united the Churches of east and west by being adopted as patron saint of the knights of Acre: but this is just an afterthought. It has been taken seriously by some historians, but what tells against it is that not one of the contemporary Lives speaks of it, Grim's 'Life' having the reference added later.

It arose perhaps for two reasons. It helped to explain things in Becket's life and character which from the first were baffling; and it could so easily be true. Contemporary writers agree that there was little sympathy between father and son, but that Thomas was devoted to his mother and was deeply distressed when she died. The Saracen blood of the adored mother could also account for his strangeness. What, after all, distinguishes Becket in his time from the stupid, powerful barons and clever clerics, and from the brilliant, hot-tempered and almost pagan king, Henry, is that they were all easily explicable while he remained a mystery. As to its likelihood, the western wanderer and the eastern maid meeting and loving is traditional, romantic and true in every century, for the crusader as for the modern soldier. Though few have had the princess's perseverance and courage, her cries of 'London! Becket!' have been echoed by centuries of dark, deserted ghosts.

When he was ten, Becket was put to be educated by the prior of St Mary's, Merton, in Surrey. This Robert of Merton was a good man, simple but wise, and faithful to Becket to the day of his murder. One of Becket's few recorded acts of gratitude was his making Robert his chaplain when he became archbishop. His second teacher, Robert of Melun, who taught him in Paris, where he presently went until he was twenty, he also remembered by getting the king to make him bishop of Hereford. It is not clear whether he was back in England before his mother died; his father seems to have got into low water, financially, and Thomas took various jobs, as clerk to a relative, Huitdeniers, and in the portreeve's office. He was, incidentally, not known as Becket until years later, since surnames did not necessarily descend; he was usually known as Thomas of London.

Gilbert, however, had influential friends, and when he wrote to Theobald, archbishop of Canterbury, Thomas was received into the household. He was twenty-five when he entered this court of brilliant young men, a court that was of paramount influence in the country in those years of Stephen and Matilda's social upheaval. He was tall, handsome and strong; dark, with a pale skin and aquiline nose. He argued well in a deep, round voice; for all his love of hunting his hands were soft and white; all his senses were abnormally acute. He was altogether chaste, and there is no evidence to show that he was ever otherwise throughout his life.

Almost at once the pattern of his future began to show. He became involved in jealousies; Roger Pont l'Evêque, who had been there for some time, intrigued to have him removed. They remained enemies to the end, when Roger as archbishop of York was accessory to Thomas's death. But his evident intelligence and grasp of affairs, his energy, ability to please when required, and a charm, which no one has been clearly able to explain but which made the old archbishop love him, established his position. He took minor orders and spent a year at Bologna and Auxerre studying law. On his return Theobald drew him increasingly into his confidence and took him on a journey to Rome. Increasing, too, were Thomas's lucrative posts, his extravagance and love of display; everything he did must be in the grand manner. His career developed logically; after becoming archdeacon of Canterbury he was sent to Rome to see that Stephen's son was not crowned, so, when Stephen died having recognized Henry, Matilda's son, as his heir, what could be more natural than for Henry II to welcome Thomas as his Chancellor? Theobald was pleased to see his protégé as a protector of the Church.

Becket was thirty-six, moving towards the height of his intellectual and physical powers. For seven years he conducted the affairs of the country, under the instructions of the king fifteen years his junior, loyally, and with great skill and prudence. The two men could not have been more different. Henry

Saint Thomas Becket of Canterbury

was square, tough and coarse, with a florid face, red hair and restless grey eyes; he could never keep still, his clothes were flung on anyhow, he bolted his food and was dirty and covered with cuts and sores from hunting. He was exceedingly blasphemous, chattered during Mass and was lecherous, violent and vicious. But he was also a hard-headed, quick-minded business man, single-minded in determination to replace anarchy by strong and stable government. Very little missed his searching eyes, and he forgot nothing: a very dangerous man.

The combination with Becket was extraordinary. Becket loved the idea of young royalty and the responsibility of the association; Henry respected the experience and intellect of the older man. Besides, there was no one else to compare with Becket as a companion, since he had both the shrewd intelligence of a political consultant and tremendous energy, high spirits, and skill in hunting and war. The two men became close friends; and as Becket's riches and honours grew with his position the magnificence with which he lived was fabulous. When sent to France to arrange a marriage for Henry's son, the court of Louis VII wondered what the king's state might be if such was his chancellor's style. When fighting later in Brittany, he had a small army of his own. At the same time he remained a devoted counsellor and as such acquired a reputation for being 'a persecutor and destroyer of holy Church', owing to his will to strengthen the king but also because he mistrusted the great lords of the Church as much as he did the barons.

But even then, as throughout his life, it seems that he was dissatisfied with himself; he gave alms lavishly and indulged in secret penances.[8] Though he pretended to ignore it, he must have been well aware of the deep disappointment of the only man besides the king who loved him, the old archbishop Theobald. One wonders what strange twist in Becket's character made him neglect Theobald's last summons shortly before his death, calling upon him to fulfil his duties.[9] John of Salisbury wrote to him at the time, telling him how distressed the archbishop was at Becket's absence and urging him to come back to England before Theobald died.[10]

The archbishop, to whom Thomas was more indebted than to any man in his life, never saw his protégé again. But he died with the continued desire for Thomas to succeed him. As the king's desire was equally strong, Becket was elected to Canterbury. It seems incredible that at this crucial point there should have been so profound a misunderstanding between two men who had lived and worked closely together. Becket could not have made it clearer to Henry that if the king insisted on his being archbishop they were bound to have serious differences. Yet Henry refused to believe that a man who as chancellor had loyally enforced his will could as archbishop oppose him. Becket, while certain there would be differences, seems to have been extraordinarily blind to all he knew of the king's violent character.

For Becket loyalty was the guiding principle. At Theobald's court he did his whole duty to the archbishop, as chancellor he bound himself to the king's interests, as archbishop he was devoted absolutely to the interests of the Church. These loyalties were single and did not affect in any way what personal feelings he may have possessed. The first time when, in this new relationship, he crossed swords with the king, Becket did not consider enmity on either side. The hot-tempered Henry felt differently. It seems as though Becket never really grasped this, even when, as the quarrel developed, it was clear that Henry was bent relentlessly on his submission or destruction. Becket himself never lost his loyalty to Henry as a symbol of kingship nor altogether his affection for him as a man.

As archbishop, Becket did not become immediately converted to asceticism. He might wear a hair shirt and drawers, which became verminous through being seldom changed and so even more penitential, but they were covered by magnificent robes, and he lived and behaved as a prince of the Church. He gave up the chancellorship to show the king that the affairs of the Church must be separate from the State. It was the first sign that Henry saw that his friend and companion was preparing to oppose him. Within a little over two years the crisis came, and, though six more years dragged out before the end, it was in 1164 that the seeds were sown from which sprang the strange growth of centuries of pilgrimage.

Though the issue may appear to us now as simple, it becomes, when considered in the light of the 12th century and of the main characters involved, extremely complex. For some time Becket had been making it clear that he regarded ecclesias-

Saint Thomas Becket of Canterbury

tical courts as superior to secular, sometimes indeed in cases where the secular would be assumed to operate. Malicious tongues made the most of this with the king, who was already disturbed. Henry was genuinely anxious to reform the position of the courts because there were far too many abuses arising from criminous clerics sheltering under the ecclesiastical wing. During the disruptive reigns of Stephen and Matilda the Church, as the only stable power capable of giving protection, had extended its jurisdiction. The king wished mainly to re-establish the usage of Henry I's reign, and many of the provisions he now put forward had been accepted from William the Conqueror's time; but where they went further than this they showed his determination to strengthen the secular arm at the expense of the Church. The nub of the whole affair was the question of jurisdiction over clerics who had committed crimes.

It is taken for granted now that one law applies to all men, and the provisions of what became known as the Constitutions of Clarendon have for the most part been written into the laws of England.[11] But the society of the 12th century to which sanctions had to be applied was very different from to-day's. Granted that the Church courts were often abused, that they seized lands on flimsy pretexts and acquitted or treated too lightly their criminals, yet by the very fact of their extraordinary power they were able also to protect the innocent against kings and barons who simply trampled on the secular law when it suited them.

There were genuine points in favour of both Becket's and the king's arguments when Becket opposed the demand that a clerk convicted of crime in a Church court should be degraded and handed to the lay court for punishment. But on both sides excess spoiled the validity of the case. The Church was the protector not only of the innocent and defenceless but also of the only educated men in the country, and its courts had over and again used this power justly. But Becket, instead of standing by this justifiable and civilized record, claimed immunity as an absolute right of the Church, and for this there was no foundation.

As immunity worked in favour of men committing crimes against clerics as well as of clerics committing crimes, there was a bitter sequel. After the acceptance of the Constitutions there was still immunity from trial in the first place in a secular court, so the murderers of Becket himself went unpunished since they were not caught by the Church and so were never tried. Becket's successor, Richard, tried in vain to have the law amended.

Meanwhile, the king became more and more enraged by the opposition. He demanded submission on every count to his Constitutions and did nothing to prevent armed knights bursting into the conclave of bishops with threats of death. Becket gave way, not out of fear for himself but on account of his colleagues. At once he regretted it and tried to leave England, wrote to the pope and for once showed indecision. The result was a complete hardening of Henry's attitude. Some weeks later at the Council of Northampton Becket was summoned to answer a number of charges which had nothing whatever to do with the main issue.

Northampton made illusory all later efforts at some sort of reconciliation. It was a horrible affair, even recognizing that in the 12th century violence was taken for granted, uncontrolled temper and words were natural in debate and the highest dignitaries gave and received public insults. As charge followed charge, most of them quite baseless, it became clear that Henry was determined on no less than Becket's absolute destruction. Becket was resolutely opposed to the right of the king's court to try him, and Henry, presumably feeling that the humiliation could do for the time being, let him depart.

The moral victory was Becket's: Henry had pursued a hateful, personal quarrel while Becket had continued to stand by a principle. It was a principle based on loyalty to the Church he served consistently with the thread of loyalties which ran through his life. However differently Becket may have appeared at different periods, there was a consistency in all he did. The scene of his leaving Northampton Castle goes some way to explain the wave of popular emotion when he was murdered six years later. The barons yelled and insulted him, trying to trip him up and throwing filth: outside, the waiting crowds, anxious for his safety, acclaimed him. He rode on giving his blessing and, finding at Saint Andrew's monastery that large numbers of his household had deserted him, he called in as many of the crowd as there was room for to eat dinner with him.

Becket had a strong sense of drama which his quick mind and resonant voice was ever ready to employ. The people who acclaimed him at Northampton and later as martyr-saint knew and cared nothing for the arguments in the case; they simply saw in this magnificent lonely figure a champion of the Church's power to save them from cruelty and oppression.

So Becket's six years' exile begins. The king makes no attempt to prevent his departure, but Becket moves secretly knowing there are many who wish him dead. He writes to the pope telling him the whole story of his persecution and how the Church in England has deserted him.[12] He asks the pope to use all his power but says that all the evil should not be imputed to the king who is the instrument, not the author, of machinations. On Christmas Eve Henry orders the seizure of all the revenues of Canterbury and the arrest of all Becket's relatives, and the fathers and mothers, brothers and sisters, nephews and nieces of all the clerks with Becket.[13] Becket's old enemy Ranulf de Broc is put in charge of this and executes it barbarously. He transports these people, some aged, some children, and most of them not remotely concerned with the case, to present their wretchedness to Becket in France. Becket sees the pope, also temporarily in exile at Sens. Louis of France refuses to grant his fellow monarch's request for help against the archbishop.[14] Becket retires to the Cistercian monastery of Pontigny.

The progressive confusion of the years shows itself in the voluminous correspondence carried on by everyone except the uneducated barons. The original issue seems lost in ecclesiastical squabbles, international politics, the intrusion of the Holy Roman Emperor and an alternately strong and wavering pope, with an anti-pope in the background, thunderings from the pulpit and excommunications. A stream of words, often expressed in splendid prose, exposes the intrigues and the bitter, uncompromising nature of the struggle.

Only Becket remained single-minded; at one point he tried in three successive letters to come to an understanding with the king, but Henry did not even reply. It was not surprising, since Becket was incapable of giving way an inch. The king showed in all the negotiations, whether with the king of France or the ecclesiastics, duplicity and obvious bad faith. In 1169, when

endeavouring to win the pope to his side, he tried to bribe him while threatening at the same time that he would make an alliance with the Mussulman rather than have Becket reinstated. Somehow a meeting was arranged between Henry, king Louis and Becket; Becket began with humility and all seemed going well until he ended with 'saving the honour of

God'. At this the king had one of his fits of rage and the meeting broke up.

So to the last attempt at reconciliation. The king, as a further insult to Becket, had had his son crowned by Roger of York. He realized then the imminence of an interdict; the pope had given Becket power to issue it and fear of this terrible punishment made him see that he had gone too far. The meeting occurred near Fréteval not far from Chartres. It must have been an extraordinary one between these men whose friendship was broken by years of hatred and distrust, the king now nearing forty, the archbishop over fifty. It seems that they talked for hours unattended, sometimes on their horses, sometimes dismounting and pacing up and down, and when at last Becket mounted to go Henry held his stirrup for him.[15]

There was an Act of reconciliation and restoration, *Henricus Anglorum Rex de pace reddita Cantuariensi;*[16] the pope exhorted the bishops to make it complete. But apart from the king's insincerity there were too many evil forces at work. The orders Henry gave for the restitution of all property before Becket's return to Canterbury were not properly carried out; land was returned wasted and goods damaged. Becket became restive, Henry equally so at Becket's delay at leaving for England. The last time they were ever to meet was at Chaumont on November 1st.

It seems that the conversation they had then was peaceful, but hopelessly sad as though lack of rancour had left them with no driving force.[17] 'Oh, why will you not do my wishes? All things would be put in your hands,' said the king with nervous familiarity, half-joking, half-serious. Becket thought of the Temptation: 'All these things will I give thee if thou wilt fall down and worship me.' Then said the king, 'Go in peace, I shall follow and see you in Rouen or in England.' 'My Lord,' answered Becket, 'my soul tells me you will never see me again in this life.' 'You think me traitor?' 'Absit a te, domine,' replied Becket.[18]

They parted without the kiss of peace. Henry, at each meeting, had avoided giving it; his reason on one occasion had been that it would be more appropriately given in England. His near-paganism caused his scant respect for Church, popes, prelates or their threats, except when they might have political implications, but it made him none the less superstitious. The *osculum pacis* was that given by the bishop to the priest between consecration and communion, and, given by the king to Becket, it would have been his seal of Becket's safety. Henry did not trust himself and he dared not risk some awful retribution. There can be no other explanation.

Becket, though urged not to depart without the kiss, let the matter pass.[19] It is likely that by then he accepted the nearness of death. While never moving from his first stand on the immunity of the Church, he had spiritualized the issue into one of far greater significance. This strange man was always aware of his sin of pride and ostentation and tormented himself with increasingly loathsome penances to atone for what he knew he could never overcome. It is surprising that in those six years of tumultuous exile he did not become even more fanatical. His judgement was certainly affected but his view by then was that judgement was God's alone. He came to see everything in terms of the scriptures, with himself as the representative of God and ultimately the sacrifice necessary to make plain His will to those who paid tribute to Caesar.

'Blessed is he that cometh in the name of the Lord', cried the people running into the water to meet Becket at Sandwich and again as they thronged the journey to Canterbury.[20] The town and cathedral were adorned, music and bells filled the air with joy. The monks had not always been on very good terms with the archbishop, but John of Salisbury had written telling them they must give him a good welcome. They responded, and if there was any hesitation it was probably due to timorous doubts of the true situation. The townspeople were wholehearted in their welcome.

The next day, Ranulf de Broc appeared again. From the first exile he had brutally executed the king's orders over everything to do with Canterbury, including taking over Becket's residence of Saltwood Castle which he still occupied. With him was the sheriff of Kent and clerks of the bishops excommunicated for their part in young Henry's coronation. There was another violent scene in which Becket declared he acted only under the pope's authority, and de Broc yelled abuse and departed.

Becket then set off to see the young Henry at Woodstock to present him with a gift of horses, but the mind of his one-time ward had been poisoned and messengers were sent telling Becket to return to his diocese. Petty indignities mounted, a consignment of French wines was seized by de Broc who also beat up the archbishop's servants, hunted over his land, intercepted food supplies and even cut off the tail of one of his sumpter horses. Worst of all, de Broc saw to it that false information reached Henry in France of Becket's marching about the country with armed bands, seizing property and inciting people against the king.

It is true that Becket was stern in ejecting those who had entered his livings, but he nowhere exceeded his rights; the enthusiasm of the people for him was spontaneous. In other ways he seemed to prepare for the imminence of death, undergoing even stricter penances, spending long hours in devotion and giving generous alms. The apex of this was reached on Christmas Day when he preached on the text 'On earth peace to men of good will' and told the congregation that just as they had had one martyr there, Alphege, soon they would have another. The church was filled with lamentation. 'Father, why do you so soon forsake us, to whom do you leave us desolate?'[21] Herbert of Bosham was there, so it should be true, but it is an odd coincidence that he puts exactly the same words, which are quoted in the Breviary lessons for St Martin's Day, into the mouths of people when Becket left Pontigny four years earlier. Grim, the Cambridge clerk who later tried to protect Becket, was also there and records only that 'after the sermon' the archbishop thundered his excommunication of de Broc and several others:[22] Herbert also tells of the anathema and emphasizes Becket's anger.

Meanwhile, the suspended prelates, Roger of York and the bishops of London and Salisbury, had crossed to see the king in Normandy. They incited him further, perhaps, than they intended. Though there are several versions of what Henry said, it is impossible to know exactly; he was certainly in such a paroxysm of rage that he did not know himself. Whatever his words, four knights, Reginald Fitz-Urse, William de Tracy, Hugh de Moreville and Richard Brito, took them as a signal to get rid of the archbishop. They left immediately, travelling separately to England where they were received by de Broc. Hardly were they gone when the King summoned a council to decide what action should be taken against the archbishop, considering that he had clearly returned to England with the intention of rousing the country, dethroning the king and asserting the supremacy of the Church over the Crown and nobility. It was decided that a commission should go at once to England with a warrant for Becket's arrest. The four knights were to be overtaken, since their absence had aroused a grave suspicion. The decision came too late.

On December 29th, the knights, having collected enough soldiers to make sure of overcoming any resistance and with their armour concealed under civil dress, arrived at the archbishop's palace about three in the afternoon, demanding audience in the king's name. Becket was still at table with some of his household and John of Salisbury, so deep in talk that he did not notice the knights' entering, until, as he paused and turned, he saw them sitting near his feet with an archer behind them. He gazed at them silently: it was some time before anyone spoke. Then Fitz-Urse asked if he would hear the king's message publicly or in private.[23] In private, Becket replied, but when the knight began he recalled his household to witness. The fabricated message was that the archbishop should at once go to swear fealty to the young Henry, absolve the suspended bishops, and, in short, make good all the wrongs of which he had been accused for years. Becket stood firm by his rendering 'unto the king the things that are the king's, and unto God the things that are God's'.

At this the knights leaped to their feet, shouting, grinding their teeth, flinging their gloves about and waving their arms. In the confusion, Becket became caught in a shouting match, reminding them that they had been his vassals and that he would assert his authority. They shouted to the monks to prevent his escape; he followed them to the door, saying that he was ready to die. As the yells of the infuriated knights faded, Becket once more became calm. John of Salisbury reproached him for answering violence with violence, reminding him that everyone was not so ready to die as he was. They were still talking when the cry came that the knights, fully armed now and with soldiers, were breaking down the doors that had been locked behind them.

The moment was approaching for which Becket had been

Saint Thomas Becket of Canterbury

preparing since Matins at midnight in his own apartment.[24] It is said that he gazed into the darkness then and asked if it would be possible to reach Sandwich by daybreak. He was reminded that it was only seven miles distant and that there was full time. 'God's will be done', he said. From then he spent hours in devotion, confessed, assisted at Mass, and three times in the day was flogged, his desire for discipline growing with the certainty with which he viewed his end. Now, with the sound of splintering wood, he is half-dragged, half-carried by the terrified monks through the cloisters. Vespers have begun, and as the archbishop is brought into the north transept the knights are already in the cloisters behind him. In that vast and intricate cathedral with winter darkness falling he could have hidden easily, but he insists on the door being left open while he turns to await the knights who rush in followed by the soldiers.

'Where?' cries Fitz-Urse, peering around in the twilight, 'is the traitor Thomas Becket?'[25] There is no answer. 'Where is the archbishop?' 'I am here, no traitor to the king, but priest. What do you want of me?' The knights fan out, clanking towards him, unrecognizable with their visors down, still arguing, threatening as the light fades. All but the Cambridge

clerk, Edward Grim, have deserted the archbishop. Becket moves down the steps that lead from the choir and stands with his back to a pillar in the transept. 'Into thy hands, O Lord, I commend my spirit.'[26]

Pilgrimage was not new to Canterbury. In the 17th century the site of a circular Roman temple was excavated, the bones of sacrifices found and several thousand votive offerings, probably of the 2nd century. The basilica of St Augustine which rose in the 6th century was following custom as well as instruction from Rome in planting Christianity in the place of a pagan shrine. There, pilgrimage had become customary, to the saints Mellitus, Alphege, Dunstan, Anselm, all of them archbishops before Becket. Now, more suddenly than ever before, a new pilgrimage began.

Pilgrimage to Becket's tomb was spontaneous and continued in spite of considerable opposition. Barbarians like the de Brocs who still occupied the primate's palace threatened to have the corpse dismembered and thrown to the dogs, intimidating pilgrims or anyone talking about miracles. To begin with, the high clergy and nobles deplored the new cult, and even some of the monks of Canterbury,[27] immediately after the murder, said that Becket's obstinacy had brought about his death. The king, after an outburst of remorse as violent as were all his emotions, was very soon receiving the murderers at court and enjoyed their company when hunting. The murderers' only punishment was their excommunication by the pope which does not seem to have worried them very much, and they lived on to found west of England landed families, except for de Moreville who was Justice Itinerant of Northumberland and Cumberland and seems to have remained in the north. Becket's life-long enemy, the vicious and quarrelsome Roger Pont l'Evêque of York, suffered no revulsion of feeling and was ready to support any endeavour to suppress the miracles.

Active opposition did not last long. The conflict between king and archbishop had for six years been one of international interest, and not only the pope but the king of France and the Emperor were fascinated by the struggle, wondering how long Becket would last and what would happen when he was killed. Debate began while he was still alive as to whether he would be entitled to be called martyr after death. The thrill of horror that ran across western Europe with the news of the murder was because such a dénouement had been anticipated for years. As Henry had more enemies than friends abroad he soon saw, whatever he felt about the criminality of what had been done in his name, that it had certainly been a blunder. The pope, who had far more to gain in the Church's cause by Becket's martyrdom than by anything in his turbulent life, accepted Henry's word that he was innocent of any part in the murder and would await papal judgement. The king then spent nearly half a year trying to conquer Ireland and making communications as difficult as possible. On May 21st, 1172 at Avranches, seventeen months after Becket's death, he at length made peace with Rome.

The attitudes and activities of king, ecclesiastics and barons were a matter of indifference to the people, and the cult of Becket grew as quickly as the news of miracles spread. One is accustomed to think of communications in the middle ages as being difficult and slow; yet there is any amount of evidence to show that news could travel very swiftly. Becket's murder is an outstanding example. On the Thursday, two days after, the wife of a knight in Sussex heard of it, prayed to the martyr of Christ and was cured:[28] on Saturday a girl in Gloucester was cured of a head complaint, on Sunday William Belet, a knight of Enborne, in Berkshire, was cured of a swelling in the arm, and so on. It also shows the immediate acceptance of Becket as a martyr-saint.

These are the earliest miracles recorded by Benedict, the monk almost at once appointed to be on duty at the tomb. His main occupation was to test those pilgrims who claimed to be healed so that accusations of fraud could be refuted. Though some of the many hundred miracles he notes strain credulity, he took great pains over his inquiries and sometimes made pilgrims indignant at being disbelieved. He reports several cases of the saint punishing fraud, sometimes rather vindictively, for example when he struck blind a man who had pretended to be blind; on two occasions he refused to help boys who had fallen asleep while praying at his tomb.

The sarcophagus stood on the floor of the crypt, and the body was covered only by the lid. Owing to the threats of de

Broc a heavy marble tomb was built around and over it. Though this has disappeared, its exact form is known from the many representations in the cathedral glass: it was a plain, low, veined marble structure with two large oval windows on each side. The top was flat with a pix for money offerings and sometimes a candlestick with votive offerings around it. Pilgrims could stretch through the portholes of this outer tomb and touch the coffin within. Between the coffin lid and the roof of the tomb was a space of about a foot, and once a poor fat madman somehow squeezed himself through and lay down on the coffin.[29] The monks thought they would have to smash the whole thing to remove him, but miraculously he squeezed himself out. There is a tomb like this in Salisbury cathedral which probably covered the coffin of St Osmund.

After desecration by the murder the cathedral was not reconsecrated for nearly a year, and services were held in the chapter-house. People were admitted singly to the crypt and spread the tale of miracles so that by Easter the monks had to open the crypt freely to all comers. From then on the crowds increased steadily. The recorded miracles vary from raising the dead to the recovery of a mislaid loaf, and the ways by which they occurred were just as varied. A mortally ill man is cured at the moment a candle is lit for him at the tomb, and a missing horse is found through a promise to present a wax figure of it to the shrine.

Cures were also caused by relics of the martyr, of his clothing and particularly of his blood. The monks had immediately after the murder collected all the blood they could and had set vessels to catch any drops that fell from the wounds. They soon saw there would be a shortage, but as the minutest drop was enough to sanctify large quantities of water they diluted it so that it lasted for centuries. It was also, they realized, far less upsetting for ladies this way. So, says Benedict, there is this remarkable circumstance that of no other holy person except the 'lamb of Canterbury' could it be said that his blood was taken as was that of the 'lamb of Bethlehem'.[30] At first the precious water was put in wooden boxes, and special ones were designed for ladies with mirrors in the lids but they were found to leak. Earthenware was too easily broken so tin or lead phials were made. It was these ampullae, hanging by a cord from the

Saint Thomas Becket of Canterbury

neck, that became the token of the Canterbury pilgrim just as the scallop-shell was that of St James of Compostella and the palm of Jerusalem. They were often miraculously refilled, and the water could be applied as well as drunk. Sometimes, even when there was no blood left in the ampulla, cures came through the pilgrim's faith.

Though the fame of the miracles spread rapidly through Europe so that Becket was soon generally regarded as a saint, he was not canonized for just over two years. Soon after the murder John of Salisbury had asked permission for veneration of him without formal papal authorization. He seems to have been unaware that not long before Becket's death Alexander III had issued the first decree reserving canonization exclusively to the pope. But compared with most others the canonization did not take long, and on Ash Wednesday, February 21st, 1172, it took place at Segni. December 29th, the day of martyrdom, became the feast of St Thomas of Canterbury.

But there were as yet no great signs of the king's penitence in spite of the reconciliation of the year before. With a lack of tact remarkable even for him he actually insisted for a while on receiving half the gifts at the tomb, but in the end he gave way to public feeling. The countless reports of miracles at last had their effect, and in a serious crisis he threw himself on the martyr's mercy. In the summer of 1174 the young Henry and his brother Richard had allied with Louis of France and the count of Flanders against their father; while fighting them in Normandy, Henry heard the news of rebellion in the north and invasion by the Scots. It seemed that only a miracle could save him.

Two days later he landed at Southampton and proceeded at once to Canterbury, fasting upon bread and water. At Harbledown, some two miles from the city, he got off his horse; at St Dunstan's church he changed his clothes for a hair-shirt and the woollen smock of a pilgrim and went on barefooted, leaving a trail of blood as he reached the High Street and entered the precincts. Having prayed in the church-porch he went to the place of martyrdom and watered it with his tears; he then made his confession and descended to the crypt where he prayed and groaned for a long time. Bishop Foliot of London announced the offerings of the king, after which Henry put his head into one of the oval openings in the side of Becket's tomb and submitted to his penance. This was severe, five strokes from each of the prelates and three from each of the more than eighty monks. He then insisted on being left there all night on the stone floor. In the small hours he visited all the altars and shrines, assisted at Mass, drank of the sanctified water and took some away with him in an ampulla.

Back in London he fell extremely sick after these excesses, but a short time later he was awakened in the night by a messenger from the north with good news. On the very day of the completed penance the king of Scots had been made prisoner, Alnwick Castle had been taken and the rebellion crushed. Moreover the Flemish fleet, bent on invasion, had been driven back by storms and his sons had at least for the moment ceased the conflict. Nothing now could hinder the glory and fame of the martyr-saint. The 20 marks of silver annually, now worth £13.6.8, which Henry vowed to the Harbledown almshouses is, after 800 years, still paid.

Soon the monk Benedict was joined by another, William, to assist in doing duty at the tomb and record the miracles. This William had been in the cathedral when Becket was murdered and tells frankly how when he heard Fitz-Urse cry 'Strike! Strike!' he thought there would be a general slaughter and, feeling unfit for martyrdom, had fled.[31] Many of the miracles he reports come from France, Italy, Germany and Holland.

But more revealing of Becket's immediate reputation are the still visible signs in works of art throughout Europe. The earliest known is a figure in the Byzantine mosaics at Monreale which was built between 1174 and 1182. Henry II's daughter, Joan, who married William the Good of Sicily in 1177, must have felt very strongly about her family connection with the murder as the mosaic can at latest be only twelve years after Becket's death. At Sens there is a high relief, also of the late 12th century, and at Sacro Speco, Subiaco, St Benedict's first foundation, before Montecassino, there is a 13th-century fresco.[32] All these show him simply in his robes, with no mitre, giving his blessing. As far apart as Lyngsjo in Sweden where there is a font, and Spoleto where there is a fresco in the church of SS. Giovanni e Paolo, there are late-12th-century representations. The most prevalent *objets d'art* are the 13th-century Limoges enamelled reliquaries. There must have been a tremendous business in these for holding either true or false relics of St Thomas, or perhaps even mementoes of him, as they have turned up in a number of places from Sweden to Sicily. A curious fact is that they ceased altogether to be made in the 14th century.

Within two months of the king's penitential pilgrimage a fire damaged the cathedral destroying Conrad's glorious choir. A great rebuilding was at once begun, the first architect being William of Sens. The work was completed by William the Englishman who was responsible for the chapel of the Blessed Trinity east of the choir and the concluding apse that was to hold the Crown of St Thomas. The Romanesque crypt in which stood the saint's tomb, east of the chapel of St Mary Undercroft, was undamaged and is still unrivalled in Europe. But as the cathedral was being extended above so the crypt was taken further east below, and a wooden casing like a miniature church was built over the tomb to protect it while the work was going on. There it remained until 1220 when rebuilding was finished and the splendid new shrine awaited the translation of the relics.

During the fifty years between the death of Becket and his translation there were there stages of pilgrimage.[33] There was the place of martyrdom in the north transept where a column was removed to open the view. The altar there was known as The Altar of the Sword's Point because on it were two pieces of Brito's sword shattered on the pavement by the last blow. There was the High Altar before which the body had lain all night after the murder, and there was the Tomb in the crypt.

The ceremony of July 7th, 1220 was so magnificent that it took some twenty years to clear the expenses of hospitality. The day of the event had been advertised for two years so that besides the king Henry III, the Papal Legate, twenty-three bishops of England and France, the earls, barons, and lesser clergy, thousands of people poured into Canterbury. Wine was free and on all the main roads vast provisions had been made ready at inns and monasteries for man and horse.[34] On the London road these were free for the asking at every stage of the journey. This prodigality probably spoiled the innkeepers because later very strict regulations were made in Canterbury about importuning pilgrims, forbidding innkeepers to run out into the road or entice them away from other inns.

Cardinal-archbishop Stephen Langton, who was more than anyone responsible for Magna Carta, was the organizer of this astonishing festival. The new shrine stood behind the High Altar in the chapel of the Blessed Trinity and from the wearing of the stones on all sides of the quadrilateral one can see how large an area it covered. No very clear description exists, but piecing together accounts it seems that the base was of pink marble some six feet high with sculptured arches on all sides. On this was a large chest, shaped like an ark, in which were the relics, the whole plated with gold and jewelled. Over it was a gold wire mesh on which were hung the offerings of brooches, rings and all manner of ornaments and precious stones. An immense painted hood fitting over the complete structure could be raised and lowered by pulleys attached to the surrounding pillars. Seven great candlesticks stood around it. Though still controversial, it seems that the main part of St Thomas's skull remained in the original Tomb above which the saint's hair-shirt and drawers were hung, and the crown, or probably the scalp, was in a gold and silver reliquary in the chapel in the new apse called the Crown of St Thomas.

Though the accounts of the monastery beginning in 1207 are remarkably complete, there are few references to the shrine during its building.[35] This may be due to funds coming to a large extent from outside. Matthew Paris in his description of the translation says that gold and gems and precious materials had been prepared and were presented together with the incomparable work of master Walter of Colchester and Elya of Derham.[36] The accounts of the Treasurer, surviving up to 1385, give a fascinating picture of the rise, and the beginning of decline, in popularity of the shrine. For the fifty years between Becket's death and translation there were six main points of pilgrimage and the order in which offerings are entered is first the High Altar, then St Mary Undercroft, The Holy Cross, St Michael, the Tomb and the Martyrdom; the Corona Sancti Thome was added in 1207, the first time that the Crown is recorded as a relic. 1220 was, of course, a special year for St Thomas, but in 1221, the first full year after the Shrine came into being, the order of offerings has hardly changed. St Thomas's four places of pilgrimage came at the end.

Saint Thomas Becket of Canterbury

It was another thirty years before the Shrine, the Corona, the Martyrdom and the Tomb, in that order, head the Treasurer's accounts. There they remain until 1336 and probably longer, though after that there are a lot of gaps; from the large sum of £330 at the Shrine in 1336 it reaches the enormous one of about £700 in 1350. This was the year following the worst devastation of the Black Death and what would have been a great drop in the number of pilgrims due to the ghastly mortality must have been made up by the gratitude of those who had survived.

But soon there comes a change. In 1373 there are once more only six pilgrimages, with the High Altar and St Mary Undercroft again in the lead, and the Shrine, Corona, Martyrdom and Tomb relegated in that order: twelve years later the position is the same. This is the period covered by Chaucer's *Canterbury Tales*. It is also a time of tremendous vitality in the growth of Englishness, in the first real revolt against the social order, in fierce criticism of the Church and the rise of Lollardry. Here is the figure of Wycliff, and Langland with his *Piers the Plowman*. The end of feudalism is coming, and if the order of the middle ages has not yet altered, the spirit of it and its attitude towards this world and the next have greatly, if subtly, changed.

Nothing illustrates this more clearly than the *Canterbury Tales* which have given to the language 'Canterbury Bells' from the bells worn on pilgrims' horses, 'canter' from the easy pace with which they moved, and 'Canterbury' as an epithet for a long and tedious story, though how this could have arisen from such vivid tales is hard to say. They are commonly accepted as the most complete and true picture of a pilgrimage. This is probably correct but with the qualification that they are true of that particular period which in terms of religion was one of disruption and decadence. The intense religious fervour of the middle ages was gone for ever though mediaeval survivals would continue until to-day with fanatics, heresies, persecutions, revivals, reformers, intolerance, superstition, and a desire for the pure word of God. But the mystical, ecstatic belief of the Age of Faith would never return.

The corruption of the Papal Curia, the universal simony, the fact that there was almost no office or privilege of the Church that could not be bought or sold, and the broadcasting of this attitude through hosts of pardoners from whom anyone could buy absolution of his sins, was one cause; the growth of national feeling and social consciousness was another. Petrarch had denounced the abominations of Avignon only a few years before Chaucer wrote his Pardoner's and Summoner's Tales. In 1381, Jack Straw marched with the men of Kent to Canterbury where the town was on their side, released the preacher John Ball and sacked the archbishop's palace. Headed by Wat Tyler, they assembled in thousands to request justice of Richard II and on being prevented by the archbishop, Sudbury, from holding a proper conference they dragged him from the Tower Chapel and beheaded him on the Hill.

This was the background to the *Canterbury Tales*. So when it comes to the characters who are connected in any way with the Church it is easy to see why the Pardoner appears as a scoundrel, the Friar a rascal, the Monk sometimes a gloomy bore sometimes a gay blade, and so on. The simple parson is, however, a completely good man. The atmosphere of the whole glorious work is set by the opening lines of the *Prologue* which sing of how when April's sweet showers have pierced to the root the drought of March, then, when small birds make melody, sleeping all night with open eye, men long to go on pilgrimage.

> And specially from every shire's ende
> Of Engeland, to Canterbury they wende
> The holy blisful martir for to seke . . .

The pilgrimage had become an excuse for a spring holiday, and it is spring vitality that infuses each tale that is told to pass the time of this immortal journey. That is the joy of it, the lack of cynicism, disapproval, preaching or scoffing. Chaucer is religious in the deep sense of understanding and loving humanity. He sees clearly the weakness and venality of the Church and that many of its members are cheats; but he knows more certainly that what it stands for is eternal. His characters are the first real people, as opposed to types, in English literature. Though typed by title – the Squire, the Prioress, the Miller, the Plowman and so on – their characters far transcend these labels. So, though there is little to be learned from these tales about a pilgrimage to Canterbury, there is a great deal to be learned about human beings. There is also little to be found

Saint Thomas Becket of Canterbury

of the great evils of the Church or of social upheavals; Chaucer's attacks are by broad and humorous implication, he has too much tolerance ever to labour a point. In this he shows the development of Englishness and growing insularity, some might say to a fault, in its mingling of laziness and optimism. The Church is decadent, pilgrimage a springtime ritual holiday, 'the holy blisful martir' – who is he? But the mercy of God is for ever, His grace has recognized the possibilities of good in man for all his sinfulness. If God does so, who am I to judge? Ultimately it will all come right provided we make an effort, not too much, but some. No one, not even Shakespeare, is more English.

Meanwhile the pilgrimage to St Thomas's shrine declined yearly, though the shrine itself glowed ever more brilliantly with jewels and was flanked now by the splendid tombs of Edward the Black Prince on the south and Henry IV, with his queen Joan of Navarre, on the north. After centuries of royal and noble pilgrims the finest jewel of all was still that given by Louis VII, the protector of Becket, who had come there to pray successfully for the life of his son. Even his old enemy Henry had not dared to interfere. Over 250 years later, on the Bohemian ambassador's visit, one of his staff described it as a carbuncle half the size of a hen's egg that shone at night. A Venetian, about 1500, gave the most real picture of the shrine. One sees it as he found it, exceeding all belief. In spite of its great size it is entirely covered with plates of pure gold which are yet hardly visible because of the sapphires, diamonds, rubies and emeralds which cover it; and not only jewels but sculptured gems as agates, onyx, cornelian and cameos. The eye wanders, everywhere alighting on something more beautiful. One thing surpasses all, a ruby the size of a thumb-nail. In the place of the shrine the church is rather dark and the writer comes there when the sun is near setting and the weather cloudy, yet the ruby glows in the shadows as though he has it in his hand. The Shrine had not been built when Louis gave this jewel, the Regale of France, to St Thomas's Tomb: still it dims all others, with a golden angel pointing at it.

The Bohemian ambassador had also described the well from which the pilgrims drew the water for their ampullae. Five times, he says, the water on St Thomas's tide has turned to blood and milk. It was a well to the north of the crypt at which it was said St Thomas had drunk each day. As the years passed there was no need for the pretence of mixing blood of the saint with the water: the well acquired a sanctity of its own.

The last pilgrim of importance to chronicle his own visit is Erasmus, accompanied by his friend Colet, Dean of St Paul's.[37] As guide to the pilgrim's progress through the cathedral he is better than anyone but uses the same form of writing as that when he went to Walsingham, a colloquy between Ogygius (himself) and his friend, Menedemus, who is welcoming him on his return. It is not so facetious as his piece on Walsingham and is more accurate, but for so great a scholar the humour at the expense of the miraculous is very heavy. He makes an interesting comment on the stone figures of the murderers on the south porch, and then invents the inscription 'Tuscus, Fuscus and Berrus' for Tracy, Fitz-Urse and Brito, omitting mention of de Morville. Hentzner, describing his visit to England in 1598, repeats this feeble joke from Erasmus's book when referring to these images which had been allowed to stay after all else pertaining to Becket had been destroyed. Reading Erasmus, one longs for Chaucer's profound wisdom and love of his fellow-men, and wishes he could have lived to complete his Tales with the arrival of the pilgrims inside the cathedral.

Of the host of legends which grew around the saint there is none more enchanting than that contained in Jacobus de Voragine's 13th-century *Legenda Aurea* printed in English by Pynson about 1520.[38] This is the 'Lyfe' referred to earlier which has the story of Becket's Saracen mother. This 'Lyfe' goes on to tell how after the disastrous scene at Northampton when Becket left England he arrives in Rome on St Mark's Day. His servant cannot find any fish so Thomas tells him to get what he can. The pope, hearing he is in Rome, sends one of his cardinals who finds Becket eating capon and reports to the pope that Thomas is not so perfect as supposed. The pope does not believe it and sends another cardinal who finds Thomas still eating capon. As evidence he slyly nips 'a legge of capon in his kerchief', but when he unfolds the kerchief to the pope there a carp is revealed and the pope says thay are not true men. When Thomas goes to see the pope he is asked what he has been eating and Thomas tells him what and why. The pope says the whole affair is a miracle and gives to all at Canterbury licence to eat flesh on St Mark's Day when it falls on a fish day, 'all which is kept accustomed to this day'.

Thomas then said mass before the pope in a white chasuble and later told him that when he, Thomas, died for the Church the chasuble would be turned from white to red. Thus it was that on the very day of Thomas's death the pope was wearing the chasuble and it turned red. So he had a great requiem sung and in the middle an angel on high began singing the Office of a Martyr, and the choir joined in singing the Mass of the Office of all Martyrs.

It seems that there is no other copy but the one in the British Museum of this work of 'Rycharde Pynson printer unto the kynges noble grace'. The reason is probably that all too soon after its appearance Henry VIII ordered the elimination of everything to do with Thomas. However long expected, the blow must have fallen with lightning suddenness.

On the last Friday in August, 1538, Madame de Montreuil went on the last recorded pilgrimage to the shrine. Sir William Penison, who was paid £40 for his attendance, wrote on September 1st to Thomas Cromwell a description of this, having accompanied her on her journey from the Scottish court.[39] Arriving at Canterbury at 6.0 in the evening together with the French ambassador and her gentlewomen, she was welcomed by the Master of the Rolls, the Mayor and sheriffs who conducted her to her lodgings and presented her with 'ypocras, and other wines, plentye, with soundry kyndes of fysshes'. Henry VIII was due at Dover any moment and Madame de Montreuil was delighted. The next morning, after more presents, she spent over an hour at the shrine. Sir William is careful to inform Cromwell that, though the lady declared that if she had not seen the richness of the place all the men in the world could never have made her believe it, she did not kneel to Saint Thomas's Head, although the prior offered it to her to be kissed. The prior sent many gifts to her in the afternoon and she invited him to dinner the next day.

Time was creeping on and arrangements had been made for the complete destruction of the shrine and the wiping out of every reminder of this saint who had opposed a king. Henry VIII was now expected at any moment, Cromwell was being kept informed and was ready to pounce. Yet here was a conducted tour, richly received, under the guidance of a knight royally appointed. It is the more sinister when one reads the entry in 'The King's Payments'.[40] There on the same page as the fee paid to Sir William Penison are payments to Wriothesley, the commissioner, to be distributed in rewards for catching some wanted men and for money laid out to 'sondry monks and chief officers of Canterbury, servants and labourers for help in disgarnishing the shrine'. No sound comes from Cranmer, the archbishop, who has toiled faithfully for the king since 1529 when he produced the plan for Henry to get rid of his first queen and later, in 1536, by a remarkable about-face found a quite different reason for having Anne Boleyn removed. Apart from his own leanings towards Protestantism he was not one to interfere with the king's designs, even in his own diocese. The only step he had taken was on August 18th when he asked Cromwell to have the blood examined, a not very helpful suggestion.

Then, within ten days, everything is over. Madame de Montreuil, for all her being 'content to stay till the king comes to Dover',[41] disappears from the scene. On September 8th the commissioners are busy dismantling the shrine and the king is at Calais. Two days later the king is at Dover waiting while the work is completed and the chests full of jewels and gold 'such as six or eight men could but convey one out of the church' removed to the Treasury. One authority thinks that the king was actually in Canterbury between September 6th and 9th, which does not agree with the evidence of contemporary correspondence: he also believes that Cromwell himself stayed on a few days to supervise the final demolition and the burning of the saint's bones.[42] There is no doubt that far greater attention was paid to Canterbury than to any other place of pilgrimage, partly because of the political significance of St Thomas, but largely because of the fabulous amount of the national wealth contained in the shrine.

If these last ten days have about them an air of mingled mystery and business-like rapine, the example of Winchester makes clearer the unscrupulousness with which such work was everywhere done. From Canterbury the commissioners went there to destroy St Swithun's shrine, and on September 21st Wriothesley reports to Cromwell that this has been done.[43] He

Saint Thomas Becket of Canterbury

evidently found its loot disappointing after Canterbury for he says he will stay on a few days 'to swepe awaye all the roten bones that be called reliques' in case it should be thought they had come more for the treasure than for 'avoiding of thabomination of ydolatry'. Then about a week later he runs into the bishop, the famous and much maligned Stephen Gardiner, returning from an embassy abroad. Their meeting is elaborately courteous and Wriothesley does not say a word to the bishop about what he has just been doing in his cathedral. He does, however, take aside the king's chaplain, Thirlby, who is accompanying the bishop, to ask him what Gardiner had thought of their doings in Canterbury through which they had just passed. Thirlby replies that Bishop Gardiner seemed rather to like it and to wish the same could be done at Winchester.[44] It sounds improbable. Anyway, the bishop, whose house Leland refers to as the seat of eloquence and special abode of the Muses, must have been angry and disgusted when he found what had happened in his absence.

In trying to find explanations of all this sort of behaviour one has only to think of Europe's recent experience of totalitarianism. What makes it so horrible is the absence of passion and the impersonal relentlessness of the men in control. Only in the north, as we have seen, was there any attempt to resist, and this was crushed by the treachery typical of such a regime. For the rest there is only the silence of terror.

In Europe, particularly in France, Italy and Spain, all moves in England were watched. On October 5th, 1538 comes a letter from France saying that 'every man that hearkeneth for news out of England asketh what is become of the Saint of Canterbury. But Master Wriothesley who played a part in that play had before sufficiently "instruct" me to answer such questions . . .'[45] As the months pass ambassadors and English travellers are continually having to find answers to more awkward questions; copies of the king's Letter to the Justices of December and relevant extracts from his Proclamation of November 16th are distributed for use as propaganda.

The purpose of these documents was to justify the King's action to people at large and to make sure that any and every reminder of Becket was erased. The Letter states simply that the king desires to dispel false rumours of future exactions and the taking away of liberties of the realm for which it was feigned that Becket died, whereas in fact Becket had only tried to prevent clergy from being punished except by himself, and had died in a wilful fray which he himself had begun. Further, his claim to be the only man to crown the king was just another of his traitorous attempts against the laws of the realm. The Proclamation is a more powerful indictment. It gives more evidence of Becket's ill-behaviour, and of his death being caused by his own violence. 'The kings majesty, by the advice of his council, hath thought expedient to declare to his loving subjects, that, notwithstanding the said canonization, there appeareth nothing in his life and exterior conversation whereby he should be called a saint, but rather esteemed to have been a rebel and traitor to his prince.'

The Proclamation had, as was intended, a sweeping effect on the whole realm. Apart from the prohibition of the name of saint, any image or picture of Becket must be done away with, there is to be no festival in his name nor mention of him in any service, and his name must be removed from all books 'to the intent his grace's loving subjects shall be no longer blindly led and abused to commit idolatry . . .' Otherwise the loving subjects would be imprisoned. These regulations were more than a threat; for example, two years later the vicar of Calne became suspect as a papist simply because he had overlooked Thomas's name in one of his books. After considerable trouble he was let off with a fine.

Meanwhile, immediately on the news of the destruction reaching Rome, Pope Paul III produced his Bull of Excommunication against the king. In this Henry is condemned for bringing St Thomas to trial, convicting him of contumacy and declaring him traitor, thereafter commanding his bones to be burned and the ashes scattered. Though it was widely believed at the time in Europe that there had been this posthumous trial of Becket there seems to be no evidence of it besides the Bull, and very little to show that the bones were burned.[46] It is argued that since the Bull was widely known the king and Cromwell would surely have denied its truth if the evidence for it had been false, and the pope could hardly have been deceived in so notorious a matter. On the other hand Cardinal Pole, then in Italy, cannot have believed the story or he would

Saint Thomas Becket of Canterbury

have used it himself, and there is no reference in the voluminous correspondence with Cromwell, nor in any contemporary letters, to this event alleged to have taken place some time before the shrine was demolished.

In 1888 a stone coffin was unearthed in the crypt in just such a place as one might expect Becket's bones to have been buried, and these bones together with a cloven head found with them may be his. There is certainly no direct evidence, even by the people at the time, that the bones were burned. It seems possible that the monks, who were a complacent lot, were allowed, as in the case of St Cuthbert, to bury them provided they did it in a way and in a place that would not attract attention. It may even have been done, as at Durham, under the direction of the Commissioners. One has the curious impression that at this last wretched moment in the history of England's most famous saint there was the same uneasy relationship between him and the monks as in his life three hundred and sixty years earlier.

In all parts of Europe the saint's fame continued through relics, statues, windows and churches dedicated to him. At Sens the vestments in which he officiated are preserved to this day; at Fourvière, near Lyons, is the chapel dedicated to Becket because four years before his death he had said it should be dedicated to the next martyr. His chalice is at Bourbourg, his hair-shirt at Douai, his mitre at St-Omer.[47]

In one respect, however, Henry VIII did accomplish what he set out to do. If Becket was any longer held to be a martyr then he was a political not a religious one, and if political then a traitor, since he had opposed the king. Ergo, anyone holding him to be a martyr was traitor also. The later Henry was as determined to destroy Becket as had his namesake been centuries before. His success was the more complete since he suffered no lapse into remorse. Pilgrimage ceased for ever.

To-day in the cathedral the sense of drama is numinous. It grows with every pace up the tremendous Gothic nave. Through the narrow doorway in the Chillenden screen at the top of the great flight of steps separating the choir from the nave there is a gleam as though beyond is some secret source of illumination. Then, as you approach, you see that at the far end of the choir and presbytery there is yet another flight of steps leading to the

High Altar. Beyond that again is the Trinity Chapel where the Shrine once stood, rounding to the apse all filled with the light that glows from 12th- and 13th-century glass.

To reach this place of the shrine you have to pass by the north transept where Becket was slain. There is no Altar of the Sword's Point now, only a plaque on the wall. Leaving it you climb the long, broad flight of steps in the north aisle of the choir which leads to the level of the shrine itself, the smooth, hollow-worn steps up which every king of England until the Dissolution has climbed, as well as unnumbered thousands of lesser pilgrims. This moving upward from one level to another, and then another, is dramatic; the absolute simplicity of the Norman crypt where Becket was first entombed provides the appropriate contrast.

One can understand the hold that this place had on the inflammable imagination of mediaeval men. The individuality of atmosphere lingers in all these great centres of religious pilgrimage, though at times the contrasts between them are strongly marked. While Durham, for all its tremendous interior, holds the sense of holiness and intimacy characteristic of St Cuthbert, Canterbury is theatrical. Above ground rises stage after stage of Becket's advancing splendour, beneath is the stark fact of St Thomas's hair-shirt. After 800 years there is still here shown the 'incurable duality' of his attitude to the relations of Church and State. He could not see that the servant of one need not necessarily be the enemy of the other. So he passed by the wonderful opportunity of renewing the work of his greater predecessor, St Dunstan, in bringing Church and State together for the common good.

But these are all aspects that emerge from centuries of study. In that age of devilish blacks and angelic whites, of flaring banners, trumpets, luxury, cruelty and squalor, Becket's great courage at the end, his committing himself and the Church to God only, stood out for the people as a superhuman gesture of protest against the oppressive power of their rulers. What appeared first as a gesture grew through pilgrimage to the reality of power which no king, until the last Henry, could wholly ignore.

> Or prium Jesu Crist le fiz sainte Marie,
> Pur amur saint Thomas, nus doinst la sue aïe,

Saint Thomas Becket of Canterbury

Que rien ne nus suffraigne a la corporal vie,
E si nus esneium de seculer folie
Qu'al muriant aium la sue conpaignie.

Amen

Ici fine la Vie saint Thomas le Martyr.

VII

SAINT EDWARD THE CONFESSOR

> 'Tis called the evil:
> A most miraculous work in this good king,
> Which often, since my here-remain in England,
> I have seen him do. How he solicits heaven,
> Himself best knows; but strangely-visited people,
> All swoln and ulcerous, pitiful to the eye,
> The mere despair of surgery, he cures;
> Hanging a golden stamp about their necks,
> Put on with holy prayers; and 'tis spoken
> To the succeeding royalty he leaves
> The healing benediction. . . .'[1]

BETWEEN THE 11TH-CENTURY SETTING and the 17th-century writing of that scene in which Malcolm and Macduff, coming to beg king Edward's help against Macbeth, see the crowds waiting to be touched for the King's Evil, English monarchs had for centuries been working this hereditary miracle. It is the best-known of the Confessor's miracles since it was perpetuated for so long by his successors. Yet the growth of his reputation for sanctity was slow.

Comparison with Becket is inevitable because the royal saint of Westminster and St Thomas of Canterbury seem to complement one another. The cults which drew pilgrims to their respective tombs grew from politics: Becket's martyrdom in the

Saint Edward the Confessor

cause of Church and people versus royalty faces the saintliness of a king who added lustre to the throne by living a legendary life of love for his people and the Church. But while Becket's leap to fame was immediate on his death it was nearly a century before Edward's was established. Becket's case, wherever one's sympathies lie, involved such intense passions that it can be understood: King Edward's was more subtle, and, as a study in the creation of a saint, is fascinating.

At first the approach seems simple. Every schoolchild has learned about the Confessor that he was the last English king, was a good man, built Westminster Abbey and was made a saint, and that he made laws which every monarch since has sworn at his coronation to keep. But almost at once the questions arise of why and how he became a saint. Soon it becomes clear that no precise answer can be found because the growth of the cult was inspired by so many imponderable and incomprehensible causes. One can only watch it happening as the Church and throne and parliament lend themselves – with occasional lapses in the 16th and 17th centuries – to the building of a fabulous mystique with no counterpart in the western world.

Though the documentation of the 11th century is scanty there are at least two contemporary recorders. The *Anglo-Saxon Chronicle* gives a vivid history with circumstantial detail of the king's doings and the activities of all the people with

Saint Edward the Confessor

whom he was dealing.[2] The other record is anonymous – part poem, part prose – begun probably in 1065, the year before the king died.[3] As it was written for the queen it must have been finished some time before her death in 1074. There has been a lot of argument about the author but it seems most likely that he was a monk of St Bertin who had been closely attached to the court for years.[4] He writes entertainingly and well, and, when being modest, seems to have his tongue in his cheek. He declares that it is the first book to be written on the subject and he is right; he hopes he will become famous because of it and he has survived nine hundred years. Subsequent 'Lives' which are better known are only embroideries of it.

Edward was born about 1003 in the middle of the Danish wars; to escape their savagery he was sent by his futile father, Ethelred the Unready, to Normandy where from the age of ten until he was forty he was at the court of his uncle Richard, duke of Normandy. Meanwhile Cnut, who had married Ethelred's widow, Emma, ruled England and then was succeeded by two unpleasant sons. The second, Harthacnut, feeble and without heir, called Edward to England just before he died. On his death earl Godwin, the most powerful man in England, saw which way the wind blew, and through the Witan restored the last English king to sit on the English throne.

England at that time was comparatively tranquil, partly from exhaustion, partly on account of the Danes' preoccupation in fighting one another or the Norwegians, and the Normans trying to set their own house in order. Embassies to the coronation came from the Emperor of Germany and the kings of France and Denmark, and comparisons are made with the glory and peace of Solomon after the wars of David. In other words the confusion and general mayhem was temporarily suspended. What is remarkable is that, but for a few brief outbreaks, this tranquillity prevailed throughout the twenty-three years of Edward's reign.

Being half-French and having spent most of his life in Normandy, he fulfilled his natural inclination by giving as many posts as possible to Normans. But except for two years when Godwin was in exile under Norman pressure the earl and his son, Harold, really ruled the country. It was an England without any sense of nationalism, for though the north, west, south

Saint Edward the Confessor

and midlands might unite in disliking Normans they disliked each other almost as much. A strong king would have taken advantage of peace from foreign wars to unite them; Edward played them off against one another. Yet by the standards of the time he was a gentle and charitable character, only occasionally treacherous and rarely deliberately cruel. When he was angry he did not burst into the customary violent abuse; he was not vain and he was moderate in eating and drinking. He always behaved well in church, and this was very different from the conduct of most mediaeval monarchs. He is usually depicted as a rosy-faced, simple creature with wavy white hair and beard and with delicate white, transparent hands and fingers. Some writers have even said he was albino. But the only writer who wrote with personal knowledge, the monk of St Bertin, knew him only in his old age. It seems improbable, in view of his indefatigable passion for hunting, that Edward always had such a frail appearance.

He was most famous for his genuine religious devotion; indeed this and hunting occupied most of his life. He liked best of all the company of monks, though he seems to have had too little interest in learning to try to raise the standard of Anglo-Saxon literature which sank to an even lower level. The aspect of his devotion which contributed greatly to his later cult was his vow of chastity. Having married earl Godwin's daughter Edith, who is reputed to have been as beautiful as she was good, he persuaded his bride to the same vow on their wedding-night. There is no evidence that what might seem an insulting trick disturbed the bride's father: it may well be that he appreciated its making his own and his son's rule more certain to continue. William of Malmesbury said later that he could not discover whether the king acted thus from dislike of his queen's family or out of pure regard for chastity, and Roger of Wendover suggested he was unwilling to beget successors of a traitor stock; but their perplexities seem ingenuous and fraught with propaganda. The subject has caused argument among later historians, but is ultimately unimportant. The fact is that he was entirely chaste; and it is the effect of his chastity, in that he perforce failed to beget an heir, rather than its cause that matters.

How was it that this dim figure acquired undying fame as

national hero, royal saint and lawgiver? As king, his policy or lack of it was to leave decisions to others; his religious fervour, though genuine, was inclined to hysteria; although monarch after monarch crowned at Westminster has sworn to observe the laws of the Confessor there is no evidence that he ever made a law or even usefully exploited existing ones.

It seems that one must read his personality between the lines of his biographers, for he surely had a stronger character than appears and one that inspired loyalty and affection; also he must have had some flair in government and in handling very tough men. It is hard otherwise to see how he ran out his twenty-three years of reign in peace. Whatever may have been the king's real personal qualities they had little or nothing to do with the development of his cult. He died on January 5th, 1066, a week after the consecration on Childermas, Day of Innocents, of the great abbey church which he had been so many years building and never saw completed. Edward was buried there on the Feast of the Epiphany and Harold was crowned there the same day, 'and he met little quiet in it as long as he ruled the realm.'[5]

This was, perhaps, the first step to glory. By restoring Westminster Edward had left a superb, visible memorial and provided the setting for his shrine when the time came. It is hard to say how much truth there is in the popular story that, when in exile, he had vowed to St Peter that when called to the throne he would make a pilgrimage to Rome and that, when the time came, the Witan said he was needed at home to rule and that the pope then absolved him on condition he restored St Peter's Abbey at Thorney. Though charters dated the last year of Edward's reign mention an embassy to Rome and relaxation of the king's vow it is doubtful if they really were contemporary and the story does not appear in full before the 12th century.[6]

Thorney, the Isle of Thorns, was not more than a mile around, a piece of solid land, half-jungle, in the fens that bordered the Thames downstream from Chelsea and some two miles from the City of London. Streams from the hills flowed on two sides into the river and on the north-west the shore dropped steep into the swamps of St James's Park. Legend has the first foundation of the abbey by Lucius in A.D. 184, and its degrada-

Saint Edward the Confessor

tion to a temple of Apollo after the Diocletian persecution.[7] The beginnings were probably in the 7th century though the accepted belief that they were made by king Sabert of the east Saxons in 616 has no support except from the monk, Osbert, in the 12th century, who must have invented it since the careful Bede does not mention it when writing of the building of St Paul's at that time.[8] Sulcard and Goscelin, writing independently towards the end of the 11th century, both tell of Mellitus celebrating the miraculous dedication by St Peter himself; Mellitus died in 624, so the period is about right.

The composite story is simple and charming. A wealthy Christian has built a church and asks Mellitus to consecrate it. Christian folk assemble from afar, setting up their tents on the island. While they sleep on the eve of consecration, St Peter appears on the far bank of the Thames and calls to a fisherman to row him over. As he goes towards the church with a more than earthly dignity, the whole island is bathed in celestial light. On the return journey, as the fisherman drops his net at St Peter's word, a great shoal of fish is caught, among which is an enormous salmon for Mellitus. The fisherman is promised good hauls, always provided he never fishes on Sunday. Mellitus, finding the walls of the church anointed with twelve crosses and with twelve burned-out candles, celebrates with joy and the Isle of Thorns becomes known as the West Monastery.

Saint Edward the Confessor

In 785 Offa of Mercia conveyed land to the monastery 'in loco terribili quod dicitur oet Westminster'.[9] Some hundred and eighty years later king Edgar under the advice of Dunstan who was establishing the Benedictines restored it. In 1039 when Cnut's son, Harold, died he was buried at Westminster; though his equally deplorable brother had him dug up and thrown into the fen the abbey church had reached the status of a royal burial-place by the time that Edward, finding it in poor condition, decided to build an entirely new one.

The construction was different from anything that had gone before in that it was the first cruciform church in England, built massively of stone with an apse at the east end, and with stained glass in the windows. The contemporary monk biographer gives the impression that here was an island of peace across the river from the rich and teeming city to which the king moved his palace in order to be near the great work in progress. Apart from building his own memorial he unwittingly set a precedent of tremendous political importance. But for this separation of the king's residence from the City of London it is unlikely that the city would have developed such independence as to cause every monarch to weigh his actions in the light of its extraordinary power.

By the time of Edward's death an aura of sanctity, to some extent promoted by courtiers and accepted by the king, already existed. He had touched the scrofulous woman, he had touched a blind man; as he lay dying he had a prophetic vision of the coming ills of England due to the wickedness of the country, and he declared an allegory of how and when the troubles would cease. The anonymous monk tells all this, not hagiologically but as facts he knew at the time, and how the archbishop Stigand whispered in Harold's ear that the old man was drivelling. By that time, 1066, only seven cures by Edward had been recorded, though his chastity remained a wonder in itself and his reputation for piety was recognized. In 1080 a history of Westminster was written by one of the monks in which there is no mention of Edward in connection with miracles. There was only the Life by the monk of St Bertin to recall his sanctity.

Meanwhile other forces of mixed politics, emotion and patriotism were at work. Edward had been half-Saxon, half-

Saint Edward the Confessor

Norman; held down by their Norman conquerors, the English looked back on the last of the English kings with sighs for good king Edward's laws as standing for an unvanquished land. William the Conqueror for his part being both a bastard and Edward's nephew, and holding to his right by descent, saw advantage in revering Edward's name from a quite different angle. The fiction of Edward as a lawgiver probably started from this time when William declared about 1070 that all men should live under the laws of Edward, meaning the laws that had prevailed when Edward was reigning, with a few additions of his own. Henry I did the same.

Once the figure of a national hero began to emerge, uniting two opposing peoples, it was natural for him to become endowed with supernatural qualities. There existed already a record of Edward's saintliness and miracles and the time came when these were bound to be exploited. The first occasion was in 1102, when monks of Westminster had been boasting that the body of Edward was uncorrupted. With only a small ceremony the tomb was opened with abbot Crispin presiding and the only important visitor the bishop of Rochester, Gundulf, who tried to pull a hair out of the dead king's beard and was rebuked by the abbot. Osbert, the only recorder, later says that there was a crown on the king's head, a ring on his finger and a sceptre at his side.

Henry I had ordered this opening, and it was he who through family relationships and coincidences brought about the first real change. He had been born in England and his queen Edith was devoted to her ancestor, the Confessor, at whose tomb, to which she often went barefoot, she made a gift of Mary Magdalene's hair. The abbey of Wilton where she was educated had over a century's connection with royalty: the nun who became St Edith towards the end of the 10th century had been the natural daughter of the abbess by king Edgar, a liaison which had been a *cause célèbre* and had brought heavy censure from Dunstan. Yet another Edith who was educated there and had later restored the abbey was the queen of the Confessor himself. A further strong reminder of Edward was the claim that Henry could cure scrofula with his touch, though it is hard to find any evidence for this.

The opportunity was not to be missed and it was taken by

Saint Edward the Confessor

Osbert de Clare, a monk of Westminster. It is not known how long he had been preparing; his was a lively and contentious character and he was away from Westminster for some years until 1134 when he returned to become prior. Four years later he produced his life of Edward.[10] As his only genuine source was the monk of St Bertin he borrowed the greater part of his work, adding another ten miracles and enlarging on the visions to make it a real piece of hagiography. With this, and a letter from Stephen who had succeeded Henry, he promoted in Rome in 1139 the canonization of Edward. On this occasion he failed owing to lack of acceptable testimony. Innocent II deferred the matter but said that Edward could be 'gloriosus'.

Osbert fell into disgrace and ceased to be prior, possibly owing to his lack of success. Nothing further seems to have been done, probably owing to the civil war and chaotic state of the country. But with Henry II, hailed by abbot Aelred of Rievaulx as the cornerstone of the English and Norman races, the matter went forward again. In 1160 the Church in England with Henry's approval declared for Alexander II in the papal schism; in return the pope accepted the new approach, supported by Henry, for Edward's canonization. On February 7th in 1161 the Bull was issued at Anagni.

Meanwhile Aelred had been working on a life of Edward, basing it on Osbert's work but adding further legends.[11] Among those he invented were the tales of Edward forgiving the thief in his Treasury, Harold and Tostig as children fighting at table, the appalling bad end of Godwin, and the recovery of Edward's ring given to a pilgrim who was really St John the Evangelist. There was also Edward's vision of the Seven Sleepers of Ephesus turning on their left sides, and the splendid story of Mimecan the champion dwarf vindicating the honour of the Emperor's wife, which is quite irrelevant. These were all recorded later on the screen in the Confessor's chapel. This biography, though it stemmed still from the contemporary 'Life', had strayed in spirit from the facts. All the same it became the official life from which all mediaeval accounts grew.

The ironical connection of Becket with the Confessor comes out in the two Translations of the king. The first Translation to follow canonization was conducted by Thomas Becket on

Saint Edward the Confessor

October 13th, 1163 when he had not long been archbishop and the tension between him and Henry II was growing. The long but simple ceremony at which the ring of St John was found on the uncorrupted body ended with the confirmation of Gilbert Foliot as bishop of London by the very man he was to assist in destroying. The second Translation was ordered by Henry's grandson, Henry III, who had attended as a boy the superb Translation of St Thomas Becket, martyr, at Canterbury.

This second Translation of the Confessor, although the cult was by then firmly established, added great lustre. On October 13th, 1269 the body was translated to the shrine behind the High Altar which was to be the focal point in the virtually new Westminster of which St Edward almost ousted St Peter as patron. The new abbey, substantially as it stands to-day, grew partly from the third Henry's intense religiosity and partly from a desire for a royal burial-place. It cost a vast amount of money and the glorious building was achieved only after a typical piece of mediaeval vandalism as reckless as ours to-day. Only a small piece of the nave was left from the Romanesque abbey which the Confessor himself had devoted years to building.

The High Altar was moved westward to its present place almost in the centre of the abbey, baring a large space between it and Henry III's Lady Chapel at the east. Into this space was brought earth, said to be from Palestine, to form a high tumulus. On the summit was set the shrine, visible from every part of the abbey. The base of the shrine was a stone structure some seven feet high covered with mosaic and enamel in elaborate patterns. In its sides were archways where pilgrims crouched to receive, by nearness to the sacred bones, relief from the King's Evil. On the twisted pillars at the western end stood gold images of St John the Evangelist and Edward the Confessor. The base stands now as it did then, though the statues and jewels are gone and the mosaic and enamel battered. The higher storey of wood, arched and painted to resemble malachite, that covers the coffin in which still lie the bones of the saint, was put there by Mary Tudor when she restored the shrine after the Dissolution. The original was a gorgeous tabernacle of gold, decorated with jewelled angels.

Saint Edward the Confessor

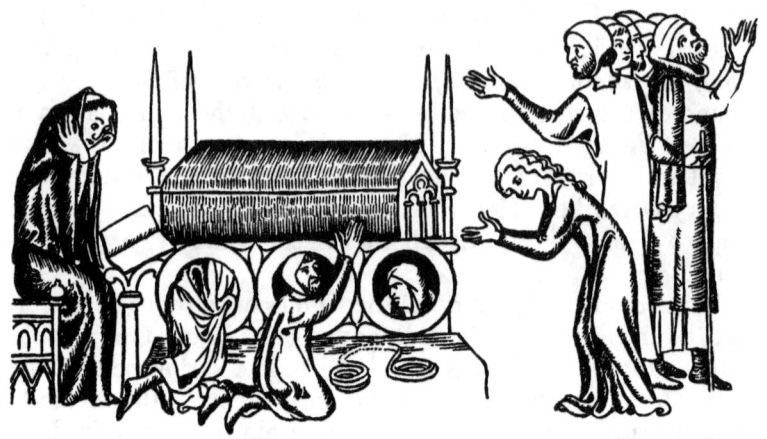

The whole design and the setting on a hill within the abbey was, and is, extraordinarily dramatic, though some of its original point was lost after Henry VI built his screen behind the High Altar. It seems strange that he, who of all monarchs most revered the Confessor, should have erected a screen that hid the shrine from the choir and nave, particularly as he had it made in honour of the saint. In its centre stands the Coronation Chair with the Stone of Fate brought by Edward I, and on its frieze are reliefs of the Confessor's miracles and visions.

Among other incidents on this frieze is that of the Confessor giving his ring to an unknown pilgrim. The story was one of the most popular ones and the ring renowned as a relic, partly owing to this representation but also to *La Estoire de Seint Aedward Le Rei*, the 13th-century and last of the great biographies of Edward.[12] This illuminated French poem was dedicated to Henry III's queen, Eleanor of Provence, and written probably by a monk of Westminster. Apart from the illuminations there are sixty-four coloured illustrations of fine quality. The story, as contained here, tells how king Edward, who was a devotee of St John, was one day at a service in a church of that saint when a beggar approached him. The king's almoner could not be found, so he drew a cherished ring from his finger and gave it to the man. Not long after this, two palmers lost at night in Palestine met an old man who led them to an inn. There he revealed that he was St John to whom Edward had given his ring, which he handed back to them to return to Edward with

Saint Edward the Confessor

the prophecy that he would meet the king in Paradise within six months, a prophecy exactly fulfilled.

This ring was the one removed at the Translation to be placed in the feretory as a relic. But it does not seem to have remained there. About 1386 the old abbot Lytlington wrote to Richard II apologizing for his inability through 'age and feblesse' to bring 'le noble relik lanel seint Edward'.[13] But it seems to have been conveyed by someone because his successor Colchester received back from the king, on November 14th, 1388, a ruby ring for the feretory. Its later history is obscure; it may have survived the spoliation of the shrine at the Dissolution and some writers have implied that it was found in the broken coffin after James II's coronation and given to the king who had it stolen from him by fishermen when he was flying to France.[14] No one really knows the truth.

The story of the broken coffin leads to that of another relic, St Edward's cross and chain. The information about this is more detailed. To begin with pure entertainment, there is a garrulous and vainglorious panegyric called *The Piety and Vertues of Edward the Confessor Reviv'd in the Sacred Majesty of King James the II*.[15] It has a long author's preface to show how clever he is, and how a Sir Winston Churchill of that time is one of his strong supporters; he has read all the old biographies and goes on to tell how someone put his stick in the hole in the coffin and hearing a 'gingle' found a gold crucifix, which was given to the king. The author remarks that now, in 1687, James II wears it, that his birthday, October 14th, is Edward's festival, that the relic was discovered on June 11th, the day of Monmouth's landing, and given to the king on July 6th when he won the battle of Sedgemoor.

This account is a fanciful version of an entirely straightforward account written at the time by the man who found the crucifix, and which is analysed in a recent paper tracing its history.[16] It appears that then, as now, Edward the Confessor's Chapel was used for robing at the Coronation. Some scaffolding there had fallen on the coffin and damaged it. Shortly after, a Mr Charles Taylour, taking round some friends, observed the hole, daringly put his hand in among the bones and drew out a chain and crucifix. He went off to the dean who was away, then took it home with him; he showed it to the archbishop of Canterbury who told him to look after it until the bishop of Rochester returned. In the end Mr Taylour presented it to James II, who was delighted and gave him a bounty, ordering the coffin to be made strong with the wood that is there to-day.

The accepted theory that James was wearing the cross when robbed by fishermen is disproved. In the inventory of his queen's belongings on her death in 1718 there was, among things subsequently sent to her son, a box containing a Cross and a Chain found in the tomb of St Edward in 1685. Two letters carry the story on. On June 4th, 1729, James III wrote to Lord Inverness from Rome saying he had left Benedict XIII at Albano too much fatigued to confirm his son; and then on the 17th he wrote again to say the pope had received him and all his family, and that his son Charles Edward behaved very well and gave the pope St Edward's Cross and Chain. In 1827 'the indubitable gold cross and collar of Edward the Confessor' was up for auction in King Street, Covent Garden and was bought for $15\frac{1}{2}$ guineas by the present owner's ancestor. But though a beautiful object, and with a cavity inscribed 'Preciosum Lignum Domini', it is 13th-century and only $1\frac{1}{2}$ inches by $1\frac{1}{2}$ inches. The original cross was Byzantine, not later than 11th-century, and described in detail by Taylour, the finder, as having the perpendicular beam 4 inches and the traverse a little over 3, trefoiled at the ends, enamelled with figures and hollowed to contain a relic, a picture of Christ in His Passion on one side and a Benedictine monk on the other.

On the evidence of the cross having been given to Benedict XIII, the Vatican has made a careful search but to no avail. The chances are that it still exists somewhere, possibly in an obscure Italian church.

The most precious relics at the shrine were, however, the stone with Our Lord's footprint made on His Ascension, presented by the Dominicans to Henry III, the Holy Blood in a crystal vase, sent by Robert, Patriarch of Jerusalem, and the Virgin's Girdle.[17] This last was most potently helpful to queens in childbirth. In 1242 abbot Crokesly and two monks took it down to Gascony for the confinement of queen Eleanor. There are records of Philippa of Hainault, Edward III's queen, using it twice, once when she left for Antwerp on July 4th, 1338 and

Saint Edward the Confessor

kept it until Lionel, duke of Clarence, was born on November 29th, and again in January 1355 when the Girdle went to Woodstock for the birth of the youngest son, Thomas, duke of Gloucester. On that occasion the queen made a gift of £6.13.4 and the king a hundred shillings. Edward I had brought back from the French wars vestments of St Peter and the head of St Benedict, presumably from the abbey of Fleury, which the monks of Montecassino still swear never left their possession.[18] The kings were on intimate terms with their royal shrine. In 1267 Henry III was short of money and borrowed some jewels from it, promising to return them the next year: he brought them back in 1269.

This royal intimacy remained a special quality of the shrine. Henry's own body was laid in the very coffin from which the saint's bones had been removed for his Translation, and only after another ten years was he moved to the splendid tomb made by his son Edward I. It was also something internationally realized: Dante, writing only thirty years after the murder of Henry's nephew at Viterbo, and the bringing of his heart in a gold cup to the shrine, records the crime and how 'Lo cor che'n sul Tamigi ancor si cola'.[19] So the Confessor became the spring of royal goodness and his authority sent his successors forward with vows to keep his laws and drew them around him when they died. It may well be that this growing tradition of Westminster as a combination of holiness, royalty and government prevented the shrine from ever becoming a focus of popular pilgrimage. One has the impression that there were so many works of all kinds going on according to the whim of royalty that the ordinary pilgrim was put off. The records tend to confirm this because the feretory accounts show that, compared with other famous shrines, the offerings at St Edward's were insignificant.

Little is heard in this early period of the popular royal gift of touching for the King's Evil.[20] Although this was held to be an English tradition, largely on the basis of the monk of St Bertin's reporting the Confessor's cure of the scrofulous woman, the French claimed the older right from Clovis in the 5th century. Only the Royal Houses of England and France had the gift, and the common belief was that they owed it to their exclusive right to be anointed with the pure chrism, not with the ordinary sacred oil. The first English king to display the gift publicly was the 14th-century Edward III, and it was said that he had it by descent through his mother from St Louis of France, Louis IX. It was he who began the practice of giving the touch-piece, a gold medal stamped with St Michael and a three-masted ship. From then the touching grew in popular recognition until by the reign of Charles II the numbers coming to be touched became such a nuisance that applicants had to obtain certificates. Charles is said to have touched a hundred thousand. The last English monarch to touch was Anne, who touched the infant Samuel Johnson; but the Old Pretender and his two sons frequently exercised their gift in Italy. Whether during this period the scrofulous pilgrims continued to crouch in the niches of the shrine is unrecorded: apart from a very early reference, the shrine and the King's Evil do not seem to be associated.

Richard II, who followed his grandfather Edward III, was devoted to St Edward. When his first wife Anne of Bohemia died his genuine grief showed itself in many extravagant ways, one of which was the removal from the Confessor's Chapel of the coffins of Edward I's grandchildren to make room for a superb tomb. It was completed with an effigy of Richard lying by that of Anne and holding her hand. No English monarch has ever received such a fantastically rich and elaborate funeral as Henry V. The great procession to Westminster started from Paris headed by king James I of Scotland and the widowed queen Catherine. At every stage a service was celebrated and when at length, following the obsequies at St Paul's, it reached the abbey of Westminster, the hooves of the dead king's chargers punctuated the shuffle of feet as the horses were led to the altar steps. To receive his body the eastern end of the Confessor's Chapel, containing all the sacred relics, had been cleared. Although Henry V had intended the relics to be kept near by, they were removed to a feretory between the tomb of Henry III and the Shrine. Over his own tomb a new chapel grew within that of the Confessor.

Henry VI spent a great deal of time and thought on where his tomb should be, and various suggestions were made by the abbot for moving the tombs of his predecessors, all of whom had been as anxious as he was to be laid near the royal saint.[21]

It was even suggested that the great tomb of Henry V should be moved a little to one side to make room. 'Nay,' said Henry VI, 'let him alone; he lieth like a noble prince. I would not trouble him.' It was then proposed that the great reliquary should be moved to make room near the Shrine, and when assured that a good place for the relics could be found at the back of the altar, he marked out the place. 'Forsooth, here will we lie, here is a good place for us!' The relics were moved and the tomb ordered. But Henry died in the Tower and was taken to Chertsey, and then, owing to embarrassment caused by miracles and pilgrims at his grave, he was removed by Richard III to St George's Chapel at Windsor.

There followed the strange development of the greatest jewel of Westminster, Henry VII's chapel. Henry, determined to rehabilitate the memory of his saintly uncle, Henry VI, who had wished to be buried near the Confessor, resolved on building of a new chapel dedicated to him and to which his bones should be translated. It is not clear what happened. There was certainly no translation, and it seems that Henry VII's growing confidence in his own position, and his reluctance to spend more than he had intended on the process of canonization and translation of his uncle, led him to let the whole matter slide. He proceeded to build 'one of the statliest and daintiest monuments in Europe'[22] to contain his tomb by Torrigiano. It thus became the chapel of Henry VII, the last mediaeval king of England, and an exclamation mark signalling the end of the middle ages from which the spirit had in fact long departed.

Inevitably, as in every abbey, the Confessor's shrine was stripped at the Dissolution and the relics destroyed. But the shrine itself was saved, owing almost certainly to its being the very symbol of royal power in Church and State. The threat that hung over the abbey was, however, nearly realized with the succession of Edward VI, and the event illustrates both the iconoclastic force of the new men and the deep-rooted strength to resist them. The Protector Somerset actually considered having the abbey destroyed and so advised the king, who, though young, was rarely averse to an exhibition of bigotry. By some it was said to have been saved by the rage of the people of Westminster, by others through the giving up of seventeen manors to the Protector; the truth is probably a combination of stubbornness and bribery.

There followed a piece of irony, almost equalling that of Thomas Becket's part in the Confessor's history. On her accession, Mary rehabilitated the shrine and saw to it that her half-brother was properly buried in the abbey, below and in front of the tomb of Henry VII. So it came about that the first Protestant monarch was buried by the enemy and persecutor of Protestants under an altar built for the Mass which he himself had abolished.[23] Moreover this altar, the supreme work of Torrigiano, was the only royal memorial destroyed by the Puritans in 1641.

Less than twenty years earlier in 1623, James I had abolished the right of sanctuary at Westminster. Pilgrimage in the usual sense may never have become popular, but the privilege of sanctuary which the Confessor had himself established certainly was, to the extent of being greatly abused. Westminster had a special charter allowing sanctuary in the whole abbey and precincts, including the Norman fortress and belfry with upper and lower churches, which made it probably the largest and most famous sanctuary in England.

While no doubt from time to time sanctuary in the abbey was sought by innocence in danger, the greater number of people taking up what sometimes amounted to residence consisted of misdoers escaping justice. They ranged from petty thieves, murderers and debtors to men of rank who brought their own guards. In 1378 the abbey's sanctuary was bloodily broken when two knights, imprisoned by John of Gaunt in the Tower, escaped to Westminster. They were pursued by the Constable of the Tower whose armed men burst in at High Mass and killed one of the fugitives in the choir. This appalling sacrilege caused the abbey to be closed for four months, and parliament, which sat in the Chapter House, was suspended from sitting within desecrated precincts.

The most dramatic and tragic case of sanctuary in Westminster was that of Elizabeth Woodville who sought it twice. The first time was when she was queen and her husband Edward IV was temporarily in exile. There, within six weeks, on November 14th, 1470, her son Edward V was born and stayed with his mother until the king returned to London. The

Saint Edward the Confessor

second time was twelve and a half years later when she was a widow and the son born in sanctuary was a boy-king deposed, confined in the Tower under the 'protection' of Richard III. Terrified, Elizabeth fled with her daughter and her second son Richard, Duke of York, to Westminster.

It seems unlikely that the truth of all that led to the disappearance of the Princes in the Tower will ever be known. The only writer to give the story at length was Sir Thomas More thirty years after the event.[24] Even Richard of Gloucester hesitated to break sanctuary directly. A deputation headed by the cardinal argued long at Westminster with the queen-mother whose resistance, it seems, was broken by the specious argument that since a child could not be capable of the crimes for which sanctuary was provided her son could not be entitled to it. 'I can no more,' she said, 'but whosoever he be that breaketh this holy sanctuary, I pray God shortly send him need of sanctuary, when he may not come to it.' And then at last. 'Farewell, my own sweet son, God send you good keeping. Let me kiss you once yet ere you go, for God knoweth when we shall kiss together again.'

One sees in this tragedy the lingering power of the mediaeval spirit as the middle ages go down in a welter of futile bloodshed. On the one hand the holding back even of Richard III from an act of desecration in the Confessor's sanctuary; on the other, the fears of a mother that she may herself be sacrilegious in claiming sanctuary for her child, fears so strong that she is persuaded to send her son out to what she knows is certain death at the hands of the man who dared not take him where he is.

Go into Westminster Abbey, climb the steps of the mound brought from Palestine behind the High Altar, and stand by the shrine of St Edward. At this extraordinary elevation you look down upon the whole building: the High Altar, the choir and soaring, gold-bossed nave seem to slide away to the white light of the western doorway; east, across as it were a moat, is the chapel of Henry VII; northward, you look down on the main entrance into the transept through which pilgrims entered and monarchs still come to their crowning. Through a south window you can see the Chapter House where parliament sat for two hundred years; and there, just out of view in the south transept, is the little side door used by Henry VI when coming from his

Saint Edward the Confessor

palace over the way, the palace built by the Confessor who set in train this whole elaborate, fantastic composition.

Here from the shrine of the saint-king, surrounded by the tombs of kings, all that you see becomes a manifestation of something far older than St Edward. The emanation of priest-king, his death and perpetual renewal, controlled by his government yet ruling, a part of his people yet inevitably separate from them, pervades the building. The shrine, the tombs, the entire structure is symbolic of the power of creative imagination over reason, of a millenium of unconscious conspiracy between the inhabitants of England and a legend. This king of legendary saintliness became the embodiment of everything that Englishmen wished, law-giving and -respecting, faithful to Church and State, builder and administrator, good and brave, a saint: ultimately, something glorious of which they might partake and shine with reflected light.

The ordinary pilgrims to his tomb, as the smallness of their offerings shows, went not so much for healing of the body or mind as to gaze on the glory and feel that it was theirs. Those English sightseers, out of the scores of thousands from all over the world who wander through the abbey and file past the Confessor's tomb to-day, come mainly for the same purpose. From the Saxon Saint-King and the mysticism of the middle ages grew the complex, ingrown yet outgoing society that spread its influence throughout the world.

VIII

SAINT ALBAN THE PROTOMARTYR

THE MASSIVE, SQUARE TOWER of the abbey is still dominant and sums up the arrogant, business-like quality of the first Norman abbot who built it of thin, pink bricks from the ruins of nearby Verulamium already a thousand years old. 'Rudes et idiotas', Paul of Caen called the Saxon nobles who had been abbots before him. Except for a few of their monolith pillars, which he built into the triforium of his south transept, he replaced entirely the abbey that had risen around the cult of St Alban. The tower frowns now on the acres of subtopia creeping over that part of Hertfordshire, but if one approaches up Holywell Hill in summer there is an illusion still of the abbey dominating a wide and wooded countryside.

At the foot of the hill the road crosses the narrow trickle of the Ver, then climbs acutely and narrowly to the town's centre between mediaeval buildings, mostly refaced. Halfway up the hill on the right is the 14th-century pilgrims' hostel, lately rescued from centuries of filth and neglect. A hundred yards further on the left is the turning up to the place where St Alban, the protomartyr of Britain, was executed. From the moment you contemplate the extraordinary building on the site of the martyrdom, and the story it commemorates, you enter a realm which is none the less a fantasy for being more worldly than spiritual.

Saint Alban the Protomartyr

The hagiographers have so elaborated St Alban's simple story that many people to-day doubt that any such man ever lived. It seems certain that Alban was real, a legionary stationed at Verulamium at the beginning of the 4th century, though whether he was British or Roman is unknown. The fact is confirmed by St Germanus, bishop of Auxerre, by his dedication of a church to St Alban in the next century. The details of why and how Alban died then began to emerge; it seems that he gave shelter to a Christian priest fleeing from the persecution inaugurated by Diocletian and was converted by him to Christianity. The priest escaped and Alban was put to death. The *Anglo-Saxon Chronicle* later put the date of the martyrdom at 286 but was certainly wrong.[1] Diocletian was very tolerant of Christians until he was persuaded of their danger to the Empire in 303. Discrepancies in dates have been explained by the suggestion that Alban did not die under Diocletian as the emperor's edict was not enforced in Britain. This may be so: the relevant point is that Alban died for his faith.

The first detailed account is given in 560 by Gildas, that vague and earliest British historian who begins the fabrications.[2] He tells how, on Alban's way to execution, the river he has to cross dries up: Gildas, never having seen the river in question, calls it the Thames though it was in fact the little Ver of which

Saint Alban the Protomartyr

the monks of St Alban's in the middle ages complained because it went dry in summer. On seeing this miracle the headsman asked to die with Alban, and they were executed together. Not long after Venantius Fortunatus, who was bishop of Poitiers for nine years from 600, included St Alban among the great saints and martyrs in a very tedious poem called 'Praise of Virgins'. An interpolation was made about the same time in Constantius' 5th-century life of St Germanus of a visit of that bishop in 429 to the place of St Alban's martyrdom and the opening of his grave. By the end of the 6th century St Alban had already become famous.

The next to record was Bede in the early 8th century.[3] As he was not an inventor of stories the two miracles he added to the basis of Gildas must have been part of the folklore that had meanwhile grown. At the place of execution a stream bubbled up to quench Alban's thirst, and, as the martyr's head fell, his executioner's eyes dropped out. Apart from this Bede gives an accurate description of the place. His mention of the saint's day, June 22nd, and of a church 'where sick folk are healed and frequent miracles take place to this day' shows that the cult was well established.

For four centuries there seems to have been no change in the legend. Then, in the latter part of the 12th century, the abbot Simon decided it should be properly written up. This was the abbot who, almost alone among ecclesiastics, showed his friendship in anxiety to help Becket at the end, asking Becket to stay with him when he returned in 1170. It must have been about the time of St Thomas's martyrdom that the sacrist William Marlet composed at Simon's request the Acta SS. Albani et Amphibali, their own particular martyrs.

But who was this Amphibalus suddenly appearing? William says his history is a literal translation from the contemporary English, overlooking that there were no English at the time of Alban. Drawing on that most imaginative of historians, Geoffrey of Monmouth,[4] he introduces Amphibalus as the name of the man whose life St Alban had saved. He goes on to give accounts of the sayings and doings of this priest whose identity has emerged for the first time after eight hundred and fifty years. There seems little doubt that Geoffrey had either misread or deliberately seized upon the mention by Gildas of

Saint Alban the Protomartyr

St Alban's cloak to discover a man called Amphibalus – the Greek for cloak – whom William identified with Alban's priest.[5]

Ussher throws more light on William's source, quoting abbot Eadmer to say that the original book was found when an old palace, presumably Roman, was being pulled down.[6] Unfortunately no one could read it as it was in 'idioma antiquorum Britonum'. Besides its history of St Alban it seems to have contained descriptions of idolatrous rites, especially of Phoebus the Sun-God. The monks rejected these devilish comments and had the history translated by an old priest, Unwona. The original then disappeared and no one knows what happened to Unwona's translation. This is the traditional account of the origin of the life of the protomartyr, which seems to have appeared some time in the 10th century.

The 12th-century Latin version of this story which William forged so badly is the original from which Matthew Paris wrote his long poem *Vie de Seint Alban*.[7] This distinguished writer's distinguished successor, Thomas Walsingham, in the early 15th century, as well as Ussher are agreed on his authorship some time between 1236 and 1250 when he was historiographer to St Alban's. It tells the story of St Alban and apart from giving many dramatic verses of conversation with Saint Amphibal gives a long description of the passion of that saint too. It has some striking illustrations, one showing Alban's head flying off while at the same time his executioner catches his own eyes in his hand as they fall out: another shows 'Amphabel' being stabbed and disembowelled while tied to a pillar. It was translated into English in 1439 by John Lydgate, a considerable poet known and much influenced by Chaucer and one of the bright lights in the literary murk before Spenser appeared. Hertford of St Albans printed it in 1534 at abbot Catton's request.[8] The text refers to this saint as 'the prince's son of Wales'. This was probably the last piece of invention attached to Amphibalus though Leland refers *ex vita Amphibali* to his being flogged and then stoned to death.[9]

It is Leland in the middle of the 16th century who presents the final metamorphosis of Alban, and it is worth quoting.

> M. *Gerard Leigh* in his accidence of armorie wryteth: "*Albon* was knight of the *Bath*, and Lord of *Verolane*, nowe called Saint *Albons*:

Saint Alban the Protomartyr

who in his youth, for the honour of this realme, made a royall chalenge of Justes at Rome, and did there other Knightly disportes in Armour, where hee had onelye the prise, and was made Knight by Dyoclesian the Emperour of Rome, who had this Realme then in subjection.

This *Albon* was Prince of Knightes, and Soveraigne Steward of *Brittaines*: and after was converted to the faith of Christ by *Amphybalus* that holy Knight, who went to *Rome* with *Bassianus* the Sonne of *Severus* in the companie of 1500. of the chiefe Lordes sonnes of *Brittaine* and *Cornewall*, where *Zepherinus* then Bishop privily instructed him in the fayth of Christ, which, at his returne, he taught to *Albon* in such sort, that openly professing the same, they were in the time of the Emperour *Dyoclesian* both martyred". Whereof you may reade in *Gildas and Bede*.[10]

Gildas and Bede would be as much surprised as we are.

There is, however, an interesting Latin manuscript life of St Alban composed especially for and dedicated to Henry VII by the abbey of St Pantaleon in Cologne.[11] The section on relics and miracles says that some of the saint's bones are in Cologne, some in England. This leads to an aspect of the cult which has never been cleared up. The centuries-long feud between St Albans and Ely over the saint's bones is famous, but there are other less known, but hardly less valid, claimants.

Saint Alban the Protomartyr

First, there is the story that when St Germanus visited the tomb of St Alban in 429 he took the relics with him to Ravenna, leaving others at St Albans in exchange, and presented them to the Empress-Mother Placidia. When Germanus died, she took the relics to Rome. Five hundred years later, Theophano, mother of Otho III, obtained the relics from Gregory V and took them to Cologne, where, placing her own circlet on the martyr's head, she deposited them in the monastery church of St Pantaleon built by Otho II's brother, the archbishop.[12] A fine reliquary was made in 1330 but was removed to the church of St Mary's in 1820 when St Pantaleon's became a Lutheran garrison church.

The tradition of Odense in Denmark has more circumstantial evidence in its streets, bridge, market, church and so on still named after Saint Alban. According to Matthew Paris, when the Danes plundered St Albans in 930 – Leland says 914 – they took the relics and deposited them in the Benedictine priory at Odense. St Alban appeared in his own abbey to Egwin the sacrist, who went over to Odense, watched his chance, bored a hole in the saint's sarcophagus and sent the relics back to England. Matthew does not seem to expect this to be believed; he says it was not known in England but feels bound to tell the story on account of the eminent men who brought it from Denmark and whose names he gives. As the plundering Danes were heathen the tale is most improbable. The usually accepted explanation is that St Canute, a great nephew of king Canute of England, had brought the bones to Denmark after fighting the Normans with Hereward the Wake and taking part in the storming of Peterborough. It is possible that the monks of Ely, believing they had the true relics, gave some to Canute for his help. 'The Passion of St Canute', reputedly the most ancient Danish historical document and written before Canute's canonization in 1101, goes far to suggest that the whole body is at Odense. There seems no doubt that at the time of Canute's murder in 1084 there were some relics of St Alban in the church of St Mary and St Alban which he had founded in Odense.

The main contest for the relics remained in England. At a Danish threat, probably that of Magnus in the Confessor's time, St Albans agreed to send the protomartyr's relics for safety to Ely, where began the double fraud. Peaceful times

Saint Alban the Protomartyr

having returned, Ely claimed possession. St Albans threatened to appeal to the pope, whereupon Ely took the saint's remains from his shrine, filled it with 'certain adulterine bones' and sent it back ostentatiously to St Albans. The abbot Leofric having marked the bones before sending them detected the fraud, but for the sake of keeping scandal from the Church nothing was said at first. But Ely proudly exhibited what they said were the original bones and everything had to come into the open. St Alban's then stated that in fact it had never sent the saint's true relics to Ely, but with considerable foresight had buried them under its own altar of St Nicholas; the bones sent for safe keeping had been of some monk. Edward the Confessor fell into a great rage with Ely but died before he could do anything. Some seventy years later when brother Anketil, the goldsmith, was working on the new shrine his assistant, Solomon of Ely, expressed doubts about the relics. To support Anketil the saint appeared and thanked him for his work, saying, 'I shall lie in this work of thine hands until the Day of Judgement.' Officially the matter was closed in 1155 when Adrian IV, Nicholas Breakspeare, issued a Bull appointing three bishops to make an inquiry which resulted in the terrified monks of Ely admitting they had grievously sinned and had never possessed the martyr's relics. Breakspeare, the only English pope, had been born in St Albans and had a special attachment to it for all his having been refused admittance there as a novice.

All this is recounted by Matthew Paris who, as chronicler of St Albans, is bound to be biased.[13] During the course of two hundred years so many lies, unconscious as well as deliberate, had been told that it must have been difficult for anyone to know who had the original bones of the protomartyr if, indeed, they had ever existed. For all the papal decision the feud continued, and one tends to believe that St Albans was in the right because the monks of Ely usually collapsed under pressure. As late as 1314 when Edward II visited Ely and saw there St Alban's shrine he taxed the bishop with it. 'By God's soul,' said the king, 'I will see in which spot I ought rather to venerate the relics of this most holy body.' The monks 'knew not how to answer or what to do', and the bishop told them they must show the king what was in the shrine. Alan de Walsingham, the sacrist, opened it only to reveal a large piece of 'hairy cloth' which they said was the cloak given to St Alban by Amphibalus.[14]

So the fantasy continues. A hundred and thirty-seven years earlier, St Alban had appeared to a certain Robert, citizen of St Albans, to tell him that the relics of his master Amphibalus were at Redbourne. The abbot Simon sent monks to confirm this and then went to Redbourne himself to see that the relics were translated to St Alban's. The date of the 'Invention of the Relics' was June 25th, 1177, and on their triumphal journey to St Albans they met a procession of St Alban's relics.[15] Wendover says that the protomartyr showed his joy at this glorious encounter after more than eight hundred years with many miracles.

Almost all contemporary writings show that the cult of St Alban and all that developed from it was more fantastical than miraculous: lacking passionate mysticism or aura of holiness, it did not inspire the breathless fear and joy experienced at other great shrines. It became famous and enormously rich, its abbot in 1237 holding the first place of all English abbots, the abbey church was superb, its ceremony splendid, its dependencies spread as far as Northumberland; but there is less here of saintly inspiration or holy purpose than may be found in almost any other great centre of pilgrimage.

The position of the abbey had something to do with this. According to Matthew Paris Offa II of Mercia wished to found a monastery to atone for the murder by his queen Quedreda of Ethelbert, king of the East Angles, who had been a suitor for their daughter. In 793 at Bath he was visited by an angel who told him to make a more worthy shrine for St Alban. At Verulamium a ray of light revealed the saint's burial place and Offa accordingly built the monastery there. Whatever the degree of truth, Offa did build it, and in a place that was bound to be involved in the world. It was not only close to the junction of the two great thoroughfares, Watling Street and the Icknield Way, but was not far from London. So in a very short time, besides being a resort of travellers and pilgrims, it attracted visitors from the court. The royal patronage and court connections greatly increased the abbey's secular prestige but they were not good for religion or learning. The Saxon abbots were of the nobility and the monks came from the same class. Wulsig, the third abbot in Athelstan's time, lived like a prince. Altogether, almost from the beginning, the inmates were far too much interested in hunting, eating well, and dressing up in lay finery.

It was not until 1077 that any sign of literary effort appeared when abbot Paul, a monk of Caen and a relation of Lanfranc, established the scriptorium. Then began a tradition of literary excellence which was maintained in varying degrees for four centuries. For a time the writers were continuous in their records with John de Cella, Roger of Wendover and Matthew Paris, a not very reliable historian owing to his strong prejudices but a man of great character. His relationship with Henry III who admired him was an example of this. He despised the king as a statesman and did not hesitate to write down his views, but he liked him as a man. In 1257, when Henry spent a week at St Albans, he had Matthew Paris at his side day and night guiding his pen 'with much good will and diligence'. Thomas Walsingham, who died about 1422, was the last of the great recorders.

For all the literary value of much that came from the scriptorium very little of it had any religious content. Its value lies in the picture presented of the times, particularly in the case of Matthew Paris. History, legend and religion are so interwoven that, although one can say by turns that the history is unreliable because the dates are wrong, the legend too inconsistent to be accepted and the religion largely superstition, one feels that the composite picture in reflecting the mediaeval mind is more reliable than that given by a scientific historian writing with the accumulated material of centuries.

A typical illustration of this is Matthew's account of the several days' stay of the Archbishop of Armenia and his suite in 1228.[16] Though mainly a transcript from Roger of Wendover, what clearly most interested Matthew was the long conversation between the archbishop and the monks about the Wandering Jew, and his report of this was the first written version of the legend to appear in England. To the chronicler of St Albans the importance of the abbey and the fame of its shrine are so obvious that comment on the visit itself by so distinguished a man as the archbishop is superfluous. The recording of a piece of folklore emphasizes this by implication. In the same sense, Matthew's detailed account of the controversy with Ely is more than a story of pious frauds; it presents a wide scene embracing court and politics, which, whether or not the chronology is faulty, has great historical value. The highly imaginative quality of his account of the life and martyrdom of Alban throws further light on the mediaeval mind, for Matthew Paris was a very intelligent man, respected by his contemporaries however much he quarrelled with them. He was sent on a mission to Norway in 1248 to reform the monasteries there, where one to St Alban was founded.

The comparative worldliness of St Albans emerges from the lack of recorded interest in what went on at the shrine which was the heart of the abbey's existence. Pilgrims came, gifts were received and the accumulation of fantastic relics was almost as great as at Durham. In the first decade of the 13th century the shrewd chaplain who later brought Bromholm to fame sold the monks a silver-gilt cross, two fingers of St Margaret and some gold rings and jewels; but the monks did not trust the piece of the True Cross he showed them.[17]

One of the few records comes from Sir Thomas More who tells of a visit of Humphrey duke of Gloucester to the shrine.[18] Seeing a man led by his wife to the shrine and declaring himself

Saint Alban the Protomartyr

cured of blindness, the duke was assured by them that the husband had been blind from birth. He therefore asked the man to tell him the colour of his gown, and then the colours of other people's gowns, always receiving the correct answer. As the man could not have named colours he had never before seen the duke had him committed to the stocks as a fraud. This duke, brother of Henry V, was a patron of Pecock who protested strongly against 'pretensed miracles'. He was also patron of Capgrave and the poets Aretino and Lydgate as well as being a close friend of Wheathamstead, the abbot. His bookcollecting, which included looting the Louvre, led to the glorious room at Oxford called duke Humphrey's Library.

This Gloucester was near-Renaissance in combining his culture and courtliness with intrigue and self-seeking. He was regent of England when young Henry VI was in France in the last struggle with Jeanne d'Arc, and later, when out of favour, his ambitions brought him to the awful point of seeing his wife condemned for sorcery against the king. In 1447, arrested for high treason, he was found dead in his bed. His splendid tomb in the abbey is a double screen filling to the apex the southern bay of the protomartyr's chapel behind the High Altar. Where there should be a sarcophagus there are three arches so that pilgrims can see the Shrine from the ambulatory. The enormous reredos raised by the extravagant abbot William of Wallingford in 1484 completely hid the shrine which, until then, had been visible from every part of the abbey.

Evidence of the steady pilgrimage is in the Watching Chamber, a charmingly carved oak construction filling the north bay across from duke Humphrey's tomb. The top storey is a gallery of Perpendicular work from which the monk on duty could look down on the shrine and the pilgrims, while another could stand by the recessed cupboards which form the lower part of the structure. These cupboards held the minor relics and probably comprised the abbey's main feretory. This monk also worked the pulley which raised and lowered the heavy canopy over the shrine.

The main relics of the saint were in the coffin high on the pedestal in the centre of the chapel. In 1123 Geoffrey of Gorham began an elaborate shrine, but after spending £60 he had a bad year and had to sell the materials and ornaments. The following year he began again with the 'incomparable goldsmith' Anketil who had been mint-master to the king of Denmark. No clear picture emerges of how the shrine looked, but it was made chiefly of silver ornamented with precious stones from the monastery's treasury. One onyx was so large that a man could not grasp it in his hand: it helped women in labour and was not attached to the shrine so that it could be taken where needed. On it was carved a figure in ragged clothes holding a spear in one hand with a snake winding up it, and in the other a boy bearing a buckler.

The Translation of the protomartyr to his new shrine took place on August 2nd, 1129. It was conducted by six bishops, and indulgences of forty days were granted to all attending. Twenty-two years later the abbot Ralph stripped the shrine of all its gold and had it melted down to buy himself an estate. True he afterwards gave the estate to the abbey, but his action shows a surprising lack of respect for his patron saint. A few years later his successor, Robert de Gorham, repaired the shrine which Simon, the friend of Becket, completed with gold. He had to borrow heavily, and Aaron, the Jew of Lincoln, boasted with humour that he had helped St Alban to a splendid new home. Early in the next century when a new west front was being built to the church, a portable reliquary was constructed and carried round the countryside supported by poles on the shoulders of monks. The procession, accompanied by a man who had been raised from the dead through the help of St Alban and St Amphibalus, 'heaped together no small sum of money' towards the rebuilding.

Abbot Simon, although given to nepotism as were most of the abbots, leaves the impression of being a good, warm man. He was simpler than the others and not so well-born as most. Though from time to time an abbot appeared who exercised restraint and restored the abbey's finances, the record over a period of some four hundred years is in general of waste and vast extravagance. Frequently an abbot inheriting the debts of his predecessor would cripple the abbey's finances for his whole term by giving an enormous installation feast. It speaks for the abbey's resources that it was able to survive such men. An example may be found of a humbler spirit at the beginning of the 13th century when the community contributed to the building of a new refectory and dormitory by giving up wine for fifteen years.[19]

There were, of course, men of the time who deplored this materialism. Yet, to read Matthew Paris is to see the futility of bringing modern criticism to bear on a purely mediaeval attitude. This most intelligent man records uncritically that the abbot John has given St Stephen's church for the kitchen of the community 'which I have always embraced in the bowels of spiritual love', that, under his successor, the bishop of Durham gave them the church of Egglinton for the improvement of their beer, and that with the next abbot the church of Norton was appropriated to make their beer even better as well as to provide for extra guests; another church is granted to increase hospitality, another for the sacristy, and yet another for the saint's day.[20] More than a hundred years later in 1395 the abbey actually obtained a papal indult on the incredible plea of the abbey being situate in the uttermost parts of the earth and with little endowment.

But more serious ultimately than the extravagance was the steady growth of 'proprietas'. The Rule of St Benedict was absolutely clear that no monk should have personal possessions of any kind. Everything was to be in common. But as the monasteries grew their revenues became allocated to different departments, first between the abbot and the monks, then to each official, sacristan, cellarer and so on. Pious donors left property for the monks' table or even sums of money to each monk. The seriously religious took a very grave view of this but they could do little to stem the waves of worldly corruption. They knew rightly that the possession of property or money inevitably led to the breaking of other essential vows and the satisfaction of fleshly lusts. In the case of St Albans it led to the conditions revealed in 1489 when Innocent VIII ordered archbishop Morton to examine the condition of religious houses. The abbey was found to contain a number of prostitutes and in two of its priories the nuns had been replaced by women of pleasure for the monks.[21]

Twenty-eight years earlier the abbey had been so thoroughly sacked by Lancastrian troops after the second battle of St Albans that the monks had temporarily moved out. Abbot Wheathampstead had put the abbey on its feet again, his successor had run into debt, and the great scandal had arisen during the abbacy of William Wallingford, who, for all his astonishing financial dealings, left the abbey solvent. From this point to the Dissolution the finances grew worse and worse, which was not wholly the abbey's fault. Wolsey held the abbey *in commendam,* a rare example in England of the ruinous practice which had destroyed countless religious houses in Europe, enabling the holder as administrator to draw on the finances to an almost unlimited extent. Thomas Cromwell completed the work.

Cromwell's Visitors found nothing to complain of in the cultural side of the abbey, nor, interestingly enough, in its moral behaviour. As in other monasteries, in the years leading to the end reforms had taken place. When the abbey was surrendered on December 5th, 1539 there were thirty-nine monks: there had been not more than a hundred in 1200, and since 1380 they had averaged a little over fifty. All those there on the Dissolution, including the abbot, received comfortable pensions.

So petered out the most aristocratic and one of the richest religious foundations in England. Owing its existence to the tomb of England's protomartyr, it had maintained almost continuously for seven hundred years a reputation for splendour. Yet except for the work of its scriptorium, at its peak in the mid-13th century, it is hard to find what the abbey and its shrine contributed to the enrichment of men's minds, let alone their souls. The architecture of the abbey depicts vividly its lack of integrity. A central block of Norman work built of flat, broad Roman tiles, some Early English bays in the nave, dogtooth ornamentation on graceful arcading in the triforium, then, a hundred years later on the other side, some overelaborate Decorated, bases of springers for a non-existent roof-vault, a nave screen that is not quite true, a bit of Perpendicular here, an uncompleted window there: nothing was ever finished and there is no sense of natural growth nor of blending; each part is simply the result of some vain man's desire to make a show. The vanity of riches reached its zenith when, after years of the church's decaying, a 19th-century baron came to its rescue with a Gothic style of striking originality. As arrogant in his views as any of the abbots, Lord

Saint Alban the Protomartyr

Grimthorpe, alone of all the builders, did not run out of funds, a fact regretted by his critics.

The abbey-church stands to-day as near to being finished as it will ever be after a thousand years, fascinating in the visual confirmation of its own history. It is significant that at the Dissolution there is hardly a mention of the shrine for which the immense building, its nave the longest in the world, had been raised. Whatever there was of value was stripped from this shrine and the pedestal smashed. The rest of the abbey buildings, except the gateway, were pulled down and the church sold to the town for a parish church. At some point the eastern arches of the saint's chapel were blocked up and the Lady Chapel, which had been the eastern terminal of the church, became a school. For three centuries a footpath ran between the two, and the area used as a church was reduced gradually as the cost of upkeep of the whole building became impossible to meet.

When the 19th-century restoration began, so many main pieces of the smashed pedestal of the shrine were found in the wall blocking the eastern arches that it was possible to reconstruct the shell of the tomb in its original position. Some of the sculpture showing the life and martyrdom of St Alban is well-preserved, and here and there are traces of colour. Parts of the smaller shrine of the fabulous St Amphibalus are in the north ambulatory. The Watching Chamber remains unscarred, owing to the blocking of the east end and the probable use of the Saint's chapel as a vestry or storage room following the Dissolution.

This Watching Chamber alone gives a sense of reality. Its shape and appearance are incongruous, like a small wooden house set down in a quarry of worked stone. But it is there for a real purpose and has a practical significance. Its simple but beautiful carving and narrow frieze of episodes in country life, the hard, smooth warmth of its wood to the fingers bring life to this dead place. Far from the pompous vanity of abbots were the pilgrims staring at the relics in the cupboards of this house and then being moved on by the duty-monk directing them towards the ambulatory and out into the open by the south door. This was the real life of the abbey, though almost totally obscured by the worldliness of the men who were there to serve it. There are still a few pilgrims there in June, and on the Sunday following the Saint's day of June 22nd there is a fine procession. Rose Sunday it is called after this rose among martyrs. Rough circles of blood-red damask, stone-absorbed, are on the pillars of his chapel showing where the painted trees once climbed.

IX

THE HOLY ROOD OF BROMHOLM

AN ARCHWAY, some fragmentary walls, a weed-tufted pillar stand among tall nettles and matted grass: half a mile off the north sea pounds the low Norfolk cliff. In winter here the world is vaporous and everything visible shivers; high gales can whirl the spray up over nearby Bacton. The summer sky is vast, the air pellucid and empty. Even to-day this edge of East Anglia feels as remote as it has always been, and it is perhaps more lonely now than in the middle ages when the Pastons ruled here, and men and women came from all over England as well as from abroad to find comfort in the piece of the True Cross at Bromholm.

> O crux salve preciosa
> O crux salve gloriosa
> Me per verba curiosa
> Te laudare crux formosa
>   Fac presenti carmine.[1]

On April 13th, 1204, the Latin pilgrim armies of the Fourth Crusade pillaged totally and systematically the capital of the Christian empire of the east. Count Baldwin of Flanders, descendant of Charlemagne and cousin to the king of France, was invested with the purple buskins of Imperial Sovereignty in the Cathedral of St Sophia. Pope Innocent III, in spite of this diversion of crusading zeal from Palestine, confirmed with pride the union of the Eastern and the Western Churches.

The following year, Calojan, chief of the Bulgarians and Vlachs, and a Christian cherished at Rome as a prodigal son, revolted against the new emperor with the help of Cumans from Scythia. Baldwin I set out with a small knightly army to chastise him. In his suite was an East Anglian priest returning from a pilgrimage to the Holy Land who, because of his diligence in singing, had become Baldwin's chief chaplain and keeper of Holy Relics. Precious among these was a small patriarchal cross made of wood from the True Cross which was carried with the army to bring victory. But in their haste against the rebels this cross had been left behind and the emperor had sent his priest back to fetch it. While the priest was gone, and almost exactly a year after the Crusaders' sack of Constantinople, the first Latin emperor of the East was defeated and captured by the rebels at Adrianople on April 15th.

Arrived at Constantinople, the priest heard of the disaster and fled, taking with him the piece of the True Cross and various other relics and jewels which he felt should be preserved. When he reached his native land he went first to St Albans where he disposed of two fingers of St Margaret and some jewels, but was rebuffed by the monks when he drew from his sleeve the cross, 'affirming that this was beyond doubt made from the very wood whereon the Saviour of the World hung for the redemption of mankind'. The rebuff may have been largely because the chaplain made his handing over this relic conditional on the acceptance into the monastery as monks of himself and two sons he seems to have had with him. He wandered on, going from monastery to monastery, offering the Cross and begging to be accepted. For a while it is said he settled quietly at Weybourne in Norfolk, but when necessity to provide for himself and his boys drove him to take the relic to the priory there he was rebuffed again.

It was then that he went to near by Bromholm, a poor, small priory to which he came in March when the wind off the sea was tearing around the bare stone buildings. There he showed his Cross 'made from two transverse pieces of wood of about the length of a man's hand' and besought in all humility that he and his sons should be received. 'So the prior and brethren,

The Holy Rood of Bromholm

rejoicing in so great a treasure, by the grace of God, who doth ever cherish honest poverty, gave credence to this chaplain, and reverently receiving this Wood of Our Lord, bore it to their church, and kept it in the most honourable place with all possible devotion.'

The events leading to the defeat of Baldwin I in 1205 are historical, the rest of the account given here is a composite of writings which vary only in detail.[2] Nothing has ever appeared to confute them so we may accept, as the poor prior and monks did, that in some such way there came to a remote corner of north-eastern Norfolk this holy relic from the imperial feretory. Originally accepted by the Greeks or looted for the greater glory of the Eastern Church, it was looted by the crusader-pilgrims of the West as a treasure for the new Western emperor, only in turn to be taken by a humbler rogue into a simple place where it acquired fame far greater than it had in its distant, exotic home.

Bromholm was a cell of Castle Acre which was itself a dependency of the Cluniac mother-house at Lewes.[3] It had been founded in 1113 by William de Glanville and dedicated to the honour of St Andrew, having at first only seven or eight monks. William's son Bartholomew increased the endowment with the gift of several churches and tithes of estates which were later confirmed by Stephen, count of Boulogne, when he became superior lord of Bromholm. Henry I gave the manor of Burgh. In 1195, pope Celestine III relieved Bromholm of most of its subjection to Castle Acre, although some dispute over authority continued; so, although it might be small and with few possessions, it had a certain independence by the time it accepted the piece of the Holy Wood.

Nothing more is heard of the emperor's chaplain and his two sons except that they stayed at Bromholm and served the Rood, nor is any date given of when they came there. But some time between the chaplain's flight in 1206 from Constantinople and 1223, when 'in this aforesaid year divine miracles began to be wrought in the aforesaid priory to the praise and glory of the life-bringing Cross', the fame of the Rood must have spread very quickly. 'For dead folk were restored to life, the blind saw, the lame walked, lepers were cleansed, those possessed by devils were freed; and whosoever might be the sick man who came to that Cross with faith in the Holy Wood, he departed whole and sound. So the aforesaid Cross is frequented, adored and worshipped not only by the English nation but also by men of far-off lands; and those who have heard what divine miracles it works do most devoutly revere it.'

Such testimony from contemporary writers must be accepted as regards the shrine's repute.[4] Within three years, in October 1226, bishop Richard de Mersh of Durham made Bromholm a grant of cut marble for the rebuilding. On April 5th of the same year Henry III had paid his first visit and next day granted the priory, by Letter Close, a fair of three days for the festival of the Exaltation of the Cross on September 14th. This event was the most important in making the pilgrimage to Bromholm fashionable.

It was from here that the king travelled some forty miles west across Norfolk to visit Walsingham for the first time. So both these shrines, the one in existence for only a handful of years, the other for a century and a half, grew all at once side by side in fame. They could hardly have been more different. The Holy House of Walsingham, rising from the vision of a country gentlewoman, remained always aristocratic in tone however much frequented. But the cult of the Holy Rood of Bromholm, growing from craftiness and superstition, ceased after the first fifty years of its history to be aristocratically fashionable but remained exceedingly popular up to the Dissolution.

There are few records of lavish gifts as in the case of many other famous shrines. In 1227 when a 'great ship' was being fitted out at Portsmouth a silver *ex voto* model was sent to Bromholm: in 1234 the king ordered an image of himself in silver-gilt to be presented, and in 1313 Edward II confirmed for 100 marks a grant of Bacton manor together with wreck at sea and other privileges.[5] Richard, earl of Cornwall, the brother of Henry III, and his son were patrons, but that is about all of royalty until Henry V on April 25th, 1416 gave the prior and monks four pipes of wine annually from the ports of Yarmouth and Kirkby. This must have been very welcome as they seem rarely to have drunk other than their home-brewed ale.

For this year there survives 'the account of dominus John Reppes, Cellarer, from the feast of St Michael the Archangel in

The Holy Rood of Bromholm

the 3rd year of Henry V after the Conquest until the same feast next following,' namely 29th September, 1415 to 29th September, 1416.[6] It appears that the income of the priory came partly from the two fairs, the Exaltation of the Holy Cross on September 14th, and St Andrew's on November 30th. There was another festival of the Holy Cross, when the Invention was celebrated and the local guild of the Holy Cross feasted with the convent, on May 3rd. Two monks who were also priests had special duties towards the Rood: the accounts do not say what were their duties but show the payment to them twice a year of 3/4 and 12d. For the purpose of accounting the oblations to the Rood the year is divided into six terms: Christmas, Easter, Nativity of St John the Baptist, St Mary Magdalene and two consecutive terms of St Michael the Archangel. During the accounted year the oblations were £32.4.5.

This seems a small sum compared with the amounts given to some of the great abbey and cathedral shrines, and is almost certainly due to the pilgrims being mostly ordinary folk; but there is no doubt of the popularity of the Bromholm pilgrimage. Langland's *Piers the Plowman*, written towards the end of the 14th century, makes nasty old Avarice and his wife swear they will go to pray to the Rood of Bromholm; no other English shrine but Bromholm and Walsingham are mentioned in this poem, which is testimony to their fame. In Chaucer's Reve's Tale the miller's wife, in most ribald circumstances,

> Out of her sleep she breyde,
> 'Help, holy croys of Bromeholme,' she seyde,
> 'In manus tuas! Lord, to thee I calle!
> Awak, Symond! the feend is on us falle.'

Another significant record of Bromholm is of an event in 1424 when Hugh Pie, chaplain of Ludney, was brought before the bishop of Norwich for the following opinions:[7]

that the people ought not to go on pilgrimage
Item, that the people ought not to give alms, but only to such as beg at their doors
Item, that the image of the cross and other images are not to be worshipped: and that the said Hugh had cast the Cross of Bromholm into the fire to be burned, which he took from one John Welgate of Ludney.

The Holy Rood of Bromholm

From the fact that there is no mention of the Cross having been produced as evidence for the defence some people have assumed that it was destroyed.[8] But as nothing very serious seems to have happened to Hugh Pie, who swore he had not thrown it in the fire, and as the pilgrimage to the Holy Rood continued, this seems unlikely. There is also the letter from Richard Southwell, commissioner at the Dissolution, telling Cromwell that he is sending the relic to him. What may have happened was the burning by the protesting churchman of one of the devotional cards sold to pilgrims, a symbolic destruction.

There is evidence for these cards in the 14th-century *Hours*

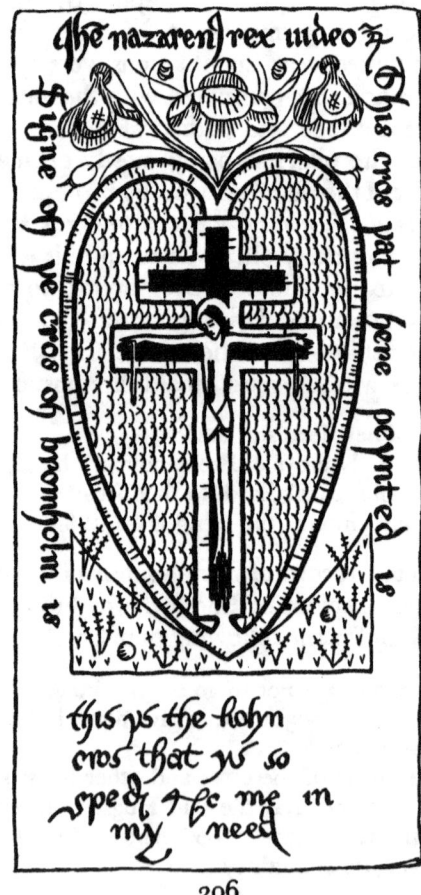

The Holy Rood of Bromholm

of Our Lady in Lambeth Library.[9] It is an illuminated leaf stuck to one of the pages: on it is a heart containing the patriarchal cross with two transverse beams, above the heart is 'Jhesus Nazarenus Rex Judeorum' and on either side

> This cros yat here peynted is
> Signe of ye cros of bromholm is

Under the cross, written in a later hand that suggests the record of a pilgrimage, is

> This ys the holy cros that ys so sped
> Be me . . . in my need.

Within the heart and all around the cross is a Latin hymn written in minute characters. Its first verse is the one beginning this chapter, and it ends,

> Me defendas de peccato
> Et de facto desperato,
> Hoste truso machinato
> Reconsignas Dei nato
>   Tuum presiduum.

The Holy Rood of Bromholm

Though there can be no certainty about it, it has the look of the kind of devotional souvenir sold at shrines.

On December 9th, 1963 Sotheby's sold to Dawsons of Pall Mall a prayer roll that does not seem to have been mentioned in any book.[10] It is an illuminated Latin and English manuscript on vellum and is four feet six inches long by seven and a half inches wide. There are four miniatures at intervals among the hymns and prayers to the Holy Cross: that of the Crucifix show Christ hanging on the 'Holy Rood of Bromholm', the next two below are of the Rood of Bromholm showing the plain patriarchal Cross surrounded by gold rays against different patterned backgrounds. Finally, there are the Three Nails, said to be the size of those used in the Crucifixion, on a Bleeding Heart with the pierced Hands and Feet in miniature. Surrounding the second Rood are the words:

> Ihesus nazarenus rex judeorum
> Filii dei miserere mei. Amen.
> Thys crosse that here peynted ys
> Synge of Crosse of Bromholme yt ys.

This roll is a century later than the Lambeth Book of Hours and probably about the same date as the *Horae* in the Fitzwilliam Museum, 1480. The same text surrounds the Holy Rood in this Book of Hours and the similarity extends to the Cross in each case having the figure of Christ added to what in the earlier manuscript was a plain patriarchal cross. Was a figure in fact ever added to the Rood itself at Bromholm? One thing that shows in the pictures is that the original Holy Wood was sheathed in the silver-gilt cross that was always apparent.

The erudite M. R. James makes a fascinating comment.[11] He points out that on page 139b of the Book there are prayers to a group of saints who seem to correspond in some way to the 'Fourteen Need-Helpers of the Tyrol':

> Egidi, Christofere, Blasi, lux divina,
> Dionisi, Georgi, in te medecina,
> Margareta, Barbara, Martha, Katerina,
> Nos ab omni sceleris purgata ruina.

They are indeed the same except for Martha: the remaining Need-Helpers are Achatius, Cyriacus, Erasmus, Eustachius, Pantaleon and Vitus. But why and how did they come there?

The Holy Rood of Bromholm

The cult is traceable in the 13th century and was especially practised in south Germany, Tyrol and Switzerland where the fourteen saints were designated powerful helpers in needs of all kinds.[12] It spread rapidly in the 15th century to Sweden, Hungary and Italy, and, as this *Horae* seems to show, to England, too. But it was almost certainly grafted on to the existing pagan ritual of Need-Fires, common to all Europe. In Scotland it had existed from time immemorial particularly at Beltane, the first of May, and continued into the late 18th century. It is not wholly extinct to this day. The fires were produced by the friction of two pieces of wood; how and by whom this was done varied all over Europe but it was essential that all neighbouring fires must be out. Need-fires were not usually associated with any seasonal fire-festival but were kindled at need, as a remedy for plague or cattle disease.[13] It was mainly a rite of purification like the other festivals of fire used for driving away evil spirits, though all were associated in some way with the power of the sun. In the early middle ages the Church denounced the rite as heathen, but the universal fear of witchcraft is so strong that it had to be Christianized. Just as Midsummer Fires were given the festival of John the Baptist, so fourteen saints were appointed as Need-Helpers. To find them associated in the late 15th century with the Holy Rood of Bromholm suggests the deep-rooted belief in the virtues of fire and of wood which can contain a synthesis of Diana's sacred grove and a piece of the True Cross. There is here an example of the fear and love of magic which was and is a compelling force in pilgrimage.

In the picture of the Rood in the manuscript of Matthew Paris's story there is a spike at the bottom of the Cross, which could be a confirmation of Coggeshall's and Wendover's stories that it was carried into battle.[14] If this is so, the spike could only have been for fixing into the top of a pole since the Cross was very small.

The evidence for the popular rather than aristocratic nature of the pilgrimage appears in the continuing modesty of the priory's life. Although Coggeshall says there was no less migration and concourse to it than had been customary to St Thomas at Canterbury and that from a poor little convent grew a 'new and noble edifice, of the highest renown, and specially noted for its expenses and its hospitality', there was certainly exaggeration with regard to its buildings. Most of the walls are so thoroughly destroyed now that it is hard to discover the plan, but it is clear that the whole place including the church must have been very modest. The largest number of monks was 25 recorded in 1298, in other recorded years it was under 20, declining steadily to the Dissolution, owing, apparently, to the revenue not keeping pace with the rise in cost of living.[15]

For example, in 1385, when the priory was in great distress because its lands had been much wasted by the sea and a part of the house had been recently burned, fifty marks were paid to Richard II for appropriation of the church of Bardwell to help. Yet only a few years later, in August 1401, Boniface IX granted the prior and his successors an indult to hear confessions and grant absolution, saving reserved cases, to the multitude who resort from afar on account of a certain 'notable piece of the Wood of the True Cross': notable because some on account of sin cannot look on it and so acquire infirmities. At the same time the priory received confirmation of appropriation of more churches for the same reasons as before: depredations of the sea, fire and pestilence. To help even more, the pope granted the distinction of an indulgence equal to that of St Mark's at Venice to penitents who on Passion Sunday or the three preceding or following days gave alms for the support of the Cluniac House. He also authorized the prior to nominate six priests to hear such penitents' confessions.

The continuing direct communication of Bromholm with Cluny and Rome is interesting. As an alien priory it came into the category of those increasingly suspect during the Hundred Years War, many of which were seized or left the country. In 1390 Bromholm became, like many others, denizen, that is to say, nationalized English. In the later middle ages, Cluny was the greatest monastery in Europe and Cluniacs, though Benedictine, were apart from the English Black Monks in that they were governed by their own code and formed an organized family of their own. It seems that even when Bromholm became denizen the close ties with the mother-house continued.

There is evidence for this in the fascinating Paston Letters. Paston, the village from which the family took its name, is only a few miles from Bromholm, and the first of the family coming

The Holy Rood of Bromholm

from France soon after the Conquest was a cousin of William de Glanville, the founder of the priory. The relationship continued through intermarriage at any rate up to the sixth generation. In 1430 William Paston wrote to the vicar of the abbot of Cluny asking authority for the prior of Thetford, a Cluniac, to profess divers virtuous young men of the 'poure house of Bromholm' who are 'monkes clad and unprofessed'. This remarkable East Anglian family, closely bound to Bromholm from the start, remained to the end its chief patron as it was of Walsingham. William was a judge of the Common Pleas as well as a large landowner, and his son John was also a member of the Inner Temple. His position vis-à-vis Bromholm appears in a letter from the prior in 1449 'addressed to my sovereyn, John Paston'. Eleven years later there is another letter, from prior Tytleshall, asking him for money and timber for the eight principal beams in the dormitory, each to be eleven yards long. He suffered a good deal from the free-booting of the upper classes let loose by the Wars of the Roses, but when he died in 1466 his funeral feast was fantastic.

Every detail of the ceremony is recorded, including the prior's bill for all the expenses attendant on the persons 'laboryng abought the enterment, begynnyng the Thursday in Pentecost weke, the vi yere of Kyng Edward the iiiith'. Among these was 8/8 for the vicar of Dullyng for bringing a pardon from Rome to pray for 'alle our frends sowles', and 8/- for a black gown for him. A few items from the supplies for the feast show the scale: apart from unnumbered geese and other fowl and 1300 eggs, were forty-one pigs and forty-nine calves. The amount of beer and wine was fabulous. The ceremony itself must have been suffocating, for there is an entry 'to the glaser for takyn owte of ii panys of the windows of the schyrche for to late owte the reke of the torches at the deryge, and sowdering new of the same xxd'.

John Capgrave, the famous Augustinian chronicler, who died two years before his Norfolk contemporary John Paston, says of Bromholm that thirty-nine had been raised there from the dead, and nineteen blind restored to sight.

There is little of interest recorded between then and the end. In 1535 the Valor Ecclesiasticus states the offerings at the Cross to have declined to £5.12.9. The net income of the priory is

The Holy Rood of Bromholm

£100.5.3¼, and everything is in very good order. Next year there came the ill-reputed Visitors of Cromwell, Legh and Layton, who noted the Holy Cross of Bromholm, the girdle and milk of the Virgin and pieces of the Crosses of SS. Peter and Andrew. They also alleged that the prior Lakenham and the three monks had confessed to incontinency. These four were all the religious of the priory and the value of the allegation may be judged by the view of the County Commissioners for the Suppression who, in the same year, had described Bromholm as a head house of the Cluniac order with four religious persons of good name and fame.

The following year on February 2nd, 1537 chief commissioner Richard Southwell writes to Cromwell saying that he has the relic in his possession; on the 26th he writes that he is sending it to him with Robert Codde, former prior of Pentney.

So the Holy Rood of Bromholm disappears. By the side of the great shrines of Glastonbury, Canterbury, Durham, St Albans, Westminster, even of Basingwerk and Walsingham, its wealth is minute. Yet in the complications of its history, in the tremendous surge of short-lived high fashion followed by three centuries of general popularity it is, perhaps, the most rhapsodical of English centres of pilgrimage. With this quality Bromholm enshrines the full expression of the mediaeval spirit.

X

CONCLUSION

IF THE JOURNEY HAS BEEN MORE COMPLICATED than was expected the reader may be sure that it could have been even more so. It should have been clear from the beginning that to take so apparently simple an action as pilgrimage in isolation was impossible: but the opening paragraphs, in which the reasons for this were given, look almost too bold now with their implication that every eventuality would be met. One's feelings on looking back at the first chapter might be compared with those of a pilgrim on returning home. He has set out with hope and fear, with hope because he believes he may discover something till then outside his experience, with fear because of the dangers that lie in wait. Now that the journey is over he realizes that, however well prepared he had thought himself, the marvels and the perilous distractions were far greater than he could have foreseen. He is lucky to be back safely at his own fireside.

The pilgrim has had to comprehend more than he had bargained for; his curiosity has taken him from shrine to shrine, and though his wonder has never abated he has learned to understand its source. But how could he have expected that going to St Winefrede's Well would have involved him in the Gunpowder Plot or that at Glastonbury his faith in St Joseph of Arimathaea would be tested by the dark god Avalloc? Wherever he has been in the length and breadth of England he

Conclusion

has been involved in danger and controversy: foreign invasion, thunder from Rome, conflict between his own Church and State, new learning to baffle him and heresies to avoid. Civil wars as well, but they do not affect his purpose since he is accustomed to violence and has learned how to keep clear of it in a thousand years of wandering. But meanwhile the world has been growing up around him. When, all at once, there comes the Dissolution of his shrines, he is resigned.

He accepts the great change that has come because he himself, having also changed without knowing it, has been in part responsible for the change. It is centuries since he had the burning, ecstatic faith of the pilgrim, though he relives something of it in his last pilgrimage to Bromholm. There, there was something constant. No politics were involved, history passed it by except for the pope's famous grant of indulgences; there had been no prettying up of a legend to make fashionable people go there. There was only the Holy Rood, a piece of the Very Wood. It was different from the bones of saints and martyrs that came and went in efficaciousness and popularity. This was the True Cross for ever to bring succour to soul, mind and body.

It is this last reflection of the pilgrim that questions the pronouncement that 'la vraie religion du moyen âge . . . c'est le culte des reliques'. It is too neat a summary to be true, like the saying of some future historian that the true religion of the late 20th century was the cult of money. A widespread belief in the virtues of relics or of money does not mean that either is the mainspring of man's faith. Each is simply a primitive manifestation of something more profound.

In the middle ages there was no possibility of escape, except for a very few, from material wretchedness; the only solace of the many was God's pity. Being simple yet imaginative, their concept of omnipotent God required tangible evidence: hence the multiplication of relics of the Cross, of the sanctified bones which could transmit the blessing of Divinity. Again and again reformers deplored that relics were becoming objects of worship. But for most men the cult of relics was the cult of the intermediary through which they could communicate with God who alone could bring liberation. Only in the last few years has there come the general opportunity for material well-

Conclusion

being. In their escape from poverty men now lay too much store by their material possessions which have become as 'relics' representing a higher life. But there is no reason to suppose that they cannot progress in spirit as others have done before them.

Not long ago I went to the abbey of Fleury at St Benôit-sur-Loire, a small but noble Romanesque building. I was gazing thoughtfully at the casket which for 1200 years the monks there have asserted contains the bones of St Benedict, when an English pilgrim came and knelt before it. Having lately come from Montecassino where I had heard a convincing counter-argument, and had been shown the very bones of St Benedict, I felt a temptation to tell the pilgrim that he was wasting his prayers. To have done so would have shown a total misunderstanding of the mediaeval mind. What did it matter whose bones were in the casket? Only a very few of the relics of the middle ages were what they were said to be, and the most fervent defenders of the authenticity of a relic were often, as at Ely, men who knew it was a fraud. Its material falseness was of no account beside the virtue it symbolized. It was an intermediary with God.

To seek such an intermediary was the real essence of mediaeval pilgrimage. If at times there has been any wonder at my choice of shrines, and the strange paths into which they have led, they have been chosen because I wished to show through their very diversity the inescapable unity of impulse that sent the pilgrim on his way.

NOTES

II
SAINT WINEFREDE OF HOLYWELL

[1] *The Life and Miracles of St Wenefrede, together with her Litanies; and some Historical Observations made thereon.* Dr William Fleetwood, 1713.
[2] *Legend of St Winefrede told by Robert of Shrewsbury.* Bodleian MS., 12C.
[3] Cottonian MS., Claudius A 5. B.M. 12th C.
[4] *Life of St Winefrede.* Fr. John Falconer, 1635.
[5] *Life of St Winefrede.* Fr Philip Metcalfe, 1712.
[6] *Itinerarium Cambrense.* Giraldus Cambrensis (Gerald de Barri), 12th C. Rolls edition.
[7] *Life of St Winefrede.* William Caxton, 1485.
[8] *The Lives of Women Saints of our Contrie of England 1610–1615.* Edited from MS. Stowe 949 by C. Horstmann, Early English Text Society, 1886; *Vitae SS*, Lippeloo, 1596 (?); *Nova Legenda Angliae*, Capgrave, 16th C.
[9] *Lives of the British Saints*, Baring-Gould and Fisher, 1907–1913, Vol. iii, pp. 192–196; also *Acta Sanctorum*, de Smedt.
[10] *History of the English Church and People.* Bede, I.30. (A modern edition is published in the Penguin Classics Series, 1964.)
[11] *Early Christian Monuments of Wales.* V. E. Nash-Williams, 1950.
[12] *Historical Atlas of Wales.* W. Rees, 1951.
[13] *Mabinogion.* Lady Guest, edition of 1838, Vol. 1, p. 115.
[14] *The Religious Houses of Mediaeval England.* Dom. David Knowles, 1940.
[15] *The Holy Lyfe and History of saynt Werburge very fruteful for all Christen people to rede.* Henry Bradshaw, 1513. Printed by Richard Pynson, 1521 (Early English Text Society, 1887).
[16] *The Worthines of Wales.* Dedicated to Queen Elizabeth. Thomas Churchyard, 1587 (Spencer Society, 1876).
[17] See Note 14 where this is given as an approximate date.
[18] *The History of the Parishes of Whitford and Holywell.* T. Pennant, 1796.
[19] See Note 2.
[20] See Note 1.
[21] *Analecta Bollandiana*, Vol. VI, 1887.
[22] *Breviarium secundum usum Sarum.*
[23] *Cal. Pap. Reg.* vii, 12.
[24] *Chronicon Adae de Usk A.D. 1377–1421.* Edited with a translation and notes by Sir Edward Maunde Thompson, K.C.B. London 1904.

Notes

[25] *Remarks and Collections of Thomas Hearne.* He notes that Bishop Fleetwood did not know who published the *Life and Miracles of St Winefrede* in 1712, but that Mr Loveday was informed when at Holywell that it was one Clayton living under the name of Metcalfe. See Note 5.
[26] *The Life of Benvenuto Cellini, written by himself.* 1559. (A modern edition is published by Everyman.)
[27] *Flint Hist. Soc. Journal.* 1919–1920.
[28] P.R.O. Patent Rolls. 21 Eliz., part 7.
[29] *Analecta Bollandiana*, Vol. VI, 1887, pp. 305–352.
[30] *Father Henry Garnet and the Gunpowder Plot.* John Hungerford Pollen, S.J., Catholic Truth Society, 1888.
The Great English Treason. George Blacker Morgan, 1931–2.
What was the Gunpowder Plot? John Gerard, S.J., 1897.
What Gunpowder Plot was (a Rejoinder). S. R. Gardiner, 1897.
The Gunpowder Plot ... in reply to Professor Gardiner. John Gerard, S.J. 1897.
Narrative of the Gunpowder Plot. (From an examination of William Handy, November 27th, 1605.) David Jardine, 1857.
[31] 'Foot out of ye Snare', *Somer's Collection of Tracts*, 17th C., Vol. III, pp. 64–65.
[32] *A Note of Papists and Priests assembled at St Winefrede's Well on St Winefrede's Day, 1629.* Record Society.
[33] *The History of the Parishes of Whitford and Holywell.* See Note 18.
[34] *The Journeys of Celia Fiennes.* Christopher Morris (Ed.), 1947.
[35] *Blundell's Diary and Letter Book*, 1702–28. Margaret Blundell (Ed.), 1952.
[36] *The Cheshire Sheaf*, vol. ii: 'Dr Johnson and Mrs Thrale', Broadley, 1909, p. 386.
[37] *The Quest for Corvo.* A. J. Symons, 1934.

OTHER REFERENCES

The Settlements of the Celtic Saints in Wales. E. G. Bowen, 1956.
Royal Commission on Ancient and Historical Monuments in Wales and Monmouthshire. Vol. II: 'Central Caernarvonshire', 1960.
Bardsey. Catherine Daniel, 1955.

III
THE SHRINES OF GLASTONBURY

[1] *De principis instructione*, 1194 and *Speculum Ecclesiae*, 1216, Giraldus Cambrensis.
[2] Bede, *History of the English Church and People*, I. 30.
[3] *De Antiquitate Glastoniensis ecclesiae* (63–1126) printed in Gales's *Scriptores*, XV, Oxford, 1691.
[4] Note to Bede's *Op. Hist.*, ii, 167, edited by Plummer, 1896.
[5] *Somerset Historical Essays et al.* J. Armitage Robinson, Oxford, 1921.
[6] *Historia Britonum.* 1st edition, 1137; existing edition apparently 1147.
[7] *Vita Gildae.* Ascribed to Caradoc of Llancarvan, 12th C.
[8] *History of Auricular Confession and Indulgences in the Latin Church.* H. C. Lea, 1896.

Notes

[9] *Hearne's Appendix to John of Glastonbury.* Oxford, 1726, Vol. II, p. 383.
[10] *Polychronicon.* Ranulf Higden (1299–1363), Rolls No. 41.
[11] *De principis instructione.* Giraldus Cambrensis, 1194.
[12] *De rebus gestis Glast.* Edited by Hearne. 2 Vols. Oxford, 1727.
[13] *History of the Anglo-Saxons,* Vol. I, Sharon Turner (*History of England from Earliest Times*), 1799–1805.
[14] *Chronica sive de hist. de rebus Glast.* John of Glastonbury. Edited by Hearne, 2 Vols., Oxford, 1726.
[15] *Monasticon Anglicanum.* Sir William Dugdale, 1655–73.
[16] *Appendix A* to the *Councils and Ecclesiastical Documents relating to Great Britain and Ireland.* Edited by A. W. Haddon and W. Stubbs, Vol. 1, 1869. See also Note 2, I. 14.
[17] *Two Glastonbury Legends.* J. Armitage Robinson, Cambridge, 1926. See also Note 14.
[18] *Joseph of Arimathie.* Vernon MS., Oxford, c. 1350 (Early English Text Society, 1871, edited by Walter Skeat).
[19] *Studies in the Arthurian Legend.* John Rhys, Oxford, 1891.
[20] See Note 18.
[21] *Here begynneth the Lyfe of Joseph of Armathia.* Printed by Pynson in 1520 (Early English Text Society, 1871, edited by Walter Skeat).
[22] *Brittanicarum Ecclesiarum Antiquitates,* 1639, Ussher. Patent an 19 Ed. III partl. membran 8.
[23] *Downside Review,* No. 16, 1897. Translation from MS. *Lives of English Saints* containing notes by Wm. Good, S.J. in English College, Rome, by F. A. Gasquet; *B. E. A.* Ussher (see Note 22). Latin text of Good taken from *Con. Angl. Ord. Benedict.* edited by Maihew, Tab. 2, pp. 118–19.
[24] *B. E. A.* Ussher. C. ii, p. 13 ff.
[25] *Histoire des Conciles.* Von Hefele, 1855. Edited and translated from the German by Leclercq, 1905. Vol. VII, pt. 1, p. 31n.
[26] Now in Trinity College Library, Cambridge.
[27] *Memorials of St Dunstan.* Edited from MSS. by Wm. Stubbs, Rolls, 1874.
[28] *Five Centuries of Religion.* G. G. Coulton, Vol. III, Cambridge, 1936.
[29] See Note 14, Vol. I, 184 ff.
[30] See Note 28.
[31] *Monasticon Anglicanum.* Dugdale, 1655–73. Edited by J. Caley, 1817–30. I. 3. n.1.
[32] Cotton. MS, Titus B i f. 446a.
[33] Cotton. MS, Titus B i f, 441a.
[34] See Note 18.

IV

SAINT CUTHBERT OF LINDISFARNE AND DURHAM

[1] *Historia de Sancti Cuthbert.* Symeon (1060–1130), Rolls.
[2] *A History of the English Church and People.* Bede. Bk. II c.5. *The Anglo-Saxon Chronicle,* Everyman Ed.: 1962 E. 616.
[3] Bede, op.cit., Bk. II. c.13 and 14 and Bk. III. c.1.
[4] Ibid., Bk. III. c.3.

Notes

[5] *The Life and Miracles of St Cuthbert.* Bede. See also Bede's *Metrical Life;* also *Vitae S. Cuthbert* by an anonymous monk of Lindisfarne, c. 699–705, edited by Bertram Colgrave, Cambridge, 1940.
[6] See Note 2, Bk. III. c. 25.
[7] *Life and Miracles of St Cuthbert.* Bede. See Note 5. c.16.
[8] Ibid., c. 17.
[9] Ibid., c. 37.
[10] Ibid.
[11] Ibid. c. 40.
[12] *The Lives of the Holy Abbots of Weremouth and Jarrow.* Bede.
[13] *Life and Miracles of St Cuthbert.* Bede. c. 42.
[14] *The Anglo-Saxon Chronicle.* Everyman Ed.: 1962 E.793.
[15] *Historia Dunelmensis Ecclesiae.* Cap. xi (1104–8), Symeon. Rolls.
[16] Ibid. Cap xiii.
[17] Ibid. Cap vii.
[18] *Libellus de Admirandus Beati Cuthberti virtutibus.* Reginaldi Monachi Dunelmensis (c. 1190), Surtees Society, Vol. I, 1835.
[19] Irish *Libellus de Ortu S. Cuthb.* Surtees Society, Vol. 8.
[20] *Nova Legenda Angliae.* John of Tynemouth in Capgrave, London, 1516 (latest edition Oxford, 1901).
[21] See Note 18.
[22] Cott. MSS., Claud. Fol. 121. b. etc.
[23] *Legend of St Cuthbert.* Hegge, 1663.
[24] *Rites of Durham* (containing 7 MSS., 1593–1660, the Rites being the earliest). First published 1672. Edited by Fowler 1902/3.
[25] Engraving in Hutchinson's *Durham,* 1787, II, 226.
[26] *Topog. Dict.* Lambarde, 1730, p. 324.
[27] See Note 18.
[28] See Note 15. Cap. xix.
[29] See Note 23.
[30] *Dunhelm Scriptores,* p. xxiv.
[31] *Capitula de Miraculis et Translationibus Sancti Cuthberti.* Symeon. Cap. vii. pp. 247–261. Rolls.
[32] *Saint Cuthbert: with an account of the state in which his remains were found upon the Opening of his Tomb in Durham Cathedral in the year MDCCCXXVII.* James Raine, Durham, 1828.
[33] See Note 24.
[34] *The History of S. Cuthbert.* Charles, Archbishop of Glasgow, 3rd edition 1887, Burns and Oates, p. 187.
[35] See Note 32, p. 110.
[36] *Five Centuries of Religion.* G. G. Coulton, Vol. 3, Cambridge, 1936, p. 463.
[37] List of Richard de Sybruk, feretrar in 1383.
[38] See Note 18.
[39] *Sanctuarium Dunelmense.* Surtees Society, Vol. V, edited by Raine, with extracts from Harl. MS., 560: 'Origins and peculiarity of Sanctuary in Durham'.
[40] See Note 18.

Notes

[41] See Note 20. Also *Hist. Eccles. Anglia*. Harpsfield, 1662. Cott. MSS. Vitell. c. 9. 12. 1st printing 1622, Douai.

[42] *Life of S Cuthbert*. Rt. Rev. Ed. Consitt, Burns and Oates, 1904, quoting Father Cressy of Douai, 1649, in his church history, Father Mannock's 18th C. *Annus Sacer Brittanicus* and Father Gregory Robinson, Ben. Prov. of the North, to Dr Lingard, 1828. Dr Consitt finds no reason to agree with them.

[43] *The Arts in Early England*. Baldwin Brown, Vol. IV, 1915, p. 509.

[44] *The Relics of Saint Cuthbert*. Studies by various authors collected and edited with an introduction by C. F. Battiscombe, O.U.P., 1956. The most scholarly work on the subject.

[45] *The Life and Miracles of S. Cuthbert*. Bede quoting Jeremy the Prophet.

OTHER REFERENCES

History of Durham Cathedral Library. Hughes and Faulkner, 1925.
'Patrimony of S Cuthbert.' Edmund Craston, in *English Historical Review*. No. cclxxi, April 1954.
The Religious Houses of Mediaeval England. Dom David Knowles, Sheed and Ward, 1940.
Lives of the Saints. Butler. 1956.
Pre-Reformation England. H. Maynard Smith. Macmillan. 1938.
Acta Sanctorum. ix. Mar. 20.
The Lindisfarne Psalter. 8th C. Surtees Society, Vol. 16.
Rituale Ecclesiae Dunelmensis. Edited by Lindelof, 1927, Surtees Society, Vol. 140.
Life of S. Cuthbert. In verse, c. 1450, from MS. in library of Castle Howard, edited by Fowler. Surtees Society, Vol. 87.
Liber Vitae. Cott. MSS. Domitian A. 7.

V

THE SHRINE OF OUR LADY OF WALSINGHAM

[1] 16th C. Anon. *Oxford Book of English Verse*. 34.

[2] Book, 1254. Pepys Library, Magdalene College, Cambridge.

[3] Pipe Roll 31 H.I. 1130/1. Pipe Roll Society, 1929, p. 94.

[4] Cott. Nero E VII.

[5] Pedes Finium. Rye's edition of Norfolk Section.

[6] Cott. Nero VII 'Vere ordinem religionis'.

[7] Cott. Nero E. VII f. 157.

[8] *The Religious Houses of Mediaeval England*. Dom David Knowles, Sheed and Ward, 1940.

[9] *Pilgrimages to Saint Mary of Walsingham and Saint Thomas of Canterbury*. Desiderius Erasmus. J. G. Nichols (Ed.). John Murray, 2nd edition, 1875.

[10] *Itineraria Willelmi de Worcestre*. Nasmith edition 1778, 303 ff.

[11] *Italia Illustrata*. Flavius Blondus. Papal Secretary, ob. 1464.

[12] *Redemptoris mundi Matris Ecclesiae Lauretana historia*. Terremanus. Contained in the *Opera Omnia*, 1576 by Baptista Mantuanus.

Notes

[13] *Annales Monastici.* RS. 36 IV. 529.
[14] Cartul. fos. 160–161 in *Arch. Journ.* XXVI (1869), 169–73 cf. *Norfolk Arch.*, XXV, 269–71.
[15] *Knighton's Chronicon.* R.S. 92. II. 183.
[16] *Repressor of over-much weeting [blaming] of the Clergie,* c. 1449. Rolls 19, I, 194. 1860 (C. Babington).
[17] *Paston Letters.* Edited by James Gardiner and published by Chatto and Windus in 6 volumes in 1904. Vols. II and III.
[18] Ibid., Vol. I.
[19] Ibid., Vol. I.
[20] See Note 9.
[21] *History of Norfolk.* Blomfield, Royal Arch. Inst., Norwich, Vol. IX.
[22] Translation by Jusserand, in his *Wayfaring Life.* 1920.
[23] *Visitations of the Diocese of Norwich 1492–1532.* Edited by Jessop, Camden Society, 1888, fo. 153, p. 57.
[24] *Anglic. Hist.* 25. cf. *Chron.* J. Hardyng, 1887, 557.
[25] *The Works of Sir Henry Spelman Kt.* Edited by Edmund Gibson, Bishop of London, 1723.
[26] *Original Letters illustrative of English History.* H. Ellis, 1834, I. 89; *Cal. of Letters & Papers.* i. (2) 2268.
[27] *Cal. of Letters & Papers.* H. VIII x No. 40.
[28] Ibid., 1. No. 1786.
[29] See Note 23. f. 33, p. 113.
[30] See Note 23. f. 53, p. 147.
[31] Ibid. ff. 67, p. 170; 47, p. 252; and 92b, p. 314.
[32] *Journal of the Royal Archaeological Inst.* 1856. Letters and Papers. VII N. 1216 (27).
[33] *Articles of Inquiry for the Monastery of Walsingham.* Harl. 791, p. 27. Also see Note 9, Appendix, p. 209.
[34] Cott. Cleop. E. iv. f. 231. Also see Note 9, pp. 213–4.
[35] *Cal. of Letters & Papers.* XI, N. 1260.
[36] Ibid. XII (i) N.1171.
[37] Ibid. XIII (i) 1177.
[38] *Chronicle.* Wriothesley. Camden, 1875, Vol. i., p. 83.
[39] N. 35. XIII (i) 1376.
[40] Ibid. XIII (ii) 86. 12th August, 1538.
[41] Close Roll. Aug. 4th, 40 H.VIII 1538. *Arch. Journ.* XIII (1856) 129–31.
[42] *Letters and Papers.* XIII (2) 529, 535.
[43] *History of Sacrilege.* Spelman. 1632(?) Re-edited by C. F. S. Warren, 1895. See also Note 9, p. 214.
[44] Bodleian Library. MS. Rawlinson (poet 219) 16.
[45] Cott. MS. Nero E. VII.

OTHER REFERENCES

Our Lady of Walsingham. Dom Philibert Feasey and Henry Curties, Weston-super-Mare, 1901.
The Shrine of Our Lady of Walsingham. J. C. Dickinson, Cambridge, 1956.

Notes

Mary's Shrine of the Holy House, Walsingham, A. Hope Patten, Cambridge, 1954.
Shrines of Our Lady in England and Wales. H. M. Gillett, Samuel Walker, 1957.
Walsingham. P. J. Goodrich. Jarrold and Sons, 1937.
The Walsingham Story. H. A. Bond, Greenhoe, Walsingham, 1960.

VI

SAINT THOMAS OF CANTERBURY

[1] *La Vie de Saint Thomas Becket.* Guernes de Pont-Sainte-Maxence, 1172–4 Walberg (Ed.), 1936.
[2] *Life and Letters of Thomas à Becket.* J. A. Giles (Ed.), 1846.
[3] Ibid.
[4] *Materials for the History of Thomas Becket.* J. C. Robertson (Ed.). Rolls. Vol. II (Ref. Annales Colonienses Maximi-Pertz. *Monumenta Germaniae Historica,* xvii 785).
[5] Harley 270 ff. 1.2°–122v°, 13th C. B.M.
[6] *Materials* . . . Vols. V, VI, VII.
[7] Harley MS., 978 ff. 114b–116.
'Appendix to Life of Edward Grim' in *1st Quadrilogus* (13th C.).
'Chronicon of John Brompton' c. 1436 (*Scriptores* x. Twysden (Ed.), cols. 1052–5. 1652).
R. Pynson. London, 1520(?) From Caxton's translation of *Legenda Aurea* of Jacobus de Voragine.
[8] 'Archbishop Thomas Becket'. Dom David Knowles, The Raleigh Lecture on History, 1949, printed in *The Historian and Character,* Cambridge, 1963.
[9] *Materials* . . . Vol. V, No. viii.
[10] Ibid., No. ix.
[11] *Select Charters.* W. Stubbs. Oxford, 1895.
[12] *Materials* . . . Vol. V, lxxiv.
[13] Ibid. lxxviii.
[14] Ibid. lxxi.
[15] Ibid. Dclxxxv.
[16] Ibid. Dclxxxvi.
[17] Ibid. Vol. III, Herbert of Bosham, Lib. V. Cap. 4.
[18] Ibid. Vol. III, William Fitzstephen (112).
[19] Ibid., Vol. III, Vita S. Thomae (109).
[20] Ibid., Vol. III, Herbert of Bosham, Bk. V, Cap. 6 & 7.
[21] Ibid., Vol. III, Bk. V, (9).
[22] Ibid., Vol. II, (74), p. 428.
[23] Ibid. Vol. III, pp. 132–5, Fitzstephen. Vol. II, pp. 480–3, Grim.
[24] *Angl. Sacr.* London, 1691, ii, pp. 423–4, G. Cambriensis. See also Rolls.
[25] *Materials* . . . Vol. II, p. 435, Edward Grim.
[26] Ibid., Vol. I, pp. 132–3, William of Canterbury; Vol. III (141) William Fitzstephen.

Notes

17 Ibid., Vol. II, Grim (84).
18 Ibid., Vol. II, Miracles of S. Thomas, Benedict, viii, ix, x.
29 *Notes on Shrines.* Add. MSS. St John Hope, Canterbury Cathedral Chapter Library.
30 *Materials* . . . Vol. II, Lib. 1, Cap. XII.
31 Ibid., Vol. I, William of Canterbury.
32 *Iconography of Saint Thomas of Canterbury.* Tancred Borenius, Oxford, 1929.
33 *The Relics of S. Thomas of Canterbury.* John Morris, Canterbury, 1888. *The Four Shrines of St Thomas of Canterbury.* Charles Wall, 1932.
34 *Polychronicon.* Higden, Rolls Society, Vol. III, p. 200.
35 *Notes on Shrines.* Add. MSS. St John Hope, Canterbury Cathedral Chapter Library.
36 *Hist. Angl.* Matthew Paris, RS ii 241–2.
37 *Pilgrimage to St Mary of Walsingham and St Thomas of Canterbury.* Desiderius Erasmus. J. G. Nichols (Ed.), 1875.
38 See Note 7.
39 *State Papers* (1831) p. 583.
40 Arundel MS 97. p. 34.
41 *State Papers*, 1538, Vol. II, Nos. 257, 317, 323.
42 Letter from John Morris, S.J. to Mr Milman. St John Hope, *Notes on Shrines*, Canterbury Cathedral Chapter Library.
43 *Letters relating to the Suppression of Monasteries*, Camden Society, p. 218.
44 *State Papers*, 1538, Vol. II, No. 442.
45 Ibid., No. 542.
46 *What became of the bones of St Thomas?* A. J. Mason, Canon of Canterbury, Cambridge, 1920.
47 *St Thomas of Canterbury.* John Morris, S.J., 1859.

VII
SAINT EDWARD THE CONFESSOR

1 *Macbeth.* William Shakespeare, Act IV, Sc. iii.
2 *Anglo-Saxon Chronicle.* Revised translation edited by Dorothy Whitelock, Eyre & Spottiswoode, 1961. Also a revised reprint in Everyman series, G. N. Garmonsway, 1962.
3 Harleian 526. B.M. Vita Aedwardi regis qui apud Westmonasterium requiescit. *Lives of Edward the Confessor* edited by H. R. Luard, Rolls, 1858.
4 *The Life of King Edward the Confessor.* Edited and translated by Frank Barlow, Nelson, 1962.
5 See Note 2. Whitelock edition C(D), p. 140.
6 *Monasticon Anglicanum.* Dugdale, 1655–1673.
7 *History of Westminster.* Prior Flete, late 15th C. (Edited by J. Armitage Robinson, Cambridge, 1909.)
8 *History of the English Church and People.* Bede II, 3.
9 Abbey Archives. Charter No. 3.
10 *Abbreviata ex tractatu domini Osberni Westmonasteriensis prioris.* 13th C. MS. Corpus Christi Coll., Cambridge, 161.

Notes

[11] See Note 3, Rolls.
[12] Univ. Lib. Cambridge, MS Ee iii 59. Also Rolls and Roxburghe facsimile edition.
[13] *The Monks of Westminster.* E. H. Pearce, Cambridge, 1916.
[14] *Historical Memorials of Westminster Abbey.* A. P. Stanley, John Murray, 1882, p. 28.
[15] *Edovardus Confessor Redivivus*-1688. J. Gibbon. B.M.
[16] 'The Quest for the Cross of St Edward the Confessor', Lawrence E. Tanner, C.V.O. Keeper of the Muniments, *Journal of the British Arch. Assoc.*, 3rd Series, Vol. xvii, 1954.
[17] *Westminster Abbey.* H. F. Westlake, Philip Allen, 1923.
[18] *Eagle Argent.* D. J. Hall, Methuen, 1956.
[19] *dell'Inferno.* Dante, Canto xii 1.120.
[20] 'King's Evil'. Herbert M. Vaughan, F.S.A. in *Enc. Brit.* (11th ed.).
[21] See Note 14.
[22] *History of Henry VII*, Francis Bacon, 1622, iii, 417 (C.U.P., 1876).
[23] See Note 14.
[24] *The History of King Richard III.* Thomas More, 1513 (unfinished). Edited by J. R. Lumby, C.U.P., 1883.

OTHER REFERENCES

Life and Times of Abbot John Islip (1464-1532). H. F. Westlake, 1921.
Historia Anglorum. Matthew Paris, c. 1253.
Norman Conquest. Vol. ii. E. A. Freeman, 1867-76.
Analecta Bollandiana. Vol. xli. 1923, pp. 5-131 (M. Bloch).
Acta Sanctorum, 13th of October volume.
Richard III. P. M. Kendall, Allen & Unwin, 1955.

VIII
SAINT ALBAN THE PROTOMARTYR

[1] *Anglo-Saxon Chronicle* (See Everyman edition, 1962.)
[2] 'de excidio Britanniae' in *Monumenta Historica Brittanica*, Petrie and Sharpe (Eds.), London, 1848.
[3] *History of the English Church and People.* Bede. I.7.
[4] 'de Gest. Reg. Brit.' ii.3. in *Historia Britonum.* Translated by J. A. Giles, London, 1842.
[5] *Acta SS. Boll.* (June) IV, 149-159.
[6] *Works of James Ussher* (1581-1656). Elrinton & Todd, Dublin, 1847-67, Vol. V, p. 183.
[7] *Vie de Seint Auban.* Robert Atkinson (Ed.), John Murray, 1876. MS. in Library, Trinity Coll., Dublin. See also Roxburghe facsimile edition.
[8] *Here begynneth the glorious lyfe and passion of seint Albon*, etc. MS. in B.M. John Hertford, St Albans, 1534.
[9] *The Itinerary of John Leland the Antiquary.* Edited by Thomas Hearne, 1710. 2nd edition 1744. Vol. VII, pt. ii, pp. 65-6.
[10] Ibid., Vol. V. p. xvi.

Notes

[11] *de incliti et gloriosi protomartyris Anglii Albani.* MS. in B.M. Martin of Werden, Cologne, 1502.
[12] *The Cult of St Alban Abroad.* W. R. Lowe, Hertfordshire Post Printing Co., 1910.
[13] V.C.H. Herts. Vol. IV. *Vitae abbatum S. Albani.* W. Watts (Ed.).
[14] *Five Centuries of Religion,* G. G. Coulton, Vol. III, p. 137, Cambridge, 1936.
[15] *Chronica Majora,* Vol. I. Edited by H. R. Luard. Rolls.
[16] Ibid. Vol. III, p. 162.
[17] See Note 16, Vol. III, p. 80. See also Bromholm.
[18] *Pre-Reformation England.* H. Maynard-Smith, 1938, quoting *Dialoge,* Thomas More, 1528, Bk. I, ch. xiv.
[19] See Note 14, p. 484.
[20] *Gest. Abb. S. Albani.* Matthew Paris, c. 1225.
[21] *The Decline of the Mediaeval Church,* A. C. Flick, Vol. II, p. 447, Kegan Paul, 1930.

OTHER REFERENCES

Chronicon Monasterii de Abingdon. Rolls, Vols. I, II, 1858.
St Alban's Chronicle 1406–1420. Edited from Bodley MS. 462, Oxford, 1937.
'St Alban in History and Legend', L. Rushbrook-Williams in *Bulletin of Dept. of History and Political and Economic Science,* Queen's Univ., Kingston, Ontario, No. 11, April 1914.
Decline and Fall of the Roman Empire. Gibbon, Chandos Classics Edition, 1898, c. xiii, xvi.
The Story of St Alban's. Elsie Toms. Abbey Mill Press, 1962.
Monasticon Anglicanum. Dugdale-Caley, London, 1846.
English Benedictine Kalendars after A.D. 1100. Henry Bradshaw Society, Vol. LXXVII. (Edited by F. Wormald, London, 1939).

IX
THE HOLY ROOD OF BROMHOLM

[1] Lambeth Lib. MS. 545, 14th C.
[2] Roger of Wendover. Rolls, Vol. II, 274. *Chron. Maj.* Matthew Paris. Rolls, Vol. III, 80. *Chron. Angl.* Ralph of Coggeshall. Rolls 202.
[3] *Mon. Angl.* Dugdale-Caley, Vol. V, pp. 59–63.
[4] See Note 2.
[5] F. Wormald in *Journal of Warburg Inst.* Vol. I, 1937–8. V. C. H. Norfolk.
[6] *The Cellarer's Account for Bromholm Priory, Norfolk, 1415–16.* Edited by L. J. Redstone, Norfolk Record Society, 1944.
[7] *Acts and Monuments.* Foxe, Sunley's edition 1870, Vol. III, 586.
[8] 'On the pilgrimage to Bromholm in Norfolk', W. Sparrow-Simpson, in *Journal of Brit. Arch. Assoc.* (xxx) 1874, pp. 52–9.
[9] See Note 1.
[10] Cat. of Sale, 9.12.63. Lot No. 120.

Notes

[11] Descriptive Cat., Fitzwilliam Museum, M. R. James, 1895, No. 55, pp. 138–40, 'Horae', acquired 1810.
[12] *Die Grosse Brockhaus*, 16th edition, 1955. *Lexikon für Theologie und Kirche*. Michael Buchberger, Vol. VII, 1963, p. 1050.
[13] *The Golden Bough*. J. G. Frazer. 1929 edition, pp. 617 ff. and 638 ff.
[14] Corpus Christi Library, Cambridge, 16 f. 59. See also Note 5.
[15] *Mediaeval Religious Houses*. David Knowles and R. Neville Hadcock, Longmans Green, 1953.

OTHER REFERENCES

Illustrations of Bromholm Priory. R. J. Simpson, 1888.
A Short Record of Bromholm Priory. Bacton, Norfolk, 1911.
The Story of the Relics of the Passion. H. M. Gillett, 1935.
Chron. Anglie. Rolls 201–3, c. 1450 and *Chronicles of England*. Capgrave, edited by Hingeston, 1858.
The Paston Letters. Edited by James Gardiner and published by Chatto & Windus in 6 vols. 1904.
English Benedictine Kalendars after A.D. 1100. Henry Bradshaw Society, Vol. LXXVII (Edited by F. Wormald, London, 1939).
Die Verehrung der hl. N. 1886. H. Weber; *Legenstudien*, H. Gunter, 1906 (for information on 'Need Helpers').

INDEX

Adrian IV, pope (Breakspeare), 191
Adrianople, battle of, 202
Aelred of Rievaulx, 174
Aidan, saint, 49, 65, 77, 79, 81, 91
Alban, saint:
    Legend, growth of, 186-187; martyrdom, 185, 186; miracles, 187; pilgrims, 192, 194, 195; relics, 189-192, 194, 195; Rose Sunday, 200; shrine, 191, 195, 196; at Ely, 191; Translation, 196
Aled, Tudor, 27, 32, 34, 44
Alexander II, pope, 174
Alexander III, pope, 132, 151
Alfred, king, 65, 78, 87, 88
Alphege, saint, 145, 148
Amphibalus, saint, 16, 187, 188, 192, 196, 199
Anglo-Saxon Chronicle, 68, 78, 84, 167, 170, 186
Anselm, saint, 148
Arthur, king, 46, 48, 53, 54. *See also* Arthurian legend
Arthurian legend, 49, 50, 52, 54, 57, 58, 59, 60, 61
Arundel, Philip, earl of: Lament, 128, 129
Ascham, Roger, 128
Athelstan, king, 65, 66, 88, 102, 193
Augustine, saint, archbishop of Canterbury, 78
Augustine of Hippo. *See also* City of God
Augustinian, canons (Black, Austin), 108-9; chronicler, 211

Bacon, Roger, 113
Baldwin I, 201, 202, 203
Bamburgh, 76, 77, 79, 82
Bardsey Island, 25, 26, 60
Basingwerk, abbey, 18, 21, 27; indulgences, 29, 30, 32; last abbot, Dissolution, 35; castle, 26, 27
Beaufort, Margaret, 19, 32, 33, 34
Beblowe, castle, 77
Becket, Thomas, saint, 97; Art, in, 152; biographies, 132; birth, 134; canonization, 151; archbishop, 138; chancellor, 136; Clarendon, Constitutions of, 139; death, 131, 147; exile, 141; Feast, 151; Henry II, final meeting with, 143; *La vie de Saint Thomas Becket*, 130, 131, 164, 165; miracles, 132, 148, 149, 150, 151, 152; murderers, 145, 148; pilgrimage, declines, 157, places of, 154; shrine dismantled, 160; sister, 132; Translation, 133, 153, 154
Bede, 10, 64, 65, 81, 82, 83, 84, 86, 90, 92, 171, 187, 189
Benedict Biscop, saint, 49, 65, 68, 83, 84
Benedict XIII, pope, 178
Benedict, recorder of Becket's miracles, 149, 150, 152
Benedict, saint, 215; Rule of, 66, 70, 108, 197
Benedictine, 26, 29, 66, 70, 87, 91, 101, 108, 112, 178, 190, 210
Benignus, saint, church of, 62

Index

Bere, abbot of Glastonbury, 71, 75, 110, 111
Beuno, saint, 19, 212, 213, 214, 215, 216, 231
Black Death, 114, 155
Bleheris, 49, 61
Blundell, Nicholas, 40, 41
Bolden Book, 95
Bollandists, 36
Boniface V, pope, 98
Boniface IX, pope, 210
Bridget, saint, 48, 51, 58, 65
Brito, Richard, 145, 153, 158
Bromholm, priory:
8, 16, 112, 118, 194, 214; Fairs, 205; founder, 203; indulgence, 210; miracles, 203; Paston family, 211; pilgrimage, 204, 206; Prayer Roll, 208; Rood, 116, 203, 204, 205, 207, 208, 209; True Cross, 201, 202; *Valor Ecclesiasticus*, 211, 212; Visitation, 212
Buckingham, earl of, 118

Caedmon, 83
Camargue, 46, 64
Cambrensis, Giraldus, 10, 21, 53
Canon Law, Roman, 117
Canterbury, 16, 210, 212; claim to St. Dunstan's relics, 50, 68; crypt, 150; Chillenden screen, 163; Conrad's choir, 153; Erasmus, 158; pilgrimage, 148, 153-5, 164; royal tombs, 157. *See also* Becket, Thomas, saint
Canterbury Tales, 1, 14, 115
Capgrave, John, 20, 195, 211
Carilef, bishop of Durham, 77, 91
Carlisle, 82
Castle Acre, 108, 203
Catherine of Aragon, 34, 122
Caxton, 21, 120
Celestine III, 203
Chalice Hill, 45, 59
Charles II, king, 180
Chaucer, 1, 14, 115, 116, 117, 155, 156, 158, 188, 205
Chester-le-Street, 87, 88

Chichele, Henry: ordains double feast of St. Winefrede, quarrels with pope Martin V, 29
Chrétien de Troyes, 50
Churchyard, Thomas, 26
Cistercians, 27. *See also* Savigny
City of God, 3, 108. *See also* Augustine of Hippo
Clarendon, Constitutions, 139, 140
Clement VI, pope, 13
Cluniac, Cluny, 52, 112, 203, 210, 211, 212
Clynnog Fawr, 26
Coggeshall, 209
Compostella, 17, 116, 151
Corrodies, 70
Corvo, baron, 42
Cotton, Sir Robert; Cotton library, 20, 21
Cranmer, 160
Crayke, 85, 113
Cromwell, Thomas, 72, 73, 100, 125, 126, 127, 159, 160, 163, 198, 206, 212
Cuthbert, saint:
Bede's Life of, 81; birth, 78; bishop, 82; called to Lindisfarne, 81; coffin found, 101; death, 83; journey of body, 85; Melrose, 79; miracles, 90-7; pilgrims, 97, 103; prophecy of Egfrid's death, 82, of sanctuary, 83; relics, 89; shrine, 93, 94, 95, 96, 100, 103; Translation, 91-3; uncorrupted body, 84, 92; visions, 79, 80; women, attitude to, 86
Cuthbertine Community, 87, 88, 90, 91

David, saint, 25, 48, 49
De Cella, John, 193
De Glanville, William. *See* Bromholm
De heretico comburendo, 117
De Montfort, Simon, 112
De Morville, Hugh, 145, 148, 158
De Tracy, William, 145, 158
Devotional card, 206-8

228

Index

Diocletian, 171, 186, 189
Domesday Book, 21, 108
Dugdale, Sir William, 54
Dun Cow, miracle of, 88, 89, 107
Duns Scotus, 113
Dunstan, saint, 47, 50, 52, 64-8, 148, 164, 172, 173
Durham, 15, 77, 84, 86, 163, 164, 194, 197, 204, 212; Carilef, bishop, 87; chapel of nine altars, 91; de Puiset, bishop, 87, 90; Galilee chapel, 90, 91, 99; Neville Screen, 95; Ranulf Flambard, bishop, 89, 91; refounding, 97; sanctuary 98-100; shrine of St. Cuthbert, 93, 94, 95, 96, 100, 103; Visitation, 100, 101. *See also* Cuthbert, saint
Durham Advertiser, 101

Ealfrid, the sacrist, 90, 92. *See also* Relics
Ebba, abbess of Coldingham, 80, 86, 90
Edgar, king, 65, 66, 67, 70
Edmund, king, 88
Edward the Confessor, 16, 97, 121, 190, 191; biographies of, 168, 174; birth, 168; canonised, 174; coronation, 168; chapel, 180; chastity, 169, 172; death, 170, 172; destruction of shrine and relics, 181; King's Evil, 166; laws, 170, 173; marriage, 169; miracles, 172, 173; pilgrimage, 182, 184; relics, 177, 178, 179, 181; shrine, 175, 176, 179; tomb opened, 173; Translations, 174, 175, 177. *See also* Westminster
Edward I, king, 113
Edward II, king, visits Ely, 191
Edward III, king, 180
Edward IV, king, 118, 182, 211; visits St. Winefrede's shrine, 32
Edward V, king, 182; born in Sanctuary, confined in Tower, 183
Edward VI, king, 181

Edwin, king, 78
Egfrid, king, 82
Elerius, saint, 20, 21
Ely, 215; feud with St. Albans, 190, 191, 194
Erasmus, 71; Colloquy, 119, 120, 125; description of Walsingham, 105, 109, 110; visits Canterbury, 158

Falconer, John, 20
Farne Islands, 76, 81, 82
Fiennes, Celia: visits Holywell, 40
Fitz-Urse, Reginald, 145, 146, 147, 152, 158
Fleetwood, Dr. William, 41, 93; polemic against cult of St. Winefrede, 20, 21, 28
Foliot, bishop, 151, 175
Forgery, 10
Franciscans, 114

Galilee, chapel: Glastonbury, 74; Durham, 74
Gardiner, bishop, 161
Garnet, father. *See* Gunpowder Plot
Gascoigne, chancellor of Oxford
Geoffrey of Monmouth, 49, 52, 187
Germanus, saint, bishop of Auxerre, 186, 187, 190
Gildas, 49, 50, 186, 187, 189
Glastonbury, 8, 15, 78, 101, 212, 213; Arthur: *See* Arthur, king; Avalon, 46, 74; Benignus, saint, church, 62; Bere, abbot, 71, 110; Chalice Hill, 45, 59; 'Charter of St. Patrick the bishop', 51; Corrodies, 70; David, saint, 48; Dunstan, saint, 64-68; Edgar chapel, 75; Gildas, 49; Grail: *see* Grail, Holy; Great Fire, 50, 62; Indulgences, 51; Joseph of Arimathaea: *See* Joseph of Arimathaea; Loreto chapel, 110; Magna Tabula, 63; Melkin, prophecy of, 55, 62; Nicodemus, 56; Patrick, saint, 48; Relics, 70; Thorn, 62, 107; Thurstan, abbot, 66, 68; Tor, 45,

Index

74; Savary, bishop, 68, 69; Visitation, 72; Whyting, last abbot, 71-74; William of Malmesbury, 47, 48
Gloucester, Humphrey, duke of: 194; library at Oxford, tomb at St. Albans, 195
Godwin, earl, 168
Gorham, Geoffrey, abbot, of St. Albans, 196-5
Gorham, Robert, abbot of St. Albans, 196
Grail, Holy, 46, 52, 54, 57, 59, 60, 61
Grim, Edward, 132, 145, 148
Grimthorpe, Lord, 199
Gregory the Great, pope, 3, 24
Gregory VIII, pope, 3, 91
Grosseteste, bishop, 113
Guernes de Pont-Sainte-Maxence, 132, 164, 165
Gunpowder Plot: conspirators pilgrimage to Holywell, 37, 38; 213
Gwynedd, Owain, 27
Gwytherin, 27, 28

Harbledown, 151, 152
Harold, king, 168, 170
Hearne, Thomas, 71
Henry I, king, 17, 139, 173, 203
Henry II, king, 131, 132, 133, 135, 136, 137, 138; Constitutions of Clarendon, 139, 140, 141, 142; final meeting with Becket, 143, 144; 145, 149; penance at Becket's tomb, 151; 163, 174, 175
Henry III, king, 112, 113, 153, 175, 176, 178, 179, 193
Henry IV, king, 96
Henry V, king, 116, 195, gift to Bromholm, 204, 205; funeral, 180; pilgrimage to Holywell, 32; tomb, 180, 181
Henry VI, king, 176, 180, 181, 183, 195
Henry VII, king, 21, 121, 189; chapel, 181; tomb, 182
Henry VIII, king, 34, 72, 121, 122, 129, 159, 161, 162; leases rights at Holywell, 35; executes abbot Whyting, 74; success in destroying Becket's cult, 163, 164
Herbert of Bosham, 145
Holy House (Walsingham), 104, 105, 106, 107, 108, 110, 119, 120, 122, 126, 129
Holy Island, see Lindisfarne
Holywell, 15, 18, 19, 23, 24, 27, 32, 33, 34, 108. See also St. Winefrede
Hugh of Lincoln, saint and bishop, 11. See also Relics
Hundred Years War, 116
Huss, 14. See also Indulgences

Illiteracy, 17, 64
Indulgences, 12-15, 51, 52, 210, 214
Innocent II, pope, 174
Innocent III, pope, 52, 69, 201
Innocent VIII, pope, 197

James II, king, 19, 40, 177, 178
Jarrow, 83, 84, 85, 90, 91, 92
John, king, 69, 112
John of Glastonbury, 55, 57, 63
John of Salisbury, 132, 137, 144, 146, 151
Johnson, Dr. Samuel: visits Holywell, 41, 42; touched for King's Evil, 180
Joseph of Arimathaea, saint, 46, 47, 52, 54, 55, 56, 57, 59, 60, 61, 62, 63, 64, 65, 69, 74, 75, 213

Katharine of Aragon, 34, 122
King's Book: See Walsingham
King's Candle: See Walsingham
King's Evil, 166, 172, 173, 179, 180
King's Lynn, 129
Kiss of Peace, 143-4
Knights Templar, 27. See also Basingwerk

La Estoire de Seint Aedward Le Rei, 176
Lanfranc, 193
Langland, William, 115, 116, 155, 205
Latimer, bishop, 127

Index

Layton, Dr. Richard, 72
Legenda Aurea, 158
Leland, John, 53, 71, 161, 188, 190
Lindisfarne, 76, 77, 79, 81, 82, 83, 84, 87, 100, 102, 103
Lindisfarne Gospels, 85, 90
Lollards, 116, 117
Loreto, 8, 110, 111
Louis VII, king, 132, 137, 141, 142, 148, 151, 157. *See also* Becket
Luther, 14. *See also* Indulgences
Lydgate, John, 188, 195

Maen Achwynfan, monolithic slab-cross, 24
Magic and Witchcraft, 118, 209
Magna Tabula, 63, 64
Map, Walter, 54
Marsh, Adam, 113
Marlet, William, 187
Martin V, pope, 27, 29, 30
Mary I, queen, 101, 175, 182
Matthew Paris, 154, 188, 190, 191, 192, 193, 194, 197, 209
Matilda, queen, 136
Mediaeval mind, 215
Melkin, 55, 57, 61, 62. *See also* Glastonbury.
Mellitus, saint and bishop, 148, 171
Melrose, abbey, 79, 80
Merlin, 25, 49, 60, 61
Metcalfe, father, 21
Middle Ages: definition 3; ending of, 117
Miracles. *See* under names of saints
Modena, Mary of, 19, 40
Money, value of, 96
Montecassino, 150, 179, 215
Montreuil, Madame de, 159, 160
More, Sir Thomas, 183, 194
Morte d'Arthur, 49, 117

Need-helpers, 208, 209
Nennius, 49
Nicaea, 2nd General Council, of 8, 32
Nicodemus, 56, 61
Northampton, Council of, 140, 141, 158

Norwich, Visitations by bishops of, 114, 121, 122, 123, 124
Nova Legenda, 86

Ockham, 113
Odense, 190
Odo of Cluny, 6. *See also* Relics
Offa of Mercia, 172, 192
Offa's Dyke, 18, 26
Oldcorne, Father, 37
Osbert of Westminster, 173, 174
Oswald, Saint and king, 78, 92, 102

Pantaleon, abbey, 189, 190
Pardoners, 12, 13, 14, 156
Paston, family, 112, 118, 201; John, 118, 211; letters, 41, 210; village, 210; William, 211
Paul III, pope, 163
Paulinus, saint, bishop of Rochester, 48, 49, 78
Pecock, Reginald, bishop, 116, 117, 195
Pelagius, 5
Pennant, Nicholas, last abbot of Basingwerk, 35; Thomas, 18th-cent. chronicler, 27
Piers the Plowman, 61, 115, 155, 205
Pilgrim and pilgrimage, 2, 149, 150, 155, 192, 194, 195, 199, 200, 204, 206, 212, 213, 214, 215. *See also* under names of saints
Pilgrimage of Grace, 72, 126
Patrick, saint, 48, 49, 51, 52, 54, 65
Pius VI, pope, 13
Pole, cardinal, 162, 163
Polychronicon, Ranulf Higden's, 52
Pomparles, bridge of, 58, 59
Pons periculosus, 58
Pontigny, monastery, 142, 145
Pynson Ballad, 105, 107, 108, 110, 114, 129
Pynson, Richard, 105, 118; life of, St. Thomas from *Legenda Aurea*, 135, 158, 159

Raine, Dr. James, 93, 94, 101, 102
Ralph, abbot of Seez, 92, 93

Index

Ranulf de Broc, 141, 144, 145, 148, 150
Reginald of Durham, 86, 89, 90, 97
Relics, 6, 7, 8, 9, 10, 11, 28, 32, 50, 90, 94, 96, 97, 177, 178, 179, 181, 189, 190, 191, 192, 194, 195, 202, 206, 214, 215. *See also* under names of saints
Renart, Roman de, 120
Rich, Edmund, 113
Richard, archbishop of Canterbury, successor to Becket, 140
Richard I, king, 68, 69, 112
Richard II, king, 114, 129, 156, 177, 180, 210
Richard III, king, 32, 113, 118, 183
Richmond, countess of, 21. *See also* Margaret Beaufort
Ripon, monastery, 80
Robert of Melun, 135
Robert of Merton, 135
Robert of Shrewsbury, 20, 27, 28, 29
Roger, Pont l'Evêque, archbishop of York, 4, 136, 143, 145
Roger of Wendover, 169, 192, 193, 194, 209
Rood, Holy, of Bromholm, 201-212, 214
Roses, Wars of, 72, 116, 118, 211
Saint Albans, abbey: 16, 202; Architecture, 198-9; Cromwell's Visitors, 198; feud with Ely, 190-1; founding by Offa II, 192; Matthew Paris, 188, 190, 191, 192, 193, 194; rebuilt by Paul of Caen, 185; reredos, 195; Saxon abbots, 185, 192, 193; Scriptorium, 193, 198; shrine of St. Alban, 191, 194, 199, 212; Watching Chamber, 195, 199
Saint Albans, 1st battle of, 118; 2nd battle of, 197
Saint Bertin, monk of: (life of Edward the Confessor), 168, 169, 172
Saint Davids, cathedral, 18, 24
Saints, vindictive, 10. *See also* Cambrensis

Sanctuarium Dunelmense, 99
Sanctuary, 83, 98, 99, 100, 182, 183
Savary, bishop of Bath, 68, 69
Savigny, 27. *See also* Cistercians
Shelley, P. B., 125
Shrewsbury Abbey: St. Winefrede, patron saint, 27, her shrine, 30; Bell, pulpit, 30
Shrewsbury Cathedral: St. Winefrede's relics, 32
Simnell, Lambert, 121
Simon, abbot of St. Albans, 187, 192, 196
Slipper chapel. *See* Walsingham
Southwell, Richard, commissioner, 125, 126, 206, 212, Robert, Jesuit poet, 125
Stephen, king, 136
Sudbury, archbishop of Canterbury, 156
Supremacy, Act of, 72, 124
Swithin, saint, 160
Symeon of Durham, 86, 88, 91, 92, 93

Taliesin, 49, 60
Theobald, archbishop of Canterbury, 136, 137, 138
Thomas, saint of Canterbury: 250th Jubilee, 29, 30. *See also* Becket
Thorny (Isle of Thorns), 170, 171
Thorn, Holy, at Glastonbury, 62, 107
Thurstan, abbot of Glastonbury, 66, 68
Tinmouth, John of, 20
Torrigiano, 181, 182
Translations: St. Alban, 196; St. Thomas Becket, 153, 154; St. Edward the Confessor, 174, 175; St. Cuthbert, 91, 92, 93, 102; St. Winefrede, 27-9
Treasure of the Church, theory of, 13
Trent, council of, 14

Usage, Celtic, 81; Roman, 80, 81, 87

Index

Usk, Adam of, 32
Ussher, James, 188

Verulamium, 185, 186, 192
Visitations, 72, 73, 100, 101, 102, 121, 122, 123, 124
Vowell, Richard, last prior of Walsingham, 119, 123, 124, 125, 126, 127, 128

Wallingford, William of, abbot of St. Albans, 195, 198
Walsingham, 112, 113, 118, 119, 122, 126, 128, 129, 211, 212; Holy House, 8, 16, 104, 105, 106, 107, 108, 110, 111, 204, 205; Inquiry, Articles of, 124, 125; King's Book, 124; *Piers the Plowman*, 115, 116; Pilgrims, 118, 122, 126; *Pynson Ballad*, 105, 107, 108, 110, 114; Rychold, 104, 106, 107, 109; Slipper chapel, 105, Surrender, 128; Visitations, 121, 122, 123-4; Wells, 119
Walsingham, Thomas, 193
Warwick the Kingmaker, 118
Wearmouth, abbey, 83, 84, 85, 91
Wendover, *See* Roger of
Werburgh, saint, abbey of, 26, 27, 52
Westacre, prior of, 122, 123
Westminster, abbey, 170, 171, 174, 175, 176, 179, 180, 181, 182, 183, 212. *See also* Edward the Confessor
Whitby, Synod of, 81, 87
Whyting, Richard, last abbot of Glastonbury, 71-4
William of Canterbury, 132
William the Conqueror, 89, 90, 91, 139, 173
William of Malmesbury, 47, 48, 51, 52, 54, 63, 64, 65, 74, 169
Wilton, abbey of, 173
Winefrede, saint, 35, 40, 41, 42, 93, 213; feast of martyrdom (June 22), of, natural death (Nov. 3), 43; double feast ordained by Chichele, 29; Fleetwood's attack on cult, 20; legend, 21, 22, 23; Miracles, 29, 36, 37, 38, 39, 42; pilgrimage of Henry V, 32; relics, 32; Translation of, 27-9
Witchcraft, *see* Magic
Wolsey, cardinal, 120, 198
Woodville, Elizabeth, 182, 183
Worcester, William of, 109, 129
Wriothesley, commissioner on dissolution of Canterbury and Winchester, 160, 161
Wyatt, James, 99
Wycliff, John, 14, 116, 155. *See also* Indulgences

York, Richard, duke of, 118

For Product Safety Concerns and Information please contact our EU representative GPSR@taylorandfrancis.com
Taylor & Francis Verlag GmbH, Kaufingerstraße 24, 80331 München, Germany

www.ingramcontent.com/pod-product-compliance
Lightning Source LLC
Chambersburg PA
CBHW071825300426
44116CB00009B/1450